WITHDRAWN

HARVARD LIBRARY

WITHDRAWN

Radical DIFFERENCE

A Defence of
Hendrik Kraemer's
Theology of Religions

TIM S. PERRY

Radical Difference
A Defence of Hendrik Kraemer's Theology of Religions

Editions SR / Éditions SR

Editions SR / Éditions SR is a general series of books in the study of religion, encompassing the fields of study of the constituent societies of the Canadian Corporation for Studies in Religion / Corporation canadienne des sciences religieuses. These societies are: Canadian Society of Biblical Studies / Société canadienne des études bibliques; Canadian Society of Church History / Société canadienne de l'histoire de l'église; Canadian Society of Patristic Studies / Association canadienne des études patristiques; Canadian Society for the Study of Religion / Société canadienne pour l'étude de la religion; Canadian Theological Society; Société canadienne de théologie; and Société québécoise pour l'étude de la religion.

GENERAL EDITORS: *H. Martin Rumscheidt and Theodore S. de Bruyn*

Editions SR

Volume 27

Radical Difference
A Defence of Hendrik Kraemer's Theology of Religions

Tim S. Perry

Published for the Canadian Corporation for Studies in Religion /
Corporation Canadienne des Sciences Religieuses
by Wilfrid Laurier University Press

2001

This book has been published with the help of a grant from the Humanities and Social Sciences Federation of Canada, using funds provided by the Social Sciences and Humanities Research Council of Canada. We acknowledge the financial support of the Government of Canada through the Book Publishing Industry Development Program for our publishing activities.

National Library of Canada Cataloguing in Publication Data

Perry, Tim S., 1969-
 Radical difference : a defence of Hendrik Kraemer's theology of religion

(Editions SR; v. 27)
Includes bibliographical references and index.
ISBN 0-88920-377-6

1. Christianity and other religions. 2. Theology of religions (Christian theology).
I. Canadian Corporation for Studies in Religion. II. Title. III. Series

BR127.P47 2001   261.2   C2001-930473-0

© 2001 Canadian Corporation for Studies in Religion / Corporation Canadienne des
 Sciences Religieuses

Cover design by Leslie Macredie. Photograph of Hendrik Kraemer courtesy of the Hendrik Kraemer Institute, Utrecht, Netherlands.

∞

Printed in Canada

Radical Difference: A Defence of Hendrik Kraemer's Theology of Religions has been produced from camera-ready copy supplied by the author.

All rights reserved. No part of this work covered by the copyrights hereon may be reproduced or used in any form or by any means—graphic, electronic or mechanical—without the prior written permission of the publisher. Any request for photocopying, recording, taping or reproducing in information storage and retrieval systems of any part of this book shall be directed in writing to the Canadian Reprography Collective, 214 King Street West, Suite 312, Toronto, Ontario M5H 3S6.

Order from:
Wilfrid Laurier University Press
Waterloo, Ontario, Canada   N2L 3C5

CONTENTS

Foreword vii
Acknowledgements ix

1. Introduction 1

Part One
Preliminary Matters

2. Typological Issues 9
3. Kraemer's Context 29
4. Kraemer's Theology of Religions 53

Part Two
Radical Difference

5. The Radical Difference of the Gospel:
   Biblical Realism 87
6. The Radical Difference of Other Religions:
   The Holistic Approach 111
7. Radical Difference and Communication:
   Adaptation and Points of Contact 135
8. Conclusion 149

Bibliography 151
Index 161

FOREWORD

The relation between the religions is one of the most important questions facing Christianity today. Tim Perry has written a very important and timely book on this subject. He makes a considerable contribution to the debate. To look at the relation between religions from a Christian point of view, he goes back to one of the neglected giants who has contributed so carefully to this debate: Hendrik Kraemer. However, he has also quite uniquely related Kraemer's approach to recent narrative theology to help support his argument that Kraemer's position has much to teach us today. Reading through Perry's work, I find that his argument is both persuasive and well presented.

Those working in this area will need to attend to Perry's claim that Kraemer's holistic and biblical approach is still valid. It stresses that any continuity between Christianity and other religions exists only within the context of greater discontinuity—wrought by Christ. Kraemer manages to overcome Karl Barth's tendency to evaporate cultural mediation and at the same time shares with Barth the epistemological and ontological priority of Christ as the only mode of our knowing God. In so doing, Kraemer provides a neo-Barthian legacy regarding the question of other religions, which Perry helps to retrieve. Hence, Perry's study is helpful both as a historical study of Kraemer's work and as a current theological contribution to the complex debate in the theology of religions.

Gavin D'Costa

ACKNOWLEDGEMENTS

It is with pleasure and gratitude that I acknowledge some of those who have contributed in various ways to the production of this book. In its earliest format this book was a Ph.D. thesis, submitted and defended in 1996. Thanks are therefore due, first, to the University of Durham, the Department of Theology and especially to Dr. Colin Crowder and Professor David Brown, all of which supported me during these initial stages. As my advisor, Dr. Crowder spilled a great deal of red ink on many preliminary drafts. I am very grateful for his investment of time and energy, not only in the project but also in my personal scholarly development. I want to mention as well Professor Ann Loades and Dr. Gavin D'Costa for their insightful criticism offered, as examiners, during my defence. Several postgraduate colleagues also contributed, albeit more informally; among these I would like to thank Christopher Devanny, Paul Fletcher, Greta Gleason, Peter Phillips, and David Weber for enriching my stay in Durham professionally and personally.

Second, Alvin Plantinga, Gavin D'Costa, Eleanor Jackson, and Lesslie Newbigin thought enough of this project to provide access to what was, at the time, rare or unpublished material. As the essays offered by Professor Plantinga and Dr. D'Costa have subsequently been published, they are cited in that form. In addition to pointing me to her published work, Eleanor Jackson copied her own private research notes that afforded greater insight into the International Missionary Council and the fledgling World Council of Churches. Finally, Bishop Newbigin's support is inestimable. His correspondence while I lived in Durham was both informative and encouraging; spending an afternoon with him at his home in London discussing Kraemer, Barth, and contemporary religious and cultural plurality will remain one of my fondest memories. While his passing saddens me, he has left me and many others an example of a life committed to the Gospel. I hope that this work does justice to his life.

Third, after I had concluded that this project had run its course, several colleagues and mentors encouraged me to re-write it and to pursue publication. I thank especially Dr. Dennis Stoutenburg, former chair of Biblical and Theological Studies at Providence College, for his persistent encouragement and enthusiastic support. It was he who introduced me to Sandra Woolfrey of Wilfrid Laurier University Press, who began the process toward publication. At the Canadian Corporation for Studies in Religion, Professor Martin Rumscheidt and Dr. Theodore de Bruyn oversaw the rewrite and guided me through the process of seeking a grant to cover publication costs. At Wilfrid Laurier, Carroll Klein and Susan Quirk were thorough editors. Any errors remaining are mine alone. Finally, this book has been published with the help of a grant from the Humanities and Social Sciences Federation of Canada, using funds provided by the Social Sciences and Humanities Research Council of Canada. I am grateful to all who supported me, both personally and professionally, during the project's gestation.

In spite of all the assistance just mentioned, this book would never have been completed without the consistent financial, intellectual, emotional and spiritual support of those to whom it is dedicated: my parents, Kathryn and Ellard Perry, and my wife, Rachel. While there are not words enough to thank them, I hope those following are a small start.

Tim Perry
Providence College

1

INTRODUCTION

"The question of Christianity's attitude and relationship to the religions of the world will not go away—and neither should it" (D'Costa, 1990: viii): so Gavin D'Costa opens a major collection of essays in the increasing body of literature falling under the rubric Christian theology of religions. That it is growing ought not to surprise anyone in North America, especially Canada. The collapse of colonialism in the years following the Second World War, increasing patterns of global immigration, and technological advances especially in telecommunications have brought the earth's inhabitants closer together than previously possible. At the same time, continuing and sometimes reviving ethnic, cultural, and religious interests throughout the world have generated issues of inter-religious tolerance and co-operation as never before. The contradictory trends toward globalism and toward tribalism have forced people of various religious faiths and/or no faith in particular to wrestle with the impact—whether real or imagined—of differing religious beliefs, practices, and world views on their own lives.

These matters are especially acute for traditional Christians, for no other religious group—not even those comprising the Muslim world—has held so consistently or fervently that its understanding of Ultimate Reality is uniquely true. Christian belief that God is encountered in a final and saving way through the person and work of Jesus Christ is the cornerstone of traditional Christian faith, whether Roman Catholic, Orthodox, or Protestant. In the past, the question of Christianity's attitude and relationship to other religions of the world has been relegated to the back of Christian minds fairly easily. From the triumph of Constantine in the fourth century until recently, Christians have been habituated into thinking that people of other faiths were remote inhabitants of far-off lands, the objects of missionary activity. Now, however, adherents to non-Christian religions are our neighbours and co-workers. Furthermore, if Christians are fortunate enough to develop friendships with non-Christians, they will likely find that they embody a lively, though very different, cultural and religious life, one from which Christians may stand to learn a great deal. Christians may discover further that they share with adherents to non-Christian religions several social and moral concerns: abortion, third-world debt, the arms trade, and genetic research are but four major social problems where Christians, Jews, Muslims, Hindus, Buddhists, and others may have common goals and shared misgivings.

Such inter-religious encounters, which are bound only to increase both formally and informally, can and should cause Christians to reflect more thoroughly on the nature of revelation (Has the Christian God made himself known to people of other faiths? if so, in what ways?), salvation (Is Jesus the only way to heaven? If so, what happens to those who never hear of him or reject him?), and ecclesiology (What does it mean to be the Church? Is the Christian Church in some sense unique, or is it one among many equally valid expressions of religious life?). A growing body of literature exploring these and similar questions is responding to religious diversity within Christian communities of faith. They are treated together under the category, Christian theology of religions.

A presupposition common to many of the works in this category is that the world religions, and many minor ones as well, are fundamentally similar; they have, at their core, a common experience of Ultimate Reality variously expressed in culturally mediated ways. This presupposition is refreshingly explicit among those who advocate for what they call a "pluralistic theology of religions." According to such scholars as British philosopher John Hick, Canadian Islamist Wilfred Cantwell Smith, and American theologian Paul Knitter, the differences among religions must be understood within this greater overall unity. They believe that Christianity especially, because it claims to have a superior grasp of religious truth and a unique path to salvation, has perpetrated many of the great evils throughout history, among them forced conversions, inquisitions, crusades, and other expressions of racial and cultural prejudice. The only way to transcend such morally bankrupt behaviour, they argue, is to "cross the Rubicon," to undergo a "Copernican revolution in theology," and see the religions as independently authentic ways of salvation, each mediating, in culturally diverse ways, experiences of the one Ultimate Reality. Christians are ethically and theologically compelled, they say, to "move away from insistence on the superiority or finality of Christ and Christianity toward a recognition of the independent validity of other ways" (1987a: viii). The irony of this position is palpable, for it claims at bottom that the only way to preserve religious diversity in practice is to deny it in theory.

Most traditional Christians have found themselves unable to undergo the philosophical, theological, and ethical "conversion" that they believe the various pluralistic approaches entail. To relinquish the beliefs that Jesus uniquely makes God known and that he alone is the savior of the world is, for them, to cease being a Christian in any recognizable sense. They therefore seek to respond to the new consciousness of religious plurality in a manner affirming traditional Christian claims concerning the uniqueness of Jesus' person and work. While the responses nevertheless occupy a spectrum of views ranging from very optimistic to very skeptical, they share a presupposition not only with each other, but also with the pluralistic approaches with which they otherwise deeply disagree. Among the more optimistic of these responses, a common claim may be that Christianity—or Jesus Christ himself—fulfils or completes all that is good in other religions. The skeptical ones, on the other hand, hold that Christianity gives a vantage point from which to designate other religions ultimately false and/or inadequate. Behind both assertions lies the presupposition that non-Christian religions overlap with Christianity to the degree that they can be judged either incomplete or incorrect with respect to it.

Another view considers that the religions are not fundamentally similar, instead presupposing a radical difference among the world's various religious communities, with each faith being defined by different beliefs, different practices, different world views and different ways of life. The Roman Catholic theologian J. A. DiNoia (1992), and the Protestant S. Mark Heim (1995, 2001), have done pioneering work in this area. Throughout subsequent chapters, their influence will be plain. The argument of this book contends that the presupposition of radical difference begins neither with DiNoia nor Heim, but more properly with Dutch Reformed theologian and missionary Hendrik Kraemer. Further, I seek to show that a critical reappraisal of Kraemer by the contemporary Christian theology of religions can only help those Christians, especially evangelical Protestants, who find themselves equally unsatisfied with current pluralisms and traditional responses, whether optimistic or skeptical. I do not intend simply to recapitulate the work of others; rather, I seek to contribute to this developing dimension of theological discussion.

1. The Scope of the Study

The scope of the study is narrow: I have deliberately confined my argument to Christian theology of religions. I do not offer it as a phenomenological study of specific religions or of certain beliefs and practices. Careful investigation into the lives of diverse religious communities is valuable, but is not undertaken here. Neither is the study an example of comparative theology, that is to say, "the detailed consideration of religious traditions other than one's own," which sometimes leads to innovative theological construction within the home tradition (Clooney, 1995: 521). Finally, this is not an exercise in apologetics, either as a defence of the truth-claims of Christianity or as a challenge to the truth-claims of other religions. Rather, the study attempts to understand, to assess, and to redeem the contribution of one member of the Christian community, Hendrik Kraemer, to the Christian understanding of other religions.

This study is thus an example of Christian systematic theology: it is a critical and ordered reflection arising out of and remaining linked to a particular community of Christian faith. Explicitly and unapologetically confessional in nature, it is written by a Christian and is intended for Christians. It is not and does not purport to be a meta-critical theory of religion to which Muslims, Hindus, Buddhists, or others should subscribe. It is incumbent upon them to construct their own theologies or atheologies of religions. This book comprises a systematic reflection on the contribution of Hendrik Kraemer to Christian theology of religions in order to show that it continues to offer insights to Christians wrestling with the problem of religious plurality.

2. The Argument of the Study

Part One of the study addresses problems that arise before a proper examination of Kraemer's contribution can begin. The first chapter offers a suspicious reading of the popular exclusivist/inclusivist/pluralist typology, showing it to be a polemical device that caricatures actual exclusivist and inclusivist theories while masking problems in pluralist ones. This analysis is undertaken to liberate Kraemer—often recognized as an exclusivist—from the highly emotive, negatively charged baggage attributed to him in part through this typology. First, an examination of its genealogy shows that this typology conceals a thesis about the inevitability of pluralism. Second, a comparison of widely accepted definitions with actual exclusivist and pluralist theories shows the definitions to be reductionistic. Finally, an attempt to rescue the typology by redefining the types in relation to matters of truth rather than related but distinct issues of salvation is shown to create more problems than it solves. The typology, then, should not prohibit reflection on openly traditional theologies of religions, of which Kraemer's is an excellent example.

Chapters 3 and 4 place Kraemer in his historical and theological contexts and offer an exposition of his position. Chapter 3 examines Kraemer's life and seeks to position him theologically with respect to the International Missionary Council, to Karl Barth, and to William Hocking. Chapter 4 then builds on this foundation, presenting a careful exposition of Kraemer's theology of religions.

Part Two defends Kraemer's contribution directly. His position deduced from his three primary works (*The Christian Message in a Non-Christian World* [1938], "Continuity or Discontinuity" [1939], and *Religion and the Christian Faith* [1956b]) and eight secondary works (1943, 1956a, 1957,

1958a, 1958b, 1960, 1962, 1966), as set out above, is analyzed thematically in three chapters. Chapter 5 begins by assessing "biblical realism," Kraemer's designation of the point from which any self-consciously Christian understanding of the great religions must begin. The analysis takes place in four steps. In the first, I summarize Kraemer's position. In the second, I raise the concern that such a position fails to take into account the rise of the historical-critical method, but rests instead on a naïve biblical hermeneutic. I hope to show that this criticism not only misunderstands Kraemer but is itself highly problematic. In the third, I deal with a cluster of criticisms focused on Kraemer's contention that the revelation of God in Christ—the starting point for biblical realism—is sui generis, or absolutely unique. Finally, I show that Kraemer's position defends the explicitly Christian nature of theology of religions adequately while affirming religious diversity as part of the Christian narrative.

Chapter 6 is a threefold consideration of the "holistic approach," or Kraemer's insistence that, while the religions can and do overlap at many points, they are fundamentally different understandings of the totality of human existence in the world. In the first section, I offer a summary of Kraemer's argument for treating the religions as holistic apprehensions of humanity's place in the cosmos. To do any less fails to consider the beliefs and practices of other religions that renders them intelligible. In the second section, I consider a very serious objection raised by Gavin D'Costa (1986: 60-76), namely, that such an approach tends to treat religions statically and ignores change arising from intra-religious and inter-religious influences. This criticism, I believe, is fundamentally accurate; nevertheless, I counter that it can be overcome from within Kraemer's own work. Finally, I conclude that this position better preserves the "otherness" of other religions than does exclusivism, inclusivism, and/or pluralism as popularly defined.

These two chapters together raise a question that threatens to scuttle the entire project: Is communication across religious traditions possible? Based on the analysis in chapter 3 of Kraemer's missionary experience it would seem that he believes it is. His years of cross-cultural experience engendered concern that indigenous members of the Indonesian churches be able to express faithfully their Christian beliefs in their own languages and cultures rather than regurgitating the vocabulary of Western missionaries. He expressed this concern in his theoretical work when considering the problems of adaptation (i.e., expressing Christian beliefs in terms understandable to an other-believer) and of the point of contact (i.e., whether there is an overlap between Christian revelation and other religions). Chapter 7 considers each in turn, showing that Kraemer offers a plausible answer, and then explores several theological implications to which they give rise.

3. The Aims of the Study

If this argument is successful, it makes a strong case, first of all, for the reintroduction of Hendrik Kraemer's theology of religions to contemporary debate. Remembering his contribution is more often than not restricted to the missiological wing of the World Council of Churches, where his pioneering spirit if not his theology is honoured. Gavin D'Costa and Lamin Sanneh are perhaps the only contemporary theologians to seriously consider and criticize Kraemer at length. This study assesses and responds to the major criticisms in order to show that Kraemer's contribution is not easily dismissed. The study seeks also to reappropriate critically Kraemer's theology of religions. In so doing, it presents a defensible position, one that is aware of contemporary and theological difficulties and how they impinge upon the theology of religions.

PART ONE

PRELIMINARY MATTERS

2

TYPOLOGICAL ISSUES[1]

For at least three decades, one could not begin seriously to unpack Christianity's relationship to other religions without reference to the work of Hendrik Kraemer. His writings in theology of mission and ecumenism were at one time widely recognized for their provocative character and theological insight. William Temple well expressed this contention in his foreword to *The Christian Message in a Non-Christian World*, writing that it was "a product of . . . knowledge, experience and vision" (Temple, 1938: ix). He further predicted that it would be "for many years to come the classical treatment of its theme—perhaps the central theme for Christian thought in this age of multiform bewilderment" (Temple, 1938: ix). It now seems that Temple's forecast was overly optimistic, for in recent literature, if Kraemer's work is mentioned at all, it is either badly distorted or summarily dismissed. The normally careful Keith Ward summarizes the opinion of many contemporary scholars when he caricatures Kraemer's thesis as: "God has spoken in the Bible and that's that" (1994: 16).

Even in the missiological and ecumenical publications of the World Council of Churches, where Kraemer is remembered as a theological, missiological, and ecumenical pioneer, his position is often misunderstood and dismissed as a historical artifact that is irrelevant to contemporary challenges. This attitude is exemplified in the July 1988 issue of *The International Review of Mission* that celebrated the fiftieth anniversary of the 1938 International Missionary Council Meeting in Tambaram, India, by publishing the proceedings of a small consultation on the "relationship of dialogue and mission, as these impact on Christian understandings of relations to people of other faiths" (Stockwell, 1988: 309). Therein, Stanley Samartha argued that Kraemer's contribution to discussion had become irrelevant in a world threatened by nuclear and environmental annihilation (1988: 315-24).[2] In what appears to be an attempt to be more

---

1 Parts of this chapter have appeared as Perry 1996b.
2 Samartha presents Kraemer himself as an intellectual and theological puzzle. He writes, "whether any scholar, whatever be the breadth of his scholarship and the depth of his understanding of other religions, can make such heavily negative judgements on other

complimentary, Wilfred Cantwell Smith asserted that had Kraemer only lived long enough, he would have adopted a more pluralist position. He writes:

> An undiscerning reader might say that he [Kraemer] was stubborn, clinging to inherited doctrine formulated in earlier, ignorant days, and deeming it important so to cling. Personally, I feel that Kraemer was not holding on so much as he was being held; he never succeeded in bringing together what his heart felt and half of his brilliant head knew, with what the other half had been taught, and from which he never managed constructively to struggle—as if God had revealed traditional Christian theology, rather than, as the best Christians have always known, that he revealed himself (to us and to others). . . . It was not only the majority of those attending the first Tambaram conference that Kraemer failed to convince of this stated thesis. He failed to convince himself. He spent the rest of his life writing further books, each of which in effect was an attempt to say that no, he had not quite meant what the last one seemed to be saying, for that was not quite right. He moved increasingly towards a more comprehensive vision. Yet he died, poor man, without ever managing to satisfy himself that he had formulated that vision adequately. (Smith, 1988: 372)

Though I, as one sympathetic to Kraemer's position, am certain no ill will was intended, it is difficult not to regard Smith's words as more condescending than conciliatory.

There seem to be few exceptions to this rather harsh assessment. First, Lesslie Newbigin did much to preserve a more sympathetic memory of Kraemer's work. In his view, Kraemer's *The Christian Message in a Non-Christian World* was a necessary and correct theological response to the more mystical proposals of William Hocking. Where the latter presented religions as possessing a common core of truths and experiences, Newbigin recalls that

> Kraemer did not claim uniqueness for Christianity, which is a changing, variegated and ambiguous human phenomenon; he claimed uniqueness for the events that form the substance of the gospel. In [his] favorite phrase, these events are *sui generis*. . . . Therefore we have no business trying to domesticate [the gospel

---

religions whose resources have provided spiritual sustenance, theological direction and ethical guidance to millions of people through the centuries and, in addition, have provided foundations for the building up of cultures and civilizations that have survived over the centuries, becomes a serious question" (1988: 312).

> story] within our cultures, or rational projects and programmes, no business trying to confuse it with the so-called Christian civilization of the west. The gospel is unique, sovereign, unbound. Our business is to bear witness to it. (Newbigin, 1988: 327)

Kraemer's thought has been considered and criticized by Gavin D'Costa (1986: 52-59) and Lamin Sanneh (1997: 555-74). While the value of these is not denied, the last serious book-length treatment of Kraemer's work was published only in 1966, and its focus was historical, regarding his early thought rather than a theological assessment of his mature ideas (Hallencreutz, 1966). As a result, a number of contextual problems must be addressed before a proper assessment can begin.

The first of these is the very theological language that is used to arrange the various Christian solutions typologically to the problem of religious plurality. This method of classification, attributed to Alan Race, has become commonplace over the last decade. John Hick, for example, states that: "the now fairly standard threefold division into exclusivism (salvation is confined to Christianity), inclusivism (salvation occurs throughout the world but is always the work of Christ), and pluralism (the great world faiths are different and independently authentic contexts of salvation/liberation) [remains] the simplest and least misleading classification" (1990: 175). That this division is fairly standard is undisputed. That it is "the simplest and least misleading" is the point with which this chapter takes issue. Indeed, I suggest that this typology tends to misrepresent non-pluralist approaches as theologically deficient and/or ethically insensitive.

The analysis takes place in three steps. The first offers a brief sketch of the typology's history and a quick summary of three previous criticisms. My primary concern, however, is to consider whether the typology functions as more than an organizing framework. Through a genealogical inquiry, I show the typology to be a subtle polemic against non-pluralist positions. If this contention were correct, it follows that there are inaccuracies in the accounts of exclusivism and pluralism, cast more often than not as typological villain and hero, respectively. The second section, therefore, compares actual exclusivist and pluralist proposals to the commonly held definitions above, in order to demonstrate that exclusivist accounts have more nuance while pluralist ones are more problematic than the typology indicates. Finally, I consider whether the typology could be rescued by shifting its axis from questions of salvation to related but distinct questions of truth. An examination of the confusion created by Race's definitions reveals that such a shift threatens the internal boundaries of the typology, rendering it useless. I conclude, therefore, that the language that too often serves as a springboard for sensationalistic stereotypes must be rejected if Kraemer's work is to be assessed fairly.

1. The Genealogy of the Typology

The exclusivist/inclusivist/pluralist typology is often said to have been inaugurated by Alan Race in the first edition of *Christians and Religious Pluralism*: "In this study I adopt the headings Exclusivism, Inclusivism and Pluralism as a broad typological framework within which most of the current Christian theologies of religions can be placed" (1983: 7).[3] Race further defined this typological framework epistemologically, according to criteria for assessing religious truth. Exclusivists, for Race, were those who counted "the revelation in Jesus Christ as the sole criterion by which all religions can be understood and judged" (1983: 11). Inclusivists, on the other hand, were more optimistic, whom Race defined as holding that "all non-Christian truth belongs ultimately to Christ and the way of discipleship which springs from his way" (1983: 38). Pluralists, for Race, were the most open-minded, believing that "knowledge of God is partial in all faiths, including the Christian. Religions must acknowledge their need of each other if the full truth about God is to be available to mankind" (1983: 72). As the definitions suggest, Race defended a version of pluralism.

In 1986, Gavin D'Costa used the typology again, contending "that three dominant paradigms [exclusivism, inclusivism, and pluralism] emerge from the recent history of theological reflection, usefully providing a conceptual matrix within which the theological issues are highlighted" (1986: 6). His approach, however, differed from that of Race in two significant ways. First, D'Costa chose to amend the definitions soteriologically—with respect to salvation—rather than epistemologically. Exclusivism, for D'Costa, holds that "other religions are marked by humankind's fundamental sinfulness and are therefore erroneous," while pluralism maintains "that other religions are equally salvific paths to the one God" (1986: 52, 22). In contradistinction to both, inclusivism, for D'Costa, affirms "the salvific presence of God in other religions while still maintaining that Christ is the definitive and authoritative revelation of God" (1986: 80). Second, D'Costa deviated in his arrangement of the positions. Where Race employed the typology to describe a shift from exclusivism to pluralism, D'Costa offered an inclusivist navigation through exclusivist and pluralist extremes.

---

[3] This observation is not quite correct. Race developed the typology while reading for an MA at Birmingham University under the tutelage of John Hick. I pursue this matter further, below.

In the decade following, the threefold typology became the standard arrangement of Christian understandings of religious plurality. Usually defined soteriologically, it can be found in a number of contemporary works seeking to defend and develop each position.[4]

None of this is to say that the typology has escaped criticism. Early on, several theologians insisted that their proposals did not fit the threefold structure, among them Schubert Ogden (1992), Ian Markham (1993), and Michael Barnes (1989). In their views, the typology is artificial and restrictive and, as Markham's title suggests they seek to shatter it with positions they believe it cannot co-opt. Later, other theologians argued that the typology is but a socio-political attempt by Western theologians, especially pluralists, to dominate and destroy the "intractable otherness" of non-Western religions and cultures. Ken Surin frames the objection well: "Traditional liberal intellectuals pride themselves on acknowledging heterogeneity and plurality, but this acknowledgment is always fatally compromised by a deployment of homogeneous logic—a logic which irons out the heterogeneous precisely by subsuming it under the categories of comprehensive and totalizing global and world theologies" (1990: 210). Surin wants not merely to shatter the typology but to abandon all such arrangements completely. Perhaps the most ironic attack comes from D'Costa who, after a decade of popularizing the typology and defending it against critics, came to regard it as redundant (1996).

As my argument below suggests, exposure of the typology's underlying aim strengthens these criticisms. First, I show curious parallels between John Hick's spiritual pilgrimage from exclusivism to pluralism and the emergence of this typology. On the basis of this genealogical inquiry, I propose, second, that the typology was not introduced by Race in 1983, but by Hick in 1972. Third, I argue that a careful analysis of Hick's language reveals the typology to be, as J. A. DiNoia has put it, "a trajectory away from exclusivism"(1992: 50), and is polemical in character. I turn first to Hick's autobiography as it is found in two recent publications (1993a: 139-45; 1995: 29-55).

Hick began his Christian journey as an extremely conservative Calvinist, after a profound conversion experience in 1941. In the two decades following, as he traveled throughout the Middle East, he had virtually no contact with other religious traditions, yet he believed that the world was slowly becoming Christianized. By his own admission, Hick was once an exclusivist. "How then," he asks, "have I come to adopt a 'pluralist' understanding of the relation between Christianity and the other great

---

4 For exclusivism, see Richard, 1994; for inclusivism, Dupuis, 1989: 104-10; and for pluralism, see Race, 1993: 149-67.

world faiths? And what is this 'pluralist' understanding? *I can only answer these questions by continuing the narrative*" (1995: 37, emphasis mine). The watershed came in 1967 with Hick's move to Birmingham, where he became involved in a variety of inter-faith organizations. In the course of this activity, he attended synagogues, mosques, gurdwara, and temples, where he was deeply impressed by the spirituality of his non-Christian colleagues. Later visits to India, Sri Lanka, and Japan confirmed these experiences. It is important to note that Hick has never spoken of a sudden switch from exclusivism to pluralism. Rather, the impression is one of a gradual process through various inclusivist stages based on his inter-faith encounters. He hints at this when describing the appeal of inclusivism: "The attraction . . . is that it negates the old missionary compulsion and yet is still Christocentric and still leaves Christianity in an uniquely central and normative position" (1993a: 143). Eventually, however, Hick came to regard this as an unsatisfactory compromise and, instead, to view the religions as independently valid ways of salvation. In these autobiographical essays, Hick deliberately links his own personal narrative with what became the threefold typology.

This gives sufficient warrant, I believe, to begin with Hick's 1972 essay, "The Copernican Revolution in Theology" (1993b: 120-32),[5] rather than with Race or D'Costa, when examining the typology's history and purpose. For it is there that the original typology, substantially if not nominally, is found. The essay opens with a description of the "Ptolemaic" understanding of religions, which takes as axiomatic the view that, outside the church, or Christianity, none is saved. For Hick, this view denies both the universal love and saving will of God: "Can we then accept the conclusion that the God of love who seeks to save all mankind has nevertheless ordained that men must be saved in such a way that only a small minority can in fact receive this salvation? It is the weight of this moral contradiction that has driven christian [sic] thinkers in modern times to explore other ways of understanding the human religious situation" (1993b: 122-23). With these words, Hick introduces several theological "epicycles," which seek to preserve the uniqueness of Christ or Christianity while extending the borders of salvation. For him, these are "fundamentally weak arguments for the sake of an intuitively accepted conclusion until better arguments are found" (1993b: 124).

Hick explains his use of astronomical language such as "Ptolemaic" and "epicycle" to label his theological survey:

---

5 *God and the Universe of Faiths*, the collection from which this essay is taken, has been reissued regularly since its first publication by the Macmillan Press in 1973.

> I have called these supplementary theories, developed to modify the original dogma whilst leaving it verbally intact, 'epicycles' because they are so powerfully reminiscent of the epicycles that were added to the old Ptolemaic picture of the universe, with the earth at the centre, to accommodate increasingly accurate knowledge of the planets. The stars, including the sun and the planets were all supposed to move in concentric circles round the earth. This was at that time a feasible theory as regards the stars; but the planets moved in paths which did not fit such a scheme. But instead of abandoning the scheme, the ancient astronomers added a series of smaller supplementary circles, called epicycles, revolving with their centres on the original circles. If a planet was thought of as moving on one of these smaller circles whilst it was in turn moving round the great circles, the resulting path was more complex and nearer to what was actually observed; and this complication of the system made it possible to maintain the basic dogma that the earth is the hub of the universe. Looking back we can see that it was theoretically possible to stick indefinitely to the conviction that the earth is the centre, adding epicycle upon epicycle as required to reconcile the dogma with the facts. However, the whole thing became increasingly artificial and burdensome; and the time came when people's minds were ready for the new Copernican conception that it is the sun and not the earth that is at the centre. Then the old Ptolemaic system was thrown aside and appeared in retrospect utterly antiquated and implausible. And much the same, I cannot help thinking applies to what I shall call the Ptolemaic theology whose fixed point is the principle that outside the church, or outside Christianity, there is no salvation. When we find men of other faiths, we add an epicycle of theory to the effect that although they are consciously adherents of a different faith, nevertheless, they may unconsciously or implicitly be Christians. In theory one can carry on such manoeuvres indefinitely. But anyone who is not firmly committed to the original dogma is likely to find the resulting picture artificial, implausible and unconvincing, and to be ready for a Copernican revolution in his theology of religions. (Hick, 1993b: 124-25)

Hick initiated this Copernican revolution in theology by calling Christians to reject the uniqueness of Christ or Christianity altogether, and to recognize that God (or, in later writings, Ultimate Reality) is at the centre of the universe of faiths.

To disclose the purpose of this early version of the threefold typology, it is important to consider first the historical context from which its language arises: that is, the most infamous instance of the Church's scrutiny of natural science. On February 19, 1616, the Holy Office in Rome submitted the following propositions to theologians for evaluation:

1. The sun is the center [sic] of the world and hence immovable of local motion.
2. The earth is not the center [sic] of the world, nor immovable, but moves according to the whole of itself, also with a diurnal motion. (Wolterstorff, 1984: 15)

The experts deemed both propositions philosophically absurd and theologically heretical; on March 5, the General Congregation declared that *De revolutionibus orbium coelestium*, by Nicholas Copernicus, and *On Job*, by Diego Zuniga, where the propagation of these ideas were found, be suspended until they were corrected. In accounts of the controversy surrounding Galileo, Copernicus, and Zuniga, Christian theology and its defenders are often presented as the great inhibitors of natural human reason on its quest to unravel the secrets of the universe. Through his use of such cosmological terms as "Ptolemaic" and "epicycle," Hick hints that the arguments of his contemporary opponents are as unenlightened as those of the Inquisition of the seventeenth century. Once more, the conclusions of Christian theology must be set aside in order to discover truth.

Furthermore, it seems also clear that Hick uses the analogy to suggest the inevitability of progress toward a Copernican (i.e., pluralist) understanding of religious plurality. This inevitability is mirrored in Hick's own journey—one he characterizes as a protracted attempt to appropriate Christian faith intellectually (1995: 32-33). Those who are willing to think theologically, Hick infers, will abandon Ptolemaic theology with its epicycles just as those who were willing to look through Galileo's telescope forsook Ptolemaic cosmology. Progress to Hick's Copernican view is restricted only by the firm but thoughtless commitment to the uniqueness of Christ or Christianity. Particularly telling in this instance is Hick's unqualified use of "fundamentalist" and its cognates to place his opponents (1995: 29, 33). Fundamentalism's noble theological heritage has in recent years been eclipsed by its constant link in Western media to terrorist activity—from the World Trade Center bombing to Waco to the Middle East. An indiscriminate use, therefore, portrays one's opponents as, at best, anti-intellectual and at worst, violently so. There is, therefore, no reason to regard Hick's initial articulation of the threefold typology as more than an attempt to deflate traditional positions as obscurantist.

Further, it seems now clear that Alan Race did not in fact develop the typology independently, but borrowed heavily from Hick. His move from Ptolemaic/epicyclic/ Copernican to the more familiar exclusivist/inclusivist/

pluralist language coupled with the shift in definition away from salvation to knowledge only mutes the polemic set out above. Indeed, while Race's definitions do differ in this respect, he continues to closely associate the two matters. Consider, for example, the following rhetorical question directed against exclusivists: "If Christianity rests on true revelation, [exclusivism] argues, then by logical inference the other faiths of mankind must be false or illusory. . . . But is it permissible in theological argument to deal with the mystery of God and man's relationship to him in so hasty a manner?" (Race, 1993: 25). Similarly, in his summary of inclusivism, Race writes: "On the one hand [inclusivism] accepts the spiritual power and depth manifest in [other religions]. . . . On the other hand, it rejects them as not being sufficient for salvation apart from Christ" (Race, 1993: 38). These citations suggest that while epistemology is Race's proper concern, issues of salvation persist. I will deal with questions surrounding the former below. I begin with the latter.

Recall Hick's definitions cited at the outset of this chapter: "exclusivism (salvation is confined to Christianity), inclusivism (salvation occurs throughout the world but is always the work of Christ), and pluralism (the great world faiths are different and independently authentic contexts of salvation/liberation) [remains] the simplest and least misleading classification" (1990: 175). The labels are different but the underlying soteriological axis is unchanged. The debate, whether articulated by Hick, Race, or, indeed some of their critics,[6] continues to centre on the question, Is the vast majority of the human race condemned to eternal conscious torment, even though they never had opportunity to hear and respond to the gospel? Exclusivists who believe this is in fact the case are portrayed as both immoral and anti-intellectual. Inclusivists are shown to be willing to wrestle with the moral dilemma, but, in so far as the salvation they proclaim is still Christian salvation, their reason remains fettered by dogma. Even when couched in more subtle language, it is clear that only the Copernican/pluralist can surmount both obstacles, morally and reasonably offering salvation or liberation to all. The polemic is preserved; the purpose is hidden but unchanged.

This examination leads me tentatively to conclude that, in addition to being an organizational framework, the typology is constructed in such a way as to blunt the edge of non-pluralist arguments and to show the inevitability of some form of pluralism. I now turn to actual exclusivist and pluralist proposals to see if this conclusion holds.

---

6 See n. 4.

2. Whose Exclusivism? Which Pluralism?

As described, exclusivism has been defined by its limiting of salvation to those within the visible boundaries of the Christian community. Further, it may be reasonable to posit that, in order for this definition to obtain, this definition must embrace all who either situate themselves or have been situated within the exclusivist position. An examination of several prominent exclusivists reveals that this is not always the case. This is not to say that such a definition is wholly inaccurate, for many do find it acceptable. A recent and lucid apology for exclusivism so defined is offered by Geivett and Phillips (1995: 213-45). Their argument is straightforward. Beginning with natural theology, they seek to show, first, that theism is a world view superior to both atheism and non-theism and, second, that Christianity is the superior form of theism. They then turn to the record of Christian revelation—the Bible—to assess the data concerning the nature and scope of salvation. "Christianity is uniquely true," they conclude, "and explicit faith in Jesus Christ is a necessary condition for salvation" (1995: 243). My complaint therefore is not that the definition does not apply; as the preceding example shows, it sometimes does. Rather, it is that the definition is too narrow and therefore possibly prejudicial to those exclusivists who simply do not fit the definition.

Though united in their desire to extend the boundaries of Christian salvation beyond explicit Christian practice, the proposals of these exclusivists are disparate. Nevertheless, solutions can be grouped into one of two sorts. Some exclusivists advance arguments for the likelihood of someone being saved by Christ apart from explicit faith in or knowledge of him tempered by the belief that eschatological destiny is known only to God. This position can be called eschatological agnosticism. Typical of this approach is Lesslie Newbigin, an exclusivist according to both Race (1993: 152-55) and D'Costa (1986: 15); it is also a label with which Newbigin himself was delighted (1994: 127). For him, the question, Can the good non-Christian be saved? is misleading for the following reasons. First, Newbigin suggests, it is one that only God can answer; it is no one else's business to presume upon divine privilege. Second, it assumes that the individual and his or her need for happiness, rather than God and his glory, is the centre of the Christian doctrine of salvation. Newbigin regards any attempt to answer this question as arrogant presumption bent on pre-empting the final judgment of God (Newbigin, 1989: 177-80).

The second sort of exclusivist is more interested in eschatological speculation. Consider George Lindbeck, for instance. Like Newbigin, he is also one of D'Costa's exclusivists (1997: 630-1). Unlike him, Lindbeck hopes all will encounter Christ after death. He argues that Christian doctrines have been understood exclusively either as "cognitive" or "experientially-expressive," the former focusing on propositional content and questions of truth, and the latter on its symbolic expression of religious experience. Against both, Lindbeck proposes a "cultural-linguistic" model that regards doctrine as enabling Christians to experience the world religiously (1984). When applied to Christian doctrines of salvation, this results in an interesting dilemma; if Lindbeck is correct, one must be fluent in the Christian language in order to experience either salvation or judgment. Thus, *extra ecclesiam nulla salus* (outside the church, there is no salvation) is balanced by *extra ecclesiam nulla damnatio* (outside the church, there is no damnation). This is not to say, however, that those unacquainted with Christian language are confined to limbo, for all, Lindbeck reasons, will be evangelized at death: "The proposal is that dying itself be pictured as the point at which every human being is ultimately and expressly confronted by the gospel, by the crucified and risen Lord. It is only then that the final decision is made for or against Christ. . . . All previous decisions, whether for faith or against faith, are preliminary" (1984: 59).

Still others hope for a universal yet distinctively Christian salvation. The most obvious representative of these thinkers is Karl Barth. For him, God's judgment on humanity—rejection and death—has been transferred from all eternity to Jesus Christ; likewise, in and through Christ, God has given salvation and life to all (1957: 94-506). This version of the doctrine of election seems to entail universal salvation, even though Barth remained enigmatic about this possibility, saying only, "I do not teach it, but I also do not not teach it" (quoted in Jüngel, 1986: 44-5). In all three examples, the exclusivist concern that salvation is found only in Christ is preserved and at the same time—whether through agnosticism, post-mortem evangelism, or universalism—the possibility of salvation is extended to those outside Christianity. The popular definition of exclusivism clearly is inapplicable.

In the light of these nuances, one option for those who wish to retain the typology might be simply to move the views of Newbigin, Lindbeck, Barth, and others from exclusivism to inclusivism.[7] This can be done, however, only if one ignores the key disagreement between those typically called exclusivists and inclusivists. In order to explore this disagreement, let us compare the views of Karl Barth (1956: 280-361) and Karl Rahner (1966) on salvation and the nature of religion. Though they are champions

---

7 Race tries to draw Barth into inclusivism as a result of David Lochhead's work (1988). Unlike many of Barth's critics, Lochhead balances Barth's early critique of religions with Barth's later expectation of "secular parables of the Kingdom," (1988: 31-9). This leads Race to observe: "This is in interesting contradiction to the usual interpretation placed on Barth, but in the typology I have adopted, it just as easily draws him into the inclusivist band" (1993: 151).

of exclusivism and inclusivism, respectively, their understandings of salvation overlap at key points. First, since both conceive of salvation in Christian terms, heartily affirming that any and all salvation is the salvation won by Christ, the quarrel is not over its nature. Second, since both men expressed hope in the universal saving will of God, the disagreement is not over its scope. They part company in their conceptions of the role of religion in salvation. Whereas Barth insisted that the Christian God saved despite it, Rahner held that the Christian God saved through it. In so far as Newbigin, Lindbeck, and others follow Barth in their reluctance to ascribe a saving role to religions, they remain exclusivists.

Shifting the debate between exclusivism and inclusivism away from the number of the saved to the role of religion in salvation, however, threatens the exclusivist/inclusivist boundary as usually articulated by the threefold typology. According to Hick, inclusivists are driven away from the morally wicked notion that exclusivist understandings of other religions reserve redemption for a few and damnation for the rest. Yet the theologians mentioned above, by retaining a distinctly exclusivist flavour without limiting the scope of salvation, undermine this contention. Ironically, close scrutiny may uncover some exclusivists extending the scope of salvation beyond that of many inclusivists, thereby rendering the labels ineffective. Here the warning of William Lane Craig is clear: "because salvation is available to more people under inclusivism . . . does not imply that more people actually *avail* themselves of salvation. . . . It is perverse to call a view inclusivistic if it does not actually include any more people in salvation" than does exclusivism (1995: 84). Therefore, while denouncing one's opponents for consigning most of humanity to hell has rhetorical flourish, it is often untrue and almost always sensationalist. I conclude that, more often than not, the typology's account of exclusivism is deficient.

The polemical character of the typology is further confirmed when one scrutinizes the arguments for various pluralist positions. As introduced, pluralism purports to offer the greatest possibility of salvation to the greatest number of people by arguing that each religion is an independently authentic avenue of salvation/liberation. In the rest of this section, I explore one ethical and one philosophical argument for pluralism. In both cases, I offer the position that the typology's account of pluralism merely combines elements of exclusivism and inclusivism.

Paul Knitter, a well-known and articulate spokesperson for the pluralist position, sets out an interesting ethical argument rooted in liberation theology (1987b). Its interest lies in the author's desire to avoid a charge commonly (and mistakenly) leveled at pluralist positions—that of relativism. Knitter believes strongly that, in dialogue with one another, religions can and should make evaluative judgments about beliefs and practices; he insists that such judgments be rooted in a liberationist understanding of the preferential option for the poor. Simply put, those beliefs and practices that promote the full humanity of the poor and oppressed and that foster a desire for economic justice are to be affirmed, while those that mitigate against these aspirations are to be condemned.

The argument begins by bringing the hermeneutics of suspicion into theology of religions. Any dogma, rite, or attitude used to justify the domination, exploitation and/or destruction of non-Christian religions and cultures must be forsaken. When applied to traditional christological beliefs, the results are startling. "Why, really, have Christians been so insistent on maintaining the doctrine . . . that Christ has to be the final norm for all other religions?" Knitter asks. "Certainly it cannot be denied that in the past . . . such christology [has] been used to justify the subordination and exploitation of other cultures and religions" (1987b: 182). Knitter continues by affirming a common context for inter-religious dialogue—*soteria*, or justice for the poor and oppressed. Finally, he posits a list of "general criteria that a variety of religions could agree to work with as a basis for grading themselves [rooted in a] common feeling of obligation to stand on the side of the poor and oppressed against the rich and oppressor." They need not lead to a new "ethical Archimedian point outside the praxis of liberation and dialogue. . . . The criteria—what elements contribute to authentic full liberation—can be known only in the actual praxis of struggling to overcome suffering and oppression, and only in the praxis of dialogue" (1987b: 189-90).

For those Christians sensitive to problems of social justice, but jarred by Knitter's rejection of traditional christology, a liberation theology of religions further enables them to affirm Christ while avoiding dogma. Beliefs about the uniqueness of Christ's person and/or work are clearly "subordinate to carrying out the preferential option for the poor and nonpersons. Orthodoxy becomes a pressing concern only when it is necessary for orthopraxis—for carrying out the preferential option and promoting the kingdom" (Knitter, 1987b: 192). It is the message of Christ that takes priority, for it "*is* a sure means for bringing about liberation from injustice and oppression . . . it *is* an effective, hope-filled, universally meaningful way of realizing *Soteria* and promoting God's kingdom" (1987b: 192-3). As long as Christians stand in solidarity with all those seeking justice, the uniqueness of Jesus is, in Knitter's words, "not that important" (1987b: 194).

Whether or not the position advanced in this argument is actually pluralist according to the accepted definition can be explored through the question, Given the different religious and cultural conceptions of justice, which is absolute? According to the argument just summarized, it is that which liberates the poor and oppressed. But this dismisses a priori rival conceptions of justice. Consider a justice rooted in a traditional understanding of karma: it may insist that the poor and oppressed are being punished for sins perpetrated in previous incarnations and that to liberate them would be to interfere with that just retribution.[8] The problems created when rival conceptions of justice collide, however, are often far more tangible than philosophical speculations. Lesslie Newbigin eloquently summarizes the dilemma: "We all long for justice, and it is these passionate struggles that tear the world to pieces" (1989: 146). He thus reminds that rival definitions translate into claims that some conceptions of justice are superior to others and that violence is often used in their support.

While admitting that there is no Archimedian arbitrator vindicating his conception of justice, Knitter holds, however tentatively, that only those resonating with his are legitimate (1987b: 187-8). He must therefore demonstrate why his idea of justice, embedded as it is in a modern Western context, transcends and evaluates all others. Knitter has committed himself to an argument for the uniqueness and supremacy of contemporary Western culture (Heim, 1995: 93).[9] I conclude, therefore, that the position he wants to advance is not pluralism. His position is exclusive in that its consciously embedded conception of justice reserves for itself the ability to evaluate accurately all other culturally embedded conceptions. It is inclusive in so far as it argues that only those religions sharing its commitment to *soteria* are ultimately saving. It is inappropriate to designate this position as "pluralist" because it does not conform to the accepted definition. The great religions are not independently authentic ways of salvation/liberation, but are effective only in so far as they embody *soteria*.

Turning from Knitter's ethical argument, it is interesting to consider John Hick's philosophical argument for pluralism, summarized as follows:

> the great world faiths embody different perceptions and conceptions of, and correspondingly different responses to, the Real from within the major variant ways of being human; that within each of them the transformation from self-centredness to Reality-centredness is taking place. These traditions are accordingly to be regarded as alternative soteriological "spaces"

---

8 Karmic law is summarized by the *Chandogya Upanishad* v.x.7 in the following way: "those who are of pleasant conduct here—the prospect is indeed, that they will enter a pleasant womb, either the womb of a *brahmin*, or the womb of a *ksatriya*, or the womb of a *vaisya*. But those who are of stinking conduct here—the prospect is, indeed, that they will enter a stinking womb, either the womb of a dog, or the womb of a swine, or the womb of an outcast (*candala*)." See Radhakrishnan and Moore (1957: 66-7).

9 For an example of such an argument, see Rawls (1981).

within which or "ways" along which, men and women can find salvation/liberation/ultimate fulfilment. (Hick, 1989: 240)

So while the Real in itself is posited as the ground of all legitimate religious experience, for Hick, it is only ever experienced indirectly as either personae (i.e., God or Shiva or Allah) or impersonae (Brahman or Nirvana or Sunyata). Ultimate Reality is such that it can be authentically experienced as both: "And these diverse *personae* and metaphysical *impersonae* . . . are not illusory but are empirically, that is experientially, real as authentic manifestations of the Real" (1989: 242). One may draw an analogy with light: though its true nature is unknowable, under certain conditions, it behaves like a particle while under others like a wave. Just so, though the true nature of Ultimate Reality is unknowable, under certain conditions—the cognitive structures of the human mind, various religious and cultural biases, etc.—the Real is experienced as personal, while under others it is experienced as impersonal. Those religions that offer authentic experiences of the Real, no matter how different from each other they may appear to be, are then said to be saving—that is, they provide independently authentic ways for their respective adherents to find ultimate fulfilment.

Thus summarized, Hick's pluralist hypothesis suggests three criteriological questions. First, one may ask, On what basis can one distinguish between authentic and inauthentic manifestations of the Real? The basis is simple: religions can and should be graded according to their ability to promote or hinder the transformation from self-centredness to Reality-centredness. This response, however, leads only to the second question, namely, How do we know when such a transformation has taken place? To this, Hick responds that the criteria lie in the spiritual and moral fruits found in the lives of exemplary believers within the respective traditions: saints (1989: 299-342). Religions, then, can and should be evaluated empirically: according to their ability or inability to produce followers whose saintly lives are commended across religious boundaries.

Thus, it is possible, for Hick, that several different and even prima facie opposing religious experiences may be valid manifestations of, and responses to, the Real. Therefore, Hick must finally address the question of the epistemological status of religious truth-claims and point to a resolution brought about by their conflict. Conflict, says Hick, arises in one of three ways. First, questions arise in which the evidence is inconclusive and admits to the formulation of several possible answers: for example, Does the Universe have a beginning? or, What happens to humans after death? Though they may arouse interest and debate, answers to these questions are not essential to salvation/liberation, and therefore disagreements should be recognized and tolerated. Second, questions arise that are theoretically capable of resolution, but practically have not and will likely never yield a consensus. For example, Whom did Abraham almost sacrifice: Isaac or Ishmael? And, Did Jesus institute the Papacy? As above, Hick suggests that these differences should be acknowledged and tolerated. Finally, questions arise, the answers to which are completely beyond the scope of human finitude. They point to realities beyond human expression. Myths are developed in response to these questions; such answers are not subject to theoretical verification or falsification, but evaluated only practically or existentially: "True religious myths are accordingly those that evoke in us attitudes and modes of behavior which are appropriate to our situation *vis-à-vis* the Real" (1989: 351). For example, the doctrine of the Incarnation is a mythical expression of the profound access to Ultimate Reality that millions of Christians have found in Jesus. He so mediates the Real to his followers that it is entirely appropriate for them to speak of him as the way of salvation (John 14:6), the Word of God come in the flesh (John 1). Once it is understood that such language expresses devotion mythically, for Hick, the conflict between Christ and other mediators of the Real disappears without in any way diminishing his significance for Christians.

Hick's objective with this philosophical argument is to construct a theory unlimited by the confines of any religious tradition. By the nature of the case, this argument is meta-critical. Because it strives to place all religious experience and activity, accepting or applying this theory requires that one must cultivate the ability to stand back from one's own religious tradition (1993b: 132). Nevertheless, the call to stand back has been answered by those from various philosophical and theological persuasions who ask, Stand where? Lesslie Newbigin suggests that the standpoint is that of a consumer-oriented society: while pluralism "owes much to the Hindu concept of *ishta devata*, the god of one's choice, there is little doubt that it is attractive to contemporary inhabitants of the affluent North because it corresponds exactly to the ethos of the consumer society where the choice of the customer is free and sovereign" (1990: 138). Similarly, DiNoia observes that pluralist hypotheses like Hick's "do not so much account for the diversely featured religious world they observe as suggest some important changes in it. They can be read as in effect inviting the Christian community and, by implication, other religious communities as well, to entertain and adopt certain revisions in their doctrines" (1990: 121). Finally, John Milbank writes: "The terms of discourse which provide both the favored categories for encounter with other religions—*dialogue, pluralism*, and the like—together with the criteria for the acceptable limits of the pluralist embrace—social justice, liberation, and so forth—are themselves embedded in a wider Western discourse become globally dominant" (1990: 175). Thus, Newbigin, DiNoia, and Milbank make clear that, when Hick asks Christians to stand back from their Christianity, he is in effect calling for a shift to another tradition entirely. Further, this tradition is not without its own absolute and potentially intolerant claims.[10]

In conclusion, the charges of epistemological exclusivism and soteriological inclusivism are established. Hick, in his generous argument for the saving validity of the great religions, insists that the Real in itself cannot be known. This, however, is a truth-claim: one that necessitates recasting of all alternatives, as is shown by his reduction of classical christology from metaphysics to mythology. With regard to soteriological inclusivism, Hick grants himself an insight into salvation/liberation that is at best obscured in the great religions. Salvation/liberation does not occur within each religion according to its own understanding, but only in so far as it conforms to Hick's description of salvation as the transition from self-centredness to Reality-centredness.

3. The Soteriological Axis

It is clear that the commonly accepted definitions of exclusivism and pluralism mask subtleties and ambiguities in each, thereby supporting the original charge: the typology is a polemical device that seems both to deny the validity of non-pluralist positions and support the inevitability of pluralism. I now consider whether the typology could be rescued by shifting its axis from salvation to related but distinct questions of truth—from soteriology to epistemology. Through an examination of the confusion created by Race's definitions, I show that such a shift dissolves the internal boundaries of the typology and renders it useless.

I begin with Race's definition of exclusivism, which "counts the revelation in Jesus Christ as the sole criterion by which all religions . . . can be understood and judged" (1993: 11). This definition, unlike soteriologically formulated ones, embraces all exclusivists—from the most conservative, who insist that knowledge and confession of Christ is a requirement for salvation, through the eschatological agnostics to even the most optimistic. This exclusivism affirms that other religions are false where their claims conflict with the claims of Scripture or the revelation of God in Jesus Christ. However, where Hick too narrowly defines exclusivism, Race is too broad. Clark Pinnock, one of a growing number of evangelical theologians who consider themselves to be inclusivists, writes: "Recognizing truth in other religions does not take any glory away from Jesus Christ. For

---

10 Though Peter Donovan rightly notes: "a cynic might well be intrigued to see the descendants of Calvin and of the Inquisition joining forces with the disciples of Nietzsche to give lessons on tolerance to the children of the Enlightenment" (1993: 219).

if all treasures of wisdom and knowledge are hid in him, the truth anyone possesses is a facet of the truth in Jesus" (1992: 139).

Race's summary of inclusivism fares little better: "To be inclusive is to believe that all non-Christian religious truth belongs ultimately to Christ and the way of discipleship which springs from his way" (1993: 38). The confusion becomes apparent when one sets the definitions together. If the revelation in Jesus Christ is the sole criterion of religious truth (exclusivism), then all religious truth belongs to Christ (inclusivism). Likewise, if all religious truth belongs to Christ, then he is necessarily the sole criterion. If the central issue is the standard of religious truth, according to Race's own definitions, there is no substantial disagreement between exclusivists and inclusivists.

Finally, consider Race's definition of pluralism: "knowledge of God is partial in all faiths, including the Christian. Religions must acknowledge their need of each other if the full truth about God is to be available to mankind" (1993: 72). The first sentence, as far as I can tell, contains one proposition—partial knowledge of God is found in all faiths—and the corollary—Christianity's knowledge of God is partial. Perhaps only the most extreme Barthian would deny that the former is in fact the case. As discussed, theologians regardless of typological position affirm the possibility of genuine religious knowledge outside Christianity. The corollary is as uncontroversial, for even the most fervent exclusivist agrees with St. Paul when he writes: "Now we see but a poor reflection as in a mirror. . . . Now I know in part" (1 Corinthians 13:12). The first half of the definition says nothing to distinguish pluralism from its interlocutors.

The point of departure then lies in Race's second sentence: Religions can and should pool their resources in order to discover the "full truth about God." There is an admirable humility about this sentence and it is certainly true that the truth is greater than any one person or any one religious tradition can grasp. Nevertheless, this humility is at best superficial. At worst, the definition deceptively makes a claim to privileged epistemic access. On this point, Newbigin is particularly eloquent:

> In the famous story of the blind man and the elephant, so often quoted in the interest of religious agnosticism, the real point of the story is constantly overlooked. The story is told from the point of view of the king and his courtiers, who are not blind but can see that the blind men are unable to grasp the full reality of the elephant and are only able to get a hold of part of the truth. The story is constantly told in order to neutralize the affirmation of the great religions, to suggest that they learn more humility and recognize that none of them can have more than one aspect of the

truth. But, of course, the real point of the story is exactly the opposite. If the king were also blind there would be no story. The story is told by the king, and it is the immensely arrogant claim of one who sees the full truth which all the world's religions are only groping after. It embodies the claim to know the full reality which relativizes all the claims of the religions (1989: 9-10).

Newbigin's point is underscored when one considers the epistemological situation of pluralists who make specific claims about the nature of Ultimate Reality. Compare, for example, Hick's central thesis with one of a typical exclusivist. Hick insists that the great religions embody independently authentic, saving responses to the one Ultimate Reality. Furthermore, he has written numerous books and articles in an attempt to convince the widest possible audience that this thesis is true. In this chapter, I have cited several theological exclusivists who counter that salvation is found in and through Jesus Christ alone (e.g., Barth, 1956: 280-361; Geivett and Phillips, 1995; Lindbeck, 1984: 46-72; Newbigin, 1988, 1990). Like Hick, they have written and published, often appealing to the same audience. It is crucial to note here that the epistemological status of both theses is the same: both make claims about reality; both marshal evidence and compose arguments to buttress them; both hold those who disagree with them to be mistaken. It is possible that both theses are false; it is possible that one is false, while the other is (at least closer to being) true. One thing is certain: both theses cannot be true, for they contradict each other. Epistemologically speaking, there is nothing pluralistic about the pluralist hypothesis.

One pluralist openly acknowledging this epistemological exclusivism is Peter Byrne (1995). The focus of his attention is, like Race's, the epistemology of religious belief. Unlike Race, Byrne far more accurately, if not exhaustively, typifies the various epistemological interpretations of religious plurality into naturalism, confessionalism, relativism, and varieties of what he calls neutralism. My point here is not to discuss the merits of Byrne's typological arrangement, but to make the following observations. First, Byrne regards exclusivism and inclusivism as soteriological variants within epistemological confessionalism, which finds "cognitive success in religion, but locates it solely or primarily within one confession" (1995: 3). Second, and more crucially, he presents epistemological pluralism as a composition of three minimal elements: "a fundamental realist commitment arising out of the faiths to the existence of a transcendent, sacred reality; a basic cognitive equality between faiths putting human beings in contact with this reality and enabling them to be vehicles of salvation; and finally, *agnosticism toward, and therefore disengagement from, the specifics of any confessional interpretation of religion*" (1995: 6, emphasis mine). In other words, for Byrne, pluralism is less about a pooling of religious resources to discover truth, as Races suggests, and more about the prescription of agnosticism in the face of religious plurality.

Thus, when the threefold typology is set out along an epistemological axis, one ends up not with three distinct approaches to religious truth but with two muddled varieties of exclusivism. On the one hand, the search for truth is defined in Christian terms. To be sure, there may be degrees of skepticism or hope as to whether or where extra-Christian truth may be found, but the criteria for discerning such truth are recognizably Christian. On the other, pluralists also make particular claims about the search for religious truth—claims that purport either to refute or reinterpret conflicting claims from other traditions. The labels are meaningless if exclusivism and inclusivism cannot be distinguished and if pluralism is simply exclusivism of a different order. Defined epistemologically, the typology is functionally incoherent.[11]

I conclude that the exclusivist/inclusivist/pluralist typology unfairly misrepresents the non-pluralist positions. As suggested by my inquiry into the introduction of the typology in the early work of John Hick, this misrepresentation is confirmed by the comparison of definitions of exclusivism and pluralism with actual exclusivist and pluralist theories. Further, I have shown that the typology cannot be delivered from these objections by shifting its axis from soteriology to epistemology. The definitions offered by Race lead to more confusion. This much is clear: it is premature—one could even say biased—to dismiss the work of a theologian in this field because he or she is or has been identified as an exclusivist. The label is too charged with sensationalistic overtones to be of much value in legitimate theological discussion. That Hendrik Kraemer is often identified as a champion of the exclusivist position does not justify ignorance or dismissal of his position on the theology of religions.

---

11 Should the typology be retained at all? I am increasingly convinced that it should not, even though I am certain that it will remain in place for some time yet. The exploding amount of literature in Christian theology of religions makes inevitable the grouping or classification of certain authors or positions. Second, this typology has enjoyed a great deal of popularity across confessional boundaries and has, despite its polemical nature, been adapted and used with mixed effectiveness by non-pluralists. Third, the attempts to transcend the typology, including my own, continue to perpetuate its language, ensuring that its unwelcome presence will endure. An analogy can be drawn with Wittgenstein's ladder (1974:74). Anyone who understands it eventually recognizes it as nonsensical, after one has used it—as steps—to climb beyond it. One must, so to speak, throw away the ladder after one has climbed it.

3

KRAEMER'S CONTEXT

While Kraemer has rightly been employed by both Gavin D'Costa and Alan Race as an exponent of the exclusivist position, he is not the only one: the most obvious, better-known alternatives are Karl Barth and Lesslie Newbigin. Nevertheless, my choice of Kraemer is deliberate. Despite his stature within Reformed theology, Barth never wrote outside the European context;[1] Kraemer did. Like Kraemer, Newbigin drew upon experience and had the added advantage of being familiar with contemporary theological problems. Yet, he acknowledges his indebtedness to Kraemer: "I find myself bracketed with Kraemer, where I am delighted to be. I would want to be an exclusivist along with Kraemer in believing that God's work in Christ is (to use Kraemer's favourite phrase) *sui generis*; that there is nothing that can be put into the same category as the incarnation, ministry, death, and resurrection of Jesus" (1994: 127).[2] In my view, Kraemer—better than either Barth or Newbigin—combines missiological experience with theological creativity and therefore merits study in his own right.

Consequently, my recovery of Kraemer begins with a careful analysis of the historical and theological context in which he lived and wrote. I begin with a general introduction to his life and works, then sharpen my focus to Kraemer's role within the missionary thinking of his time by critically examining the first three ecumenical conferences: Edinburgh 1910, Jerusalem 1928, and Tambaram 1938. Finally, I present the argument that to regard Kraemer as Barth's mouthpiece is too simplistic and that a far more important influence, albeit negatively, was the American philosopher and mystic, William Hocking.

---

1 Barth's famous reply to D. T. Niles typifies his lack of interest in other religions: When asked by Niles how he knew that Hinduism was unbelief when he had never known a Hindu, Barth replied, "a priori." (1969: 10-11).

2 This is not to say, however, that Newbigin and Kraemer are theological clones. On their differences, see, for example, Hunsberger (1998: 45-6) and Sanneh (1997: 568-72).

1. Kraemer's Life and Works

Born in Amsterdam on May 17, 1888, Hendrik Kraemer suffered the death of his father when he was six years old and his mother only six years later. With his sister, he was then placed in a Nederlandse Hervormde Kerk orphanage where he was first exposed to Christian faith (Gloede, n.d.: 204). At sixteen, after hearing a missionary speak of the need for workers in Papua New Guinea, Kraemer resolved to become a missionary, thereby embarking on a career that would alter ecumenical Protestantism greatly (Nicholson, 1978: 64).

In the autumn of 1905, Kraemer took the first step toward his goal when he was enrolled in the newly opened Nederlandse Zendingshooge school in Rotterdam. Although he had not completed his secondary education, he was admitted as a candidate for the Utrechtsche Zendings-Vereniging. His years at the school should not be underestimated, for there he became familiar with influential Dutch missiologists, among them, J. H. Gunning (the school's principal), Nicolaus Adriani, and A. C. Kruyt (Hallencreutz, 1966: 47ff). More importantly, Kraemer was initiated into international missiology by serving as J. H. Oldham's guide during his visit to the Netherlands in 1907 in preparation for the World Missionary Conference, which was to take place in Edinburgh three years later. Most notably, though, Kraemer was influenced in his theological development by two Leiden University professors who lectured at the school periodically: W. Brede Kristensen and Pierre Daniël Chantepie de la Saussaye (Nicholson, 1978: 65). Kraemer failed his final examinations in 1909 because of an unsatisfactory result in systematic theology. While preparing to rewrite them, he began to study languages and displayed an uncanny ability (Nicholson, 1978: 66). This impressive linguistic capacity caught the attention of Adriani, who encouraged Kraemer to specialize in Eastern languages. After passing his examinations with honours three months later and another two years of intense study, Kraemer passed his state examinations. In the autumn of 1911, after joining the Netherlands Bible Society, Kraemer acted on Adriani's suggestion and enrolled in Leiden University.

At the time, Leiden was the leading centre of Indology in the Netherlands (Hallencreutz, 1966: 48), and Kraemer's work in Arabic, Javanese, Malay, and oriental literature left him few free moments (van Leeuwen, 1962: 13). Though his primary field of study was linguistics under the Islamist, Snouck Hurgronje, Kraemer spent much of his limited spare time in Kristensen's lectures on comparative religions and Chantepie's on Islam. What remained was spent working closely with Chantepie in the missionary and administrative work of the Dutch Student Christian

Movement (DSCM) (Hallencreutz, 1966: 50). J. R. Mott, the key figure behind Edinburgh 1910 and the entire ecumenical movement, addressed a study conference of the DSCM in November 1913. When commenting on the mission efforts in the (then) Dutch East Indies, he outlined the "tremendous possibilities" for mission activity among Javanese students (Hallencreutz, 1966: 43). Sparked by this presentation, Kraemer's interest grew through his friendship and work with Chantepie, until eventually he relinquished his dream of going to New Guinea and focused instead on Indonesia. After completing his sixth term, Kraemer left Leiden for Hamburg to continue his linguistic work with Karl Meinhoff. In January 1915, however, he was compelled by the outbreak of war to return to Leiden, where he continued his studies and assumed the chair of the Leiden DSCM (Hallencreutz, 1966: 67).

It was as chair that Kraemer attended and delivered the opening address at the Nunspet conference in July 1915. His former teacher, Nicolaus Adriani, contributed a paper calling for a reorientation of missions on Java by cultivating relationships with Javanese nationals who, having benefited from a Western education, took up important positions in the colonial civil service and later were among the leaders of the Indonesian drive for independence (Adriani, 1917). Those taking up the challenge would require extensive training in the field to become familiar with ideological developments and the indigenous press. Kraemer contributed to the discussion by expanding on Adriani's themes and indicating his willingness to direct the operation (Hallencreutz, 1966: 70-1). With the encouragement of Adriani and Chantepie, and with the support of A. W. F. Idenburg—a former Governor General to Indonesia—Kraemer proposed a "policy of association" to the Netherlands Bible Society (Nicholson, 1978: 67). In March 1916, the board of the society approved the proposal and finalized it by November. Kraemer was to be sent to Java to bring the Christian message to Muslim intellectuals.

In that same year, Kraemer passed his "candidaats" examinations cum laude (van Leeuwen, 1962: 14), and began study for a doctoral degree in languages, science of religion and ethnology (Lathuihamallo, 1958: 15). During postgraduate study, Kraemer persisted in his activities with several missionary societies, including the DSCM. He contributed to its journal and in 1919, the same year in which he married Hijke van Gemeren, he became its national president (van Leeuwen, 1962: 17). Finally, on January 28, 1921, Kraemer successfully defended his thesis on rare Javanese Islamic mystical writing (Kraemer, 1921).

Rather than travel directly to Indonesia, Kraemer undertook a three-month study in the history of religions at the Sorbonne with Louis Massignon and Marcel Maus (Nicholson, 1978: 69), then a four-month study of Islam at El-Azhar, the Muslim University in Cairo (van Leeuwen, 1962: 22-25). While there, his colleagues "because of his perfect Arabic and his deep understanding of the Moslem faith" dubbed him "Sheikh Kraemer" (Weber, 1966a: 7). Finally, in 1922—over a year after completing his Ph.D. and several months after leaving the Netherlands—Kraemer arrived in Java. It must be emphasized here that just as Kraemer was not a theology student at Leiden, neither was he a missionary in Indonesia. His role, in addition to Bible translation, was to report regularly to the Netherlands Bible Society concerning the cultural and spiritual situation in the colony. The society, in turn, passed this information on to the many missions operating in the islands. To accomplish this task, Kraemer travelled widely and immersed himself in the indigenous press and other writings.

Throughout the 1920s, as Indonesia edged toward independence, Dutch missions shifted their focus from conversion to strengthening the indigenous Christians and their responsibility for leading the dialogue with Islam (Hallencreutz, 1966: 140-4). In June 1923, at the Conference of the Utrechtsche Zendings-Vereniging, Kraemer asked for a special conference to address the cultivation of indigenous leadership. The next year, when working with the East Java Mission, he called for contacts between the mission societies and major nationalist organizations, including the moderate Budi Utomo and the more extreme Sarekat Islam. At the conference of Javanese-speaking missionaries in Djokjakarta in August 1924, Kraemer expressed particular concern for Christian nationalists who were being portrayed by their Muslim counterparts as colonialist collaborators. To counteract these accusations, he argued for a thoroughly Indonesian expression of Christianity and unity among indigenous Christians (Hallencreutz, 1966: 144 ff).

Kraemer's concern for the indigenous Christian population dominated his thought and work throughout his first term in Java. His colleague, W. A. Visser't Hooft, recalls that:

> Some small Christian groups had been formed there [on Bali] and the Church of East Java had been requested by these Christians to send pastors. But then came a reaction. A number of anthropologists and artists were strongly opposed to any form of Christian work on the island. . . . Hendrik Kraemer had taken up this challenge with his customary energy. He had shown that no culture could live any longer in complete isolation. The invasion by Western tourists was a much more disturbing element than Christianity. And missions had learned their lesson. Nobody wanted to westernize the Balinese. What the Church of East Java and he himself had in mind was to help the small church in Bali to

work out its own forms of life in the light of its own cultural background (Visser't Hooft, 1973: 54)

Kraemer further envisaged an autonomous Indonesia where missions, independent of the Dutch government, could be both positive toward and critical of nationalistic elements and could prevent the isolation of indigenous Christians. Increasingly, this vision forced Kraemer to expose the growing Islamization and anti-missionary trends within nationalistic organizations (Visser't Hooft, 1973: 54). In addition, this vision brought him under scrutiny at home where the Netherlands Bible Society suggested he was becoming too politicized. Yet there were also some significant achievements: in 1925, the indigenous congregation at Djokjakarta (now Yogyakarta) welcomed their first Javanese minister and at Whitsuntide 1928, Javanese ministers were first permitted to administer the sacraments (Visser't Hooft, 1973: 54; see also Weber, 1966b).

That year also marked an interlude in Kraemer's missionary activity when he left Indonesia to chair the session on Islam at the International Missionary Council held on the Mount of Olives, between March 24 and April 8. After the conference, Kraemer returned to the Netherlands instead of Java, owing to ill health. Persistent insomnia led him to Christian psychologist Alphonse Maeder for treatment. Though his contact with Maeder was brief, it was significant, for Maeder introduced him to Emil Brunner (Nicholson, 1978: 73). It was also during this furlough that Kraemer first encountered the work of Karl Barth, whom he regarded with cautious optimism (Hallencreutz, 1966: 224). He spent most of 1928 and 1929 convalescing. On November 11, 1929, however, Kraemer embarked on a hectic schedule again, beginning with a four-month tour of India, during which he studied Islam for the Indian YMCA, followed by a return to Indonesia, where the found the Church in a delicate situation.

As a result of the national elections of 1929, the right-wing majority in the Dutch parliament increased; in 1930, the Vaderlansche Club, made up of Europeans in Indonesia, became the dominant party in the Indonesian People's Council. Moderate and radical nationalists reacted to these conservative developments by increasing opposition to the colonial government, which imprisoned and exiled nationalist leaders with increasing frequency. Kraemer, like many other missionaries, found himself in the middle of this potentially explosive situation, opposing both radical nationalist and conservative colonial elements while sympathizing with the moderates (Hallencreutz, 1966: 230-6). Kraemer expressed both his views in regular contributions to the Dutch periodical *De Stuw*, which sought to co-operate with the moderate Indonesian nationalists (Visser't Hooft, 1973: 54). Also, during this second stay, Kraemer was instrumental in establishing a theological school in Djakarta. In 1935, however, ill health again took Kraemer back to the Netherlands.

Shortly thereafter, W. Brede Kristensen retired from Leiden University and recommended Kraemer to succeed him in the Chair of History and Phenomenology of Religion. Kraemer accepted and, on December 3, 1937, delivered his inaugural lecture. It foreshadowed much of *The Christian Message in a Non-Christian World*, which was published the following year. Over Christmas 1938, he was at the centre of controversy at the International Missionary Council Conference, held at Madras Christian College, Tambaram, India. When he returned, he found a Dutch Reformed Church sharply divided along liberal and conservative lines. Hence, in addition to his university responsibilities, Kraemer also began to work in Church renewal. Once again, however, his activities were hampered by the outbreak of a world war.

During the occupation of Holland, Kraemer actively opposed the Nazis in print and, eventually, by resigning his University Chair in 1941.[3] As a result he was interred in the prison camp at St. Michielgestel (Edwards, 1970: 385). Yet, when the war ended, his was an early voice calling for reconciliation between the German and other European churches. In 1945, when delegates of the embryonic World Council of Churches met with the Council of the Evangelical Church of Germany, Kraemer represented the Netherlands. It was in this capacity, Visser't Hooft recalls, that Kraemer

> said there was no hatred in the hearts of Christians in Holland. Those who had suffered much had learned to be merciful in their judgment. He hoped we could speak together as standing before God. . . . He understood this as a call to his own church also, that it could only live by the forgiveness of sins. It could not be a matter of bartering. In the light of what had been said the other churches could now say to the German church that they were also ready to accept their responsibility for what had happened in Germany (Visser't Hooft, 1973: 192).

After the war, Kraemer returned to Leiden, but his post-war University career was short-lived. In 1947, he resigned in order to become, in co-operation with Suzanne de Dietrich, the first director of the World Council of Churches' Ecumenical Institute at Chateau de Bossey (near Geneva). As director, he was the driving force behind the creation, in Willingen in 1952, of the WCC's regional study centres. Despite these successes, Kraemer's

---

3 Both the pamphlets and the resignation were Kraemer's response to Jewish persecution. He resigned along with fifty-three other members of faculty when two Jewish colleagues were removed. See Kraemer (1943).

stay in Geneva was also brief: three years later, he returned to live in the Netherlands in Dreibergen, and devoted himself to lecturing, travelling, and writing. The immediate result was his classic restatement of his theology of religions, *Religion and the Christian Faith* (1956b).

Over the next nine years, Kraemer travelled, lectured, and wrote extensively, producing two smaller works and one larger one: *The Communication of the Christian Faith* (1957), *World Cultures and World Religions: The Coming Dialogue* (1958), and *Why Christianity of All Religions?* (1962). On November 11, 1965, at his home in Dreibergen, Hendrik Kraemer died. Stephen Neill's tribute, written when Kraemer was still alive, stands as a fitting epitaph:

> Everything in the career of this outstanding man is paradoxical. He has never been a missionary; he went to Indonesia as an expert in languages and Bible translation on behalf of the Bible Society of the Netherlands. Yet no living man has exercised a deeper influence on missionary thinking. He is a layman. But no minister has had more to do with shaping the pattern of life of the Dutch Reformed Church. He is not a theologian. Yet he has read more theology than many of those who make it their profession, and by his writings and his work as the Director of the Ecumenical Institute near Geneva he has influenced the theological thinking of many leaders of the younger generation. (Neill, 1960: 113-4)

2. Kraemer and the International Missionary Council

Having completed this introduction to his life and works, I now focus on Kraemer's role within the early ecumenical movement. Though he was active in the 1928 and 1938 meetings of the International Missionary Council, the survey begins earlier to set the stage. The World Missionary Conference, convened in Edinburgh in June 1910, is rightly seen as the birthplace of ecumenical Protestantism and, more specifically, of the International Missionary Council (IMC) and the World Council of Churches.[4] Edinburgh itself was the climax of a succession of conferences beginning with New York and London in 1854, and continuing in London, 1878 and 1888, and New York in 1900 (Robson, 1910: 3-7). And, while it was ecumenical in intention, the Edinburgh conference's 1,356 attendants were mainly British and American, with European delegates a distant third (at 175), and only 14 members of the "younger" churches (1910: 18-19). It

---

4 In fact, the site of the birth can be narrowed further to the report of Commission VIII, which was ecumenical in intention, title, and content. See World Missionary Conference (1910d: 131-50).

is also important to remember that the delegates were predominantly Protestant and almost overwhelmingly evangelical.

Overseen by J. R. Mott, the conference proper dealt with the following subjects through eight commissions: carrying the gospel to the non-Christian world; the church in the mission field; education in relation to the Christianization of national life; the missionary message in relation to the non-Christian religions; the preparation of missionaries; the home base of missions; missions and governments; and co-operation and the promotion of unity. These topics had been selected by an international committee, of which J. H. Oldham was executive secretary, in 1908. Each commission produced a report, which became a separate volume of the full conference records on publication.

True to its evangelical heritage, Edinburgh 1910 was indeed a "missionary conference," as Commission I made clear in its findings: "This is a decisive hour for Christian missions. The call of providence to all our Lord's disciples, of whatever ecclesiastical connections, is direct and urgent, to undertake without delay the task of carrying the gospel to all the non-Christian world" (World Missionary Conference, 1910a: 363). Nevertheless, Commission IV, without sacrificing any of this missionary fervour, displayed unusual openness to other religions. Chaired by D. S. Cairns and Robert E. Speer, the commission sought an informed discussion by sending a detailed questionnaire to missionaries throughout the world. Impressed by the quality of the 185 responses, it condensed and divided them into five categories: animistic religions, Chinese religions, Japanese religions, Islam and Hinduism (World Missionary Conference, 1910b: 28). Wesley Ariarajah comments that "the work of Commission IV shows a remarkable degree of thinking that was in many ways ahead of its time" (1991: 28). This is especially evident in the first of two general conclusions drawn by the commission, which stated: "the practically universal testimony [is] that the true attitude of the Christian missionary to the non-Christian religions should be one of true understanding and, as far as possible, of sympathy. [While not denying that] in some forms of religions the evil is appalling [the] missionary should seek for the nobler elements. . . and use them as steps to higher things" (World Missionary Conference, 1910b: 267). Yet, the second conclusion was equally clear: "along with this generous recognition of all that is true and good in these religions, there goes also the universal and emphatic witness to the absoluteness of the Christian faith" (World Missionary Conference, 1910b: 268). Furthermore, the commission believed the tension created by the juxtaposition of these conclusions was both good and necessary:

> All down through the history of Christian missions from the earliest days, there have been two types of thought on the question of the relation of the Gospel to existing religions—the types exemplified by Tertullian and Origen—the one dwelling for the most on the evils of religions and the newness of the Gospel; and the other seeking to show that all that was noblest in the old religions was fulfilled in Christ. . . . There is no reason whatever for Christian propaganda unless the missionary has something new to proclaim; but it is equally certain that there is no basis whatever for the missionary appeal, unless the missionary can say, "whom therefore ye worship in ignorance, Him I declare unto you." (World Missionary Conference, 1910b: 279)

On the whole, Edinburgh 1910 stressed the expansion of Christianity and the decline and death of other religions. Yet Ariarajah mentions three points deserving attention. First, the conference, and especially Commission IV, sought to understand non-Christian religious experience and doctrine theologically rather than apologetically. It therefore displayed a remarkable lack of defensiveness (Ariarajah, 1991: 28). Second, there was no attempt to judge these religions "based on unacceptable manifestations of their religion in social life, even though such manifestations were taken seriously and criticized" (Ariarajah, 1991: 29). Third, doctrines of other religions were not ruled out a priori as incompatible with the gospel (Ariarajah, 1991: 29). A unifying theme in Ariarajah's three points is the conference's belief that Christianity was the fulfilment of the world's religions. Combined with it was the certainty that, as Christianity progressed, other religions, cultures, and peoples would become visibly Christian. Eighteen years later, at the International Missionary Council Conference in Jerusalem, this certainty had evaporated under the combined pressure of the First World War, the rise of secularism and nationalism, and a world-wide religious renaissance in which anti-missionary sentiment was expressed. The concept of fulfilment, however, remained.

The International Missionary Council was formally constituted in 1921 and met for the first time on the Mount of Olives in 1928. It incorporated several advances over Edinburgh. First, rather than Edinburgh's many questionnaires and commissions, preliminary papers were prepared by experts to serve as springboards for more focussed discussion during the plenary sessions. Second, Jerusalem 1928 saw Christian missions touching on many areas of life including, but not limited to evangelism.[5] Last and

---

5 For example, the only Edinburgh volume not focussed specifically on traditional missionary activity was Volume VII (World Missionary Conference, 1910c). On the other hand, four of the seven Jerusalem 1928 volumes (International Missionary

most importantly, delegates from the "younger" churches increased greatly in number and made their presence known through significant contributions to the meeting.[6] Still, Jerusalem 1928 is rarely remembered for these improvements. It is more often recalled for the controversy surrounding the seven preparatory papers, which make up Part I of *The Christian Life and Message* (International Missionary Council 1928a: 3-338).

Prepared in advance of the meeting and not submitted to the Council for approval, the papers were under the direct supervision of J. H. Oldham. His desire to decrease the evangelistic fervour of Edinburgh and to focus instead on the positive values inherent in non-Christian religious experience and doctrine is evident in this excerpt from a letter written on February 19, 1927, to Martin Schlunk, one year prior to the meeting:

> What we propose is to ask ourselves, not in terms of *theological formulation or definition*, but in terms of the *interpretation of spiritual experience*, is what men live by and rely upon for support in the non Christian systems and secondly, what Christianity has to offer *in enrichment of and addition to the insights and help, which they attain from their own religious systems*. We are thus not raising a discussion as to what is and what is not important in Christianity, but are inviting the co-operation of Christians, whatever their individual views may be, *in a common effort to discover what respect the Christian faith transcends the best that other religious systems can offer.*
> (J. H. Oldham, cited in Hallencreutz, 1966: 170; emphasis mine)

From the papers themselves, it seems that Oldham's ideas were not clearly communicated to the contributors. Nicol Macnicol's submission on Hinduism, for instance remained firmly within the "fulfilment theology" of Edinburgh 1910.[7] J. Leighton Stuart's paper, however, pushed the limits of

---

Council, 1928b-1928e) moved beyond missionary problems. One centres on ecclesiology (1928b), while the rest relate missions to specifically secular areas of life.

6 According to William Paton: "The most important change by the Rättvik Committee in the Atlantic Committee proposals was in the decision to make the Jerusalem meeting representative in approximately equal numbers of the missionary organizations of the 'sending' countries, and of the Christian councils and missionary organizations on the mission field not less that two-thirds of the delegates from the latter religions being nationals of the countries they represented" (International Missionary Council, 1928f: 7-8).

7 Macnicol, for instance, writes: "The Christ whom we preach does not destroy any gracious and beautiful trait in the character of the Hindu, or deprive him of anything of which he is justly proud in his cultural inheritance. . . . If Hinduism will let Christ enter within its ancient walls, then it will be found that he is no stranger, but One who has sojourned there before, and who will find within it those who will recognize his Lordship and set Him upon its throne" (Macnicol, 1928: 11, 34).

"fulfilment."[8] Going yet further, K. J. Saunders hinted at an ineffable mystical core common to all religions.[9] The clear lack of agreement and direction among the authors left many participants alarmed and confused by the tone and contents of their papers.

In this light, it is ironic that the flash point for controversy was provided not by a paper dealing with a religion at all, but with secularism. On May 6, 1927, during a committee meeting in London, J. H. Oldham urged that greater attention be paid to the religious confrontation with secular civilization, proposing that secularism be treated as another non-Christian religion akin, for instance, to Hinduism or Buddhism. The committee agreed and assigned the preparatory paper to Charles Raven and Rufus Jones, although Jones alone finally composed the paper (Hallencreutz, 1966: 173). Jones's paper, "Secular Civilization and the Christian Task," argued that, while Christianity fulfilled the longings of secular culture, an interfaith alliance was necessary to oppose the creeping influence of secularism. Jones concluded his contribution with this challenge:

> Go to Jerusalem, then, not as members of a Christian nation to convert other nations which are not Christian, but as Christians within a nation far too largely non-Christian, who face within their own borders the competition of a rival movement as powerful . . . as any of the great historic religions. We meet our fellow Christians in these other countries in terms of equality, as fellow workers engaged in a common task. More than this, we go as those who find, in the other religions which secularism attacks as it attacks Christianity, witnesses of man's need of God and allies in our quest for perfection. (Jones, 1928: 338)

---

8 Stuart, for instance, writes: "We welcome all the spiritual intuition or ethical enthusiasm that may come through any of the world's great sages as part of the 'light that lighteth every man coming into the world.' [We seek to] blend the experience with any such racial heritage, believing that the resultant gain to all will be greater. . . . We gladly if humbly anticipate that the specific emphases of Oriental culture will bring fresh understanding of Him and help us correct or supplement our one incomplete appreciation of His transcending greatness" (Stuart, 1928: 62-3).

9 Saunders, for instance, writes: "Whatever our Christologies or our Buddhologies may be, the great fact remains that behind all religions there is Religion and the religious consciousness of man. The mystics are the experts who experience the truth by which the rest of us live. According to their upbringing and environment, they give the ineffable a local habitation and a name. But the missionary must get behind the names to the realities; and there is a growing recognition among such Buddhist scholars as D. T. Suzuki and such Christian scholars as Rudolf Otto that what the German mystic calls *Das Nichts* and the Upanishad seer, *Neti*, the Buddhist calls *Sunyata*: it is 'that from which the words turn back' " (Saunders, 1928: 128).

The strong reaction of European delegates to what they perceived to be the syncretistic tone of the preparatory papers threatened to scuttle the meeting before it began. Consequently, an emergency was convened in Cairo to resolve the situation.

William Paton, the International Missionary Council representative, remembered that the Cairo meeting gave those delegates whose first language was not English the opportunity to acquaint themselves with the contents of the preparatory papers. Kraemer, who acted as both secretary and interpreter for the meeting, assessed it differently. In his view, the German delegates were most concerned that the papers had failed to consider sufficiently the uniqueness of Christianity in its relation to other systems of thought and life. Other European delegates expressed similar concerns, though in more muted language. On the whole, however, the various delegates shared the desire "to see stated, in a more unequivocal way than seemed to be done by the papers, the fact that Christianity was a religion *sui generis* in the most pregnant sense of the word" (International Missionary Council, 1928a: 418). Finally, the Cairo meeting agreed on the following four points: first, that the concerns raised by the various delegates should be made known to the committee of the International Missionary Council; second, that this uneasiness about the syncretistic tone of the papers be presented to the council in written form; third, that the papers had not shed sufficient light on the essence of Christianity; and, fourth, that even the best elements in the non-Christian religions need to be "converted and regenerated" through an encounter with Jesus Christ (International Missionary Council, 1928a: 418-19).

At the opposite extreme, some American delegates were enthusiastic about the tone of the papers, and especially Jones's call for an interfaith alliance. These found a voice in the philosopher and mystic, William Ernest Hocking. He proposed "a form of hospitality to the experience and thought of other religions . . . which was demanded by the new situation in the world of thought to-day" (Hocking in International Missionary Council, 1928a: 369). This new situation brought about by the spread of "scientific materialism or naturalism [was] opposed to all religion . . . [and] required a new alignment of religious forces, a recognition of alliance with whatever was of the true substance of religion everywhere" (Hocking in International Missionary Council, 1928a: 369). He went on to speak somewhat cryptically of a "world religion," into which the religions would merge "in the universal human faith in the Divine Being" (Hocking in International Missionary Council, 1928a: 369). Finally, he suggested three reasons for Christian openness to other religions: Christianity must speak the language of other religions if it is going to be understood; Christianity, like other religions, is a product of particular historical events in specific cultures; and Christianity's conceptions of truth need to be enlarged (Hocking in International Missionary Council, 1928a: 370).[10]

Somewhere in between fell members of the British and Asian delegations. Representing the British, Edwyn Bevan emphasized not the uniqueness of Christianity, but the uniqueness of Christ, calling for Hindus, Jews and Christians alike to "bow to the Hebrew Jesus as the supreme Lord" (International Missionary Council, 1928a: 436). The Indian delegation also struck a more Christ-centred position embodied in the words of Pandipeddi Chenchiah: "The Hindu does not want a way of life, but life; not the preaching about Christ, but Christ. If you have Christ, pass him on" (International Missionary Council, 1928a: 361). The Chinese, on the other hand, saw Christianity as fulfilling Confucianism and combating secularism: according to Francis Wei, "Christianity is to fulfil Confucianism, not to destroy it" (International Missionary Council, 1928a: 358), while for T. C. Chao, "the battlefield of Christianity in China is not the realm of the non-Christian religions, but the realm of secularism" (International Missionary Council, 1928a: 358). For his part, Kraemer tried to set out the points shared by both extremes. First, God is the world's Creator and Redeemer and human beings, though sinful, are in relationship with him. Second, the world as God's creation, has been corrupted by sin, but will again become God's world. Third, Christianity was "the most paradoxical and the most matter-of-fact religion in this world. Paradoxical because it combined in real communion of life two opposites . . . the Holy Personal God and sinful man. . . . It was matter-of-fact because it took into account the stern facts of life: sin, pain, disappointment, and unrest" (International Missionary Council, 1928f: 348).

William Temple was presented with the daunting task of drafting the "Statement by the Council" in such a manner that it would be supported by all delegates. In *The Christian Message*, he ended up offering a twofold missionary approach. First, missions should call the "religious man" to fight against secularism and to study Christ—although not necessarily Christianity. Second, when approaching the "secular man," missions should acknowledge the values of secular culture, while seeking to expose its inadequacies and joining with other religions to oppose it. Temple also recognized the value of other religions, but in a manner that did not threaten the uniqueness of the Christian faith:

---

10 See also Hocking's "Psychological Conditions for Growth in Religious Faith" (International Missionary Council, 1928f: 138-61). For a full statement of Hocking's mystical philosophy of religion, see his Gifford Lectures, entitled *The Meaning of God in Human Experience: A Philosophic Study of Religion* (1912).

[W]e recognise as part of the one Truth that sense of the Majesty of God and the consequent reverence in worship, which are conspicuous in Islam; the deep sympathy for the world's sorrow and unselfish search for the way of escape, which are at the heart of Buddhism; the desire for contact with Ultimate Reality conceived as spiritual, which is promised in Hinduism, the belief in a moral order of the universe and consequent insistence on moral conduct which are inculcated in Confucianism; and the disinterested pursuit of truth and human welfare which are often found in those who stand for secular civilization, but do not accept Christ as their Lord and Saviour. (Temple in International Missionary Council, 1928f: 491)

That *The Christian Message* was accepted unanimously probably had more to do with Temple's political ability than a genuine bridging of the American/European gulf. It denied neither some value in other religions nor the uniqueness of the gospel and therefore was acceptable to those espousing either view.

With regard to the world religions, Jerusalem 1928 attempted to accommodate almost opposing points of view. Though not all were prepared to go to Hocking's extreme, American delegates spoke of values, fulfilment, and collaborations against secularism. On the other hand, European delegates eschewed the language of the preparatory papers— charging them with syncretism—and spoke instead of proclamation, conversion, and the sui generis character of the gospel. Not even Temple could reconcile the two positions. Indeed, the distinction between the two became more pronounced when the council met at Tambaram between December 12 and 29, 1938.

Tambaram 1938 incorporated two significant differences over the previous conferences, which both focused explicitly on Christian missions. Edinburgh 1910 attempted to articulate what missions were and Jerusalem 1928 attempted to discern the relationship between missions and other areas. From the planning stages, it was determined that Tambaram should take a wider perspective and consider the relationship between the Church and the world, as reflected by the titles of the six discussion themes: the authority of the faith; the growing Church; evangelism; the life of the Church; the economic basis of the Church; and the Church and the state. Carl Hallencreutz attributes this shift from missions to Church primarily to the publication of *Re-Thinking Missions: A Layman's Inquiry After One Hundred Years* (Hocking, ed., 1932), a critical restatement of the American position expressed at Jerusalem. Two other factors were the rise of nationalism especially in Germany and Italy and the growth of Barthian and biblical theologies (Hallencreutz, 1966: 257-60). All three factors forced the council to consider the role not only of missions but also of the Christian Church in relation to all spheres of life. This time, instead of a number of preliminary papers, the planning committee opted for the work of one author on one specific issue. They then commissioned Hendrik Kraemer to "state the fundamental position of the Christian Church as a witness bearing body in the modern world . . . and to deal in detail with the evangelistic approach to the great non-Christian religions" (Kraemer, 1938: v). During the early stages, J. R. Mott and William Paton were of particular importance in shaping what would become *The Christian Message*.

Mott, while completing the arrangements of Kraemer's appointment, suggested he go to the United States in order to become better acquainted with American missiological thought. There, Kraemer experienced the aftermath of *Re-Thinking Missions* first-hand and concluded that American missiology was in danger of being compromised by relativism, pragmatism, and subjectivistic idealism.[11] Paton, on the other hand, was a constant source of encouragement: "This involved finding a salary for Kraemer while he wrote [*The Christian Message*] and taking the decision to permit him to write double the amount commissioned, which meant that someone (Nicol Macnicol) had to be found to produce a summary of it, and to help Kraemer write in readable English" (Jackson, 1980: 85). Although it was intended to be just one of several contributions to Tambaram 1938, Kraemer's work, because of its size and quality, became the centre of debate.

This is not to say that Kraemer's contribution was the sole source of controversy. Because of discord, first, between the Chinese and Japanese

---

11 Kraemer recalled that: "In America, which takes a large share in the world-wide missionary enterprise at home and abroad, the scene is much more confusing. The relativistic spirit of a Christianity which in the case of thousands of people is all too much assimilated to a humanistic conception of life undermines the missionary understanding of Christianity. If it were not for the fact that the American temperament, for natural and historical reasons, is youthfully aggressive and prone to a crusading type of idealism, the missionary temperament in the Churches of America would be still lower than it is. To be sure, there is to be observed a turning away from the roads of subjectivistic idealism and an expectant returning to the bed-rock verities of historic Christianity. The rank and file in the Churches, however, are wholly at sea about the Christian faith and the Christian obligation in the world. An all-pervading pragmatist attitude, which naively takes the practically demonstrated value of a certain attitude in life as the standard of reference for truth, naturally causes a very diluted conception of what religion and Christianity really are. This is the more easily so because the religious and moral quality of life of many of those who think in this line is strikingly pure and novel and is still emotionally centred around the Personality of Jesus Christ. However, if there should not occur in the future a real re-discovery of Biblical Christianity, the next generation will lack this emotional connection with the realm of Christian faith and worship, and become definitely unchristian and anti-christian." (1938: 46-7)

delegations and, second, between both them and the British, the proposed site for the meeting was moved in 1935 from Kowloon to Hangchow, China. Two years later, as a result of Sino-Japanese conflict, this site was abandoned for Tambaram, India (Jackson, 1980: 148-49). As late as May 1938, the German delegation sought a postponement or cancellation because of European crises (Jackson, 1980: 149). Nevertheless, the controversy aroused by Kraemer seems to be the only one left unresolved by the conclusion of the meeting. One of its participants later recalled that: "within the fellowship of the meeting, the very real tensions among the conference members—Chinese and Japanese, British and Indian, South African whites and South African blacks, Germans and other continental Europeans—were transcended by the common purpose" of emphasising the universality of the Church (Visser't Hooft, 1973: 59). Nevertheless, he continued: "The conference was less successful in dealing with the basic theological conflict for which Hendrik Kraemer's book . . . provided the focus" (1973: 59).[12] For better or worse, the debate aroused by Kraemer's book had forced the whole missionary movement to examine again its basic assumptions—a fact to which all participants agreed.[13]

Tambaram 1938 is rightly interpreted as attempting to put mission theology back on its rails after Jerusalem 1928 (Ariarajah, 1991: 85). In the aftermath of the European/American division, *Re-Thinking Missions*, and the very intense political climate, a clear statement of the Christian faith and a convincing apologetic for missions and evangelism were necessary. This is what Kraemer was asked to, and did, provide: he was "in a strong position to do this for no one could accuse him of failing to study. This had started at Cairo. . . [and had] continued in the same way in Central Java, in Bali, among the Bataks in Sumatra and in India" (Visser't Hooft, 1974: 58-9).

---

12 Visser't Hooft's assessment is widely shared. For instance, according to another delegate, "This proved to be the only theological issue upon which the conference did not achieve unanimity". (Van Dusen, 1948: 193).

13 The concluding statement, endorsed unanimously, reads in part: "There are many non-Christian religions that claim the allegiance of the multitudes. We see and readily recognize that in them are to be found Values of deep religious experience, and great moral achievements. Yet we are bold enough to call men out from them to the feet of Christ. We do so because we believe that in Him alone is the full salvation which man needs. . . . Everywhere and at all times [God] has been seeking to disclose Himself to men. He has not left Himself without witness in the world. Furthermore, men have been seeking Him all through the ages. Often this seeking and longing has been misdirected, but there are evidences that His yearning after His children has not been without response. . . . As to whether the non-Christian religions as total systems of thought and life may be regarded as in some sense or to some degree manifesting God's revelation Christians are not agreed. This is a matter urgently demanding thought and united study" (International Missionary Council, 1939: 194).

Kraemer's Context   45

Indeed, none of Kraemer's opponents accused him of misrepresenting or misunderstanding non-Christian religions—although such accusations did come in later years. Rather, as will be seen in the following chapter, the controversy revolved around the presuppositions upon which his argument was based.

3. Kraemer's Theological Development

An unfortunate result of the failure to consider Kraemer's work from within his particular context is that he is often equated with Barth regarding the theology of religions.[14] Before Kraemer's position can be examined, therefore, I must situate him theologically.

Pierre Daniël Chantepie de la Saussaye and W. Brede Kristensen were major figures in Kraemer's early development. Chantepie's phenomenology of religions resembled that of C. P. Tiele, the first professor of comparative religion at Leiden. Although he was a member of the theological faculty, he wanted to avoid a Christian theological interpretation of religion. In his Gifford Lectures, Tiele proposed instead a two-tier approach, the foundation of which was the comprehension of religion in its cultural and historical manifestations (Tiele, 1897: 8). This evolutionary analysis posited the ethical consciousness, as opposed to theological categories, as the criterion by which other religions were to be judged (Tiele, 1897: 58-149). From there, he moved to a metaphysical inquiry into the nature of religion itself (Tiele, 1899). Like Tiele, Chantepie sought to avoid theological evaluations of the various aspects of faith and life under consideration. He argued that theology had a different object in view. George Alfred James summarizes the two-tier approach: "On the one hand, the a-theological trait is expressed in an acknowledgement that, as such, the inquiry does not and cannot meet the qualifications of a genuine theological inquiry. On the other hand it is expressed in the effort to preserve the integrity of the study of the object from the encroachment of the theological agenda" (James, 1995: 57). Chantepie also broke sharply with scholarly consensus at the time that insisted that Christianity represented the highest form of religion along an evolutionary scale: "[h]e proceeds systematically from the religious object to the religious subject without reference to any inherent chronology or advancement among the phenomena" (James, 1995: 81).

In 1901, W. Brede Kristensen, then newly appointed Chair of History and Phenomenology of Religion, delivered his inaugural lecture in which he set out his approach to the study of religions. Like Chantepie, he opposed

---

14 See, for example, Knitter (1985: 82, 11, 138); Dupuis (1989:105-6, 109); Pinnock (1993: 108).

any evolutionary grading of religions, insisting that this rendered any kind of sympathetic understanding of a religion impossible. Religious evolutionary theory insisted that religions could be graded from lower to higher in terms of value and could progress or regress along this continuum as they developed in history. The problem with this approach, rightly perceived by Kristensen, is that different interpreters could apply different criteria when ranking religions as "lower" or "higher." Also, every evolutionist presupposed his or her own position at the highest rung of the evolutionary ladder. Kristensen adamantly asserted that to investigate religions in this way was highly prejudicial and proposed instead a totalitarian (i.e., holistic) approach which spoke not of religion as a genus, but of religions as complex, indivisible unities. James observes that: "While theology inquires after the knowledge of God given by revelation, Kristensen inquires into the religious value the believers attach or have attached to their faith, what their religion meant for them" (James, 1995: 158). Kristensen's interest lay in understanding a religion's specific beliefs and practices in their relationship to the social and cultural whole.

Kraemer follows his teachers in his phenomenological treatment of the religions as total systems of thought and life. Any sympathetic understanding of a religious belief or practice explores its relationship to the religio-cultural matrix in which it arises rather than according to some evolutionary model, which is itself historically and culturally situated. While Kraemer is not as skeptical about the value of a theological interpretation of religions as either Chantepie or Kristensen, he also follows them in refusing to confuse phenomenological and theological studies. These two presuppositions—the holistic approach to religions and the distinct nature of theology of religions—underlie *The Christian Message* and became the sources of controversy at the Tambaram Meeting. They are diametrically opposed to those who confuse phenomenological and theological studies by regarding the religions as stages culminating in Christianity or in some other "essence of religion." Furthermore, as has been demonstrated, these presuppositions are not rooted—as some commentators infer—in Barth's *Church Dogmatics*, but in Dutch phenomenology of religion, particularly as it developed at Leiden University, prior to and during Kraemer's tenure.

When Kraemer arrived in Indonesia, he retained an optimism inherited from the Dutch ethical theology of J. H. Gunning and Nicolaus Adriani. Prior to the First World War, ethical theology assumed that Asian and African religions, as part of a greater social collapse, would disintegrate. In the light of this assumption, it conceived Christian missions as renewing whole cultures according to Christian principles. It further located the uniqueness of Christianity in conversion—humanity's experience of "new divine life powers" given by God though Jesus Christ (Jathanna, 1981: 64). Kraemer followed his early mentors in emphasising conversion and predicting the demise of other religions. Yet, Kraemer's mature position bore no resemblance to the optimistic appraisal of the early 1920s. His emphasis on conversion remained, but instead of "divine life powers," Kraemer spoke of recognition of what God had done for humanity in Jesus Christ (1938: 45). In addition, he relinquished any idea of the future disintegration of other religions; in his opinion, religious plurality would persist until the consummation of history (1956b: 366-76). In the light of both factors, Kraemer regarded indigenous expressions of Christianity as vital (1960, 1962). This reversal emanated from his experience of the Islamic renaissance in Indonesia.

Contrary to expectations, Kraemer did not find Islam disintegrating before the advance of Western technology and values. In fact, quite the opposite was taking place: Islam was growing rapidly and finding expression in such organizations as the radical nationalist party, Sarekat Islam, and the anti-missionary organization, Muhammadijah.[15] Attendance at the pan-Islamic conferences at Cheribon in 1922 and Garaut two years later confirmed Kraemer's suspicions that, while some of the nationalists may have been using Islam as a means to end colonialism, the religion was especially healthy (Hallencreutz, 1966: 130-6). He therefore began to emphasize he importance of indigenous expressions of Christianity. Although the mission agencies were bound to educate and strengthen indigenous congregations, Kraemer held that the responsibility for the dialogue with Islam and the conversion of Indonesian Muslims lay not with Dutch missionaries but with Indonesian Christians (Hallencreutz, 1966: 144).

Perhaps the most frustrating aspect of Kraemer's theological context relates to scholars linking him to dialectical theology and, specifically, to Karl Barth.[16] This linking is not new, being first employed immediately after Tambaram (Hogg, 1939: 102-25). Whether developed by contemporary scholarship or by Kraemer's contemporaries, the criticism of Kraemer as a Barthian, as I have shown above, disregards the fact that the skeleton of his mature position was in place prior to his first encounter with Barth in 1929. Carl Hallencreutz has countered that Kraemer should be understood against his missionary background, and that Barth should be relegated to a position of minimal influence (1966: 99). This, it seems to me, runs to the other extreme. Instead I propose a median position based on Kraemer's writings.

---

15 For a detailed analysis of these and other Islamic organizations in Indonesia in the early twentieth century, see Hallencreutz, 1996: 21-121.
16 Some contemporary examples of this strategy were cited in n. 14, above.

Kraemer wrestles with the Swiss giant in both early and later works. In *The Christian Message*, Kraemer praises Barth's theology as an attempt to set forth the uniqueness of Christ—although not necessarily Christianity—with clarity in a hostile atmosphere (1938: 115-6). He is not, however, completely uncritical. For Kraemer, Barth's refusal to discuss how God works in other religions "savours too much of theological and logical consistency and breathes not sufficiently the free atmosphere of Biblical realism. This self-willed refusal to move further," he declares, "will in the long run appear to be untenable" (1938: 120). To Barth's declaration, "There is no point of contact between Christianity and other religions," Kraemer counters that "the fact that faith in God's revelation occurs presupposes that it can be communicated to man and apprehended by him as revelation coming from God" (1938: 131).[17] This sympathetic criticism continues in *Religion and the Christian Faith* where Kraemer distances himself from both Barth and Emil Brunner. On the subject of Christianity and other religions Kraemer is closer to Brunner's position, which, in his view, deals very well with religions in their concrete manifestations, rather than speaking of an abstract "essence of Religion" (1956b: 185).[18] Yet, notwithstanding his persuasive arguments and appeals to scripture, Kraemer is reluctant to side with Brunner because of the latter's defence of natural theology. On the other hand, while Barth rightly rejects the classical concepts of general revelation and natural theology, Kraemer believes he goes too far. Specifically, Kraemer rejects Barth's contention that "accepting the self-disclosure of God in the past, the present and the future, through nature, history and conscience, which is clearly taught by Paul in Romans 1 and 2, must mean accepting the current concepts of General Revelation and Natural Theology" (Kraemer, 1956b: 357). He concludes:

> *Christomonismus* is a horrible word, but one must judge discriminatingly what Barth does and does not say. If Barth says— and he does—that the Bible knows no other mode of revelation than Christ, he has the Bible against him. If he says that all modes of revelation find their source, their meaning and criterion in Jesus Christ, and that the revelation of God's righteousness in Christ is the final revelation in the light of which Jesus Christ is the Truth, the *only* Truth, without whom no man comes to the Father—then he is quite right and we ought all to be *Christomonists*. (Kraemer, 1956b: 158-59)

---

17 See also Brunner and Barth (1946).
18 See also Brunner (1947: 218-71).

In a review written for *Theology Today*, Kraemer expresses his admiration for and distance from Barth: "it ought to be an obligation on everyone who claims to be a theologian to seek an encounter with Barth's theology, not in order to become a 'Barthian', but in order to learn in our twentieth century what it means to be a theologian" (1956a: 398). On Kraemer's own list of influences, Barth ranks only fifth: "The only ones to whom I know myself to be deeply indebted as far as theological thinking is concerned are Paul, Pascal, Kierkegaard and also, although in a lesser way, Blumhardt and Barth."[19] These examples clearly illustrate the simplistic nature of the solutions of those who either equate or sunder Kraemer and Barth. They were quareling brothers in the Reformed family. Kraemer was a theological ally who was neither a clone nor completely independent of Barth.

My analysis has provided a general theological context within which Kraemer's ideas developed. Yet, without the influence of Hocking's *Re-Thinking Missions*, Kraemer could not have written *The Christian Message*. Much of the work is practical in nature and reflects the insights of a number of important American missionaries. My focus on is the transcendental idealism found in the opening four chapters of the book—drafted by Hocking alone—under the heading, "General Principles." In these chapters, Hocking outlines three factors that he believes all religions share: namely, a common mystical core, search for truth, and uniqueness.

Hocking defends his first factor by stating that: "if there were not at the core of all creeds a nucleus of religious truth, neither Christianity nor any other faith would have anything to build on" (1932: 37). He was convinced that within the religious life of every culture, at the core of the beliefs and rites—many of which are vulgar and superstitious—lay the religious intuition of the human soul. Further, the God of this common intuition is the true God. Therefore, he averred: "universal religion has not to be established, it exists" (1932: 37). This starting point leads Hocking to affirm belief in a common search by all religions for truth. Accordingly, missionary activity should continue but, instead of seeking converts, the missionary should look for opportunities for inter-religious inspiration and improvement. Hocking urged the missionary to "look forward not to the destruction of these religions, but to their continued co-existence with Christianity, each stimulating the other in growth toward the ultimate goal, unity in the completest [sic] religious truth" (1932: 44). These two factors logically require Hocking to present a new understanding of the uniqueness

---

19 Hendrik Kraemer, (1942) "Theologie en het kerlijk vraagstuk," in *Onder eigen vaandel*: 17, 17 (cited and translated in Garon, 1979: 43).

of Christianity. For him, Christianity is unique in its interpretation and expression of the "inalienable religious intuition." He writes:

> In respect to its theology and ethics, Christianity has many doctrines in common with other religions, yet no other religion has the same group of doctrines. . . . [What] is true belongs, in its nature, to the human mind everywhere. . . . From this treasury of thought, however, Christianity proffers a selection which is unique. The principle of selection is its own peculiar character: its individuality lies in the way in which it assembles these truths, and leads them to clarity, certainty, exemplification and therefore power. Its features, like the features of a person, are unmistakably its own. (1932: 49)

This is to say that, while Christianity may overlap with other religions at many points of belief and practice, its peculiar selection and arrangement of these is unique. Hocking extends this uniqueness from theology and ethics to embrace symbolism and history. "The uniqueness of Christianity does not consist solely in its interpretation of religious truth. It consists also, perhaps chiefly, in those things which make religion different from philosophy . . . its symbolism, its observances, its historical fellowship, and especially the personal figure to whom it points . . . as its highest expression of the religious life" (1932: 51). Therefore, for Hocking, Christianity is unique just as every historically and culturally embedded expression of the essence of religion is unique.

For Kraemer, Hocking's transcendental idealism combined an admirable devotion to missions as a Christian responsibility and an incredibly underdeveloped sense "apostolic consciousness" (1938: 36). Kraemer regarded it as relativism masked by the language of tolerance, which failed to take the Christian obligation to proclaim the gospel seriously. In *Religion and the Christian Faith*, Kraemer recalls this objection bluntly:

> The point of view advocated by *Re-Thinking Missions* and its chairman [Hocking] is devoid of any real theological sense and is, though intended to be the contrary, a total distortion of the Christian message, its content and real meaning. Religion and Christianity are simply reduced to immanent cultural phenomena. Nowhere is that maintained. Nor is the case stated in this way, because none of the writers had that in mind. In fact, however, the whole argument amounts to that. Its consequence is a suicide of missions and an annulment of the Christian faith. . . . With the bombshell of this Report in my mind my book *The Christian Message in a Non-Christian World* was written, and acted, at least

for a great part of the American missionary world, as another bombshell. (1956b: 223-4)

On the basis of these words, one can conclude that, in part, *The Christian Message* was Kraemer's attempt to exorcise what he perceived to be Hocking's theological demons. Ariarajah reports that Bishop Sabapathy Kulandran, although he disagreed with Kraemer at a fundamental level, felt that Hocking had "proposed with sardonic frankness the question whether [the Christian Church] had anything left to preach." In this light, the bishop considered Kraemer's work to be both necessary and beneficial.

> What Kraemer did was to seize hold of the main idea of the book with both hands and throttle it to death. Its ghost still occasionally haunts the theological field here and there. But as a full-blooded and serious figure to be reckoned with it certainly died with the appearance of Kraemer's book. . . . It is this punitive aspect of Kraemer's book that made the deepest impression on people. It was not that there was no constructive aspect, but once the chief item in the show was over, whether people stayed through the rest of the programme or not they paid little attention to it. [20]

Unfortunately it is this punitive aspect of which Kulandran spoke that is most often the only aspect of Kraemer's work to be remembered and, regrettably, even these memories are faulty.

This chapter is a step toward correcting this imbalance. I have presented Kraemer, the lay missionary and theologian, surveyed his life and works, and placed him in his historical and theological contexts. I have shown how Kraemer's thought was influenced by a number of factors, including but not limited to Karl Barth, and have concluded that either to herald or to dismiss Kraemer as a Barthian is unfair. I now wrestle directly with Kraemer's theology of religions.

---

20 Sabapathy Kulandran, "The Renaissance of Non-Christian Religions and a Definition of Approach to Non-Christians," mimeographed paper presented to *The Study on the Word of God and Men of Other Faiths* (WCC Archives, Box 26.32.19), 26 (cited in Ariarajah: 1991, 86).

4

KRAEMER'S THEOLOGY OF RELIGIONS

This chapter analyzes Kraemer's theology of religions through his three major works. *The Christian Message in a Non-Christian World* (1938) was Kraemer's first attempt at a theology of religions. "Continuity or Discontinuity" (1939), his contribution to the post-Tambaram documents, was his response to the initial criticism directed against the earlier work. Finally, *Religion and the Christian Faith* (1956b) represents his most sustained and thought-out presentation.[1] This analysis is the final preparation for Part Two—a defence of this position.

1. The Early Work

Kraemer opens *The Christian Message* with a description of two interrelated crises. The first is global, caused in the West first by the collapse of the quest for certainty and the growth of relativism and second, by the rise of the "pseudo-absolutes" of communism, fascism and national socialism (1938: 11-6). The loss of belief in the possibility of truth to the notion that all systems of thought are but projections of the mind had paved the way in Europe for totalitarian governments that sought to force on their citizens their visions of the world by whatever means necessary. Regardless of their ostensible power, however, Kraemer felt that these systems were "to be compared with Baron von Munchausen's endeavor to draw himself by his own hair out of the swamp in which he is sunk" (1938: 11). In the East, Kraemer believed that a similar crisis had been triggered by colonialism and the promulgation of Western technology and values, which had destroyed many political, social, economic, and cultural structures. While technological ingenuity had enabled Western nations to dominate others in many ways, Kraemer wondered whether the creators had become the servants and victims of their own inventions (1938: 17-8). Ironically however, colonialism had also produced a worldwide religious and cultural

---

[1] As mentioned in the first chapter, these are not his only writings. Nevertheless, because of their timing in Kraemer's career, they serve as important organizers of his thought. Other works will be cited when appropriate.

renaissance, one in which Kraemer felt once geographically limited religions had expanded to become truly global phenomena.[2] For Kraemer, it was this global situation that had provoked the identity crisis in the Christian churches.

Philosophical relativism, totalitarian regimes and the resurgence of non-Christian religions prompted Kraemer to raise the troubling question: "What is the Church's 'relation to the world and all its spheres of life . . . '?" (1938: 30). This question was especially acute for Kraemer in the missions, where he felt that the Church must forsake the colonial assumption of Western moral and religious superiority and instead proclaim its message within a deliberate encounter with other faiths. In Kraemer's analysis, non-Christian religions, which seemed to be undergoing a renewal, could no longer be treated as objects of study, but must by recognized by Christians as helping to shape the spiritual life of the human race, as they impinged on the development of Christian belief and practice (1938: 38). Moreover, for Kraemer, the responsibility for this encounter could no longer rest solely with Western churches, but also with Asian and African ones. Indeed, Kraemer regarded Eurocentrism as past or passing; the future of the Christian Church, for him, would be written "in the life-books of Africa and Asia, and these new chapters will be of decisive importance for the life and development of the Christian Church in its older domains" (1938: 39).

Kraemer was certain that the answer to his pressing question, if there was one, would be found not in assumptions of the superiority of Western culture but, rather, in the foundation common to all Christians: "Therefore, to the Bible we will turn, because there the witness of the prophets and the apostles is to be found on which the Church is built" (1938: 61-2). For this basis, Kraemer is unapologetic. For him, biblically grounded Christian faith is irreducible to the canons of coherence or rationality, not because it is in some way incoherent or irrational, but because it has its own internal coherence and rationality (1938: 64). He did not advocate an uncritical reading of the scriptures, for Kraemer noted that the severe testing to which Christian scriptures, beliefs, and practices had been both necessary and beneficial, preparing Christians for the oncoming interreligious encounter

---

[2] Toward the end of his life, Kraemer confirmed his early assessment when he wrote: "The lightning-like change of a great part of Asia from the status of being colonies of Western powers to the status of political independence and sovereignty is a fact of cataclysmic importance. . . . Until World War II . . . [it] had no power, influence or voice in its own right. . . . Since the great landslide toward independence broke loose in 1947 with the independence of India, this has radically altered. Notwithstanding the central place of the U.S.A. in world affairs, it is possible to defend the thesis that the world has not shifted from Europe-centredness to America-centredness, but to Asia and Africa-centredness" (1966: 236).

(1938: 62-3). For Kraemer, for a Christian to begin from a position other than the Bible was, whether deliberate or not, to begin from a position outside the Christian Church; further, to do so was to force Christian faith on to the Procrustean bed of an alien philosophy. Instead, Kraemer offers biblical realism—his "fundamental starting-point and criterion of all Christian and theological thinking" (1938: 66)—as the only adequate point of departure when discerning the relationship between Church and world.

Kraemer's biblical realism, in turn, presupposed a peculiar concept of revelation, one that eschewed both the liberal Protestant conception of revelation as immediate inner experience of the divine and the conservative Protestant and Catholic idea of revelation as propositional communication. Instead, Kraemer understood revelation as an event or encounter in which God's essence is revealed to be inaccessible and the human religious imagination is exposed as idolatrous, declaring that revelation is "what is by its nature inaccessible and *remains so even when it is revealed*" (1938: 69, emphasis his). These encounters, recorded in the Bible, reach their climax in the incarnation. "Nowhere is the genuine meaning of revelation maintained so consistently.... God was truly revealed in Jesus Christ, but at the same time He hid and disguised Himself in the man Jesus Christ. The universal revulsion from and protest against the Incarnation at all times is a clear indication of how completely hidden God's revelation remains from the eye of natural man" (1938: 70). This reaction against the incarnation, for Kraemer, exposed the deepest of human instincts—the desire to be God. Revelation above all, however, is not about the mystery of God's essence or the idolatry of the human imagination for Kraemer; rather it is about the proclamation of God's will and acts to restore human beings and the world. It is always and everywhere "a tale about 'the wonderful things God has done' (Acts II.ii) which remain 'wonderful' and incomprehensible despite their being told" (1938: 30).

Kraemer's Christocentrism was, nevertheless, not monolithic. The reality of the incarnation may be described in various ways because of the inexhaustible wealth of images and metaphors contained in the gospel. In the Johannine account, for example, the incarnation is an unthinkable and mysterious act in which God makes himself known as the One who loves, redeems, and restores the world. Kraemer noted especially that the world, which includes the human race, is of such value to God that he surrenders himself in Christ to death on the Cross (1938: 74). The Pauline doctrine of justification by faith declares that God in Christ opened a way of reconciliation where there was no way: for Kraemer, "Christ must be called the crisis of all religions and philosophies [for to do so exposes humanity's] wilful maintenance of self in the face of God [and counters that] God Himself can only make possible the impossible by His sovereign, creative act of salvation in Jesus Christ" (1938: 76). In the synoptic proclamation of God's Kingdom, biblical realism reminds that human beings cannot create the ideal society, but that "God has begun in Jesus Christ a new divine order of life, of which Christ is the centre and the head" (1938: 77). People called to this new way of life, described by Kraemer as the way of the cross, relinquish all self-assertion: "It is the way of the 'obedience of faith' and fellowship with Christ, of joy and of service, of living by divine forgiveness and therefore loving God and loving men" (1938: 77-8). And yet, while there is indeed variety, in each of the portrayals, the initiative of God in salvation is stressed as the heart of the *"radical religious realism of the Bible"* (1938: 82, emphasis his). Kraemer noted that although the biblical authors display "many varying, individual accents, [the] Christ they proclaim is always the incarnate Son of God, whose life and work meant the execution of God's plan of salvation. . . . The Holy Spirit to whom they testify is always the creator and sustainer of the new life in Christ, and the guarantee of God's dealing with those who are new creatures in Christ" (1938: 84-5). This, concluded Kraemer, was the only way to express adequately the radical difference of the religion of biblical realism (Kraemer's Christianity) from all the other spheres of life.

Kraemer wanted to express the relationship of the Christian Church to the world in which it is found from the openly confessional perspective of biblical realism (1938: 103). In contemporary terms, Kraemer's theology of religions occurs not as a sub-doctrine of fundamental theology but of ecclesiology. He hoped to safeguard the importance of Christian missions by stressing the apostolic nature of the Church.[3] For Kraemer, Christianity existed only through the proclamation of the message of the Bible, while maintaining a positive attitude toward non-Christian religions and stressing God's presence in all creation:

> whether the attitude is one of renunciation, of reserve or of intimate relation, it has to be essentially a *positive* attitude, because the world remains the domain of God who created it. After its rebellion against Him, He did not let it go but held it fast in His new initiative of reconciliation. It must be a positive attitude also because the Christian Church, as the witness to and representative of the new order of salvation and reconciliation, has been set by God *in* this world in order to be and work for the sake of this world. Jesus taught us to pray, 'God's will be done on earth as it is

---

3 He later added that the Christian message "is not a message about which the hearers have the right to decide whether it should be communicated or not. . . . It must be communicated because it issues from the consciousness that is the Word of the Lord of the Universe" (1957: 22).

> in heaven,' and this petition will always be the Magna Charta [sic] of the Church's obligation to occupy itself strenuously and positively with the world and its spheres of life, including the non-Christian religions. (1938: 104)

By combining a thoroughly apostolic consciousness of the Church's mission with an equally profound appreciation that God remains committed to the world and its religions, Kraemer underscored "the dialectical relation in which Christianity, if true to its nature and mission, ought to stand to the world—the combination of a fierce 'yes' and at the same time a fierce 'no' to the world: the *human* and *broken* reflection of the divine 'no' and 'yes' of the holy God of reconciliation who held the world under His absolute judgment and at the same time claimed it for His love" (1938: 104). Furthermore, in so doing Kraemer wishes to avoid arguments attempting to prove the superior value of a religion.

Such proofs flounder, for all religions can give detailed, impressive accounts of "psychological, cultural and other values, and it is wholly dependent on one's fundamental axioms of life whether one considers these non-Christian achievements of higher value for mankind than the Christian" (1938: 106). By framing theology of religions within ecclesiology, Kraemer sought entirely to bypass the discussion of religious values. Focussing instead on the relationship between the Church and the world, he orients his work around that which separates the Church from the world, that which he "claimed to be the standard of reference for all truth and all religion [namely] the faith that God has revealed *the* Way and *the* Life and *the* Truth in Jesus Christ and wills this to be known to all the world" (1938: 106-7). Thus Kraemer's attitude toward other religions is to be seen within the broader framework of the doctrine of the Church and, specifically, the relationship of the Church to the world. Kraemer insisted that for a Christian, the only vantage point enabling a legitimate evaluation both of non-Christian religions and what he called empirical Christianity is that of biblical realism, and its climax, the revelation of God in Christ. Further, Kraemer eschewed all feelings of superiority: "A missionary or a Christian who harbours the tiniest spark of spiritual arrogance and boasts of 'his' superiority by being a Christian and 'having' the truth grieves the Spirit of Christ and obscures his message" (1938: 110-1). From the foundation of these three major points, Kraemer attempted to answer the question, "Does God—and if so, how and where does God—reveal Himself in the religious life as present in the non-Christian religions?" (1938: 111).

Borrowing from Kristensen, Kraemer began by asserting that all philosophies and world views reflect the various human efforts to understand humanity and its place in the universe. In Kraemer's words, the totality of existence was one in which every theology or a/theology "is an effort to reflect in a system of coherent thinking the religious apprehension of existence" (1938: 111). Although they may at times share hopes, beliefs, practices, and institutions—these cannot be distilled into Hocking's essence of religion. On the contrary, he insisted that phenomenological inquiries into the various religions has demonstrated clearly that there is no natural religion, but only a universal religious consciousness which has produced various concrete religions, each fundamentally different from the rest: "there is no 'natural' religion . . . there are religions, each with its peculiar structure and character" (1938: 112). He continues by interpreting this holistic view of religions theologically; humans, he wrote, are "dual beings": of divine origin, but corrupted by sin (1938: 112). The divine origin, the root of all religious creativity, is evident "in the lofty religions and the ethical systems that [humans have] produced and tried to live by" (1938: 113). At the same time, Kraemer believed that even the most sublime religious achievements are tainted by sin. As a result, every religion—Christianity included—is a record of great achievements and terrible wickedness.

Against these rival apprehensions of the totality of existence stands the Christian revelation. Echoing the early Barth, Kraemer contended that revelation is "an act of God, an act of divine grace for forlorn man and a forlorn world by which he condescends to reveal His Will and His Heart" (1938: 118). As a result, general revelation—the notion that God makes himself known in compelling ways in nature, history, and reason—is self-contradictory, "for what lies on the street has no need to be revealed. By its nature revelation is and must be special" (1938: 119). While Barth was content to stop here, however, Kraemer wants to take the issue further.

The emphasis on the unsurpassable nature of the revelation of God in Christ cannot be employed prematurely to end reflection on the relationship of the Church to the world and its religions. Insofar as Barth does just this, he surrenders biblical realism to "sterile intellectualism" (1938: 120). While, for Kraemer, the revelation of God in Christ is sui generis—in a class by itself—the world remains the creation of God:

> "who does not abandon the work of His hands," but continues working in it. . . . Even in this fallen world God shines though in a broken, troubled way: in reason, in nature and history. Otherwise the urge for truth, beauty, goodness and holiness stirring in science, philosophy, art, religion are incomprehensible. The community of the believers in Christ belongs to this world and lives and works in it, and even for the sake of self-comprehension

> it needs light on the subject of this world as it is and its relation to God. (1938: 120-21)

Therefore, for Kraemer, the universally observed religious consciousness of human beings, along with the systems of thought and life it has produced, cannot be dismissed as outside discussion a priori. Kraemer asserted that John Calvin's *sensus divinitatis*[4] and Emil Brunner's natural theology[5] affirm the uniqueness of the revelation in Christ, while speaking about the world and its religions "in a deeper, more realistic, freer way" than does Barth (1938: 121). In their analysis, one can rejoice over "every evidence of divine working and revelation that may be found in the non-Christian world [while maintaining that these are not] of the same sort and quality as the revelation in Jesus Christ" (1938: 122).

Unlike Barth, Kraemer did not reject terms such as "general revelation" and "natural theology." He redefined them so that general revelation was characterized as follows:

> General revelation can henceforth only mean that God shines revealingly through the works of His creation (nature), through the thirst and quest for truth and beauty, through the conscience and the thirst and quest for goodness, which throbs in every man in his condition of forlorn sinfulness, because God is continuously occupying Himself and wrestling with man, in all ages and with all peoples. (1938: 125)

Thus recast, general revelation is not a foundation—whether of information or religious experience—to be completed by the revelation of God in Christ, the continuous disclosure of God's self to the world. Kraemer also recharacterized natural theology:

---

[4] Calvin writes: "There is within the human mind, and indeed by natural instinct, an awareness of divinity [*Divinitatis sensum*]. . . . To prevent anyone from taking refuge in the pretense of ignorance, God himself has implanted in all men a certain understanding of his divine majesty. . . . Men of sound judgment will always be sure that a sense of divinity that can never be effaced is engraved upon men's minds." Calvin hastens to add, however, that "proud vanity and obstinacy, and carnal stupidity" have corrupted this "seed of religion" Human beings "do not therefore apprehend God as he offers himself, but imagine him as they have fashioned him in their own presumptions."(1960: 43-47)

[5] Brunner writes: "Man is a culpable sinner because he rejects the revelation in the creation which God gives him; because he 'holds down the primal truth in unrighteousness'; and because, in his madness, he transforms that which the Creator reveals into the form of idols. Of himself, he can no more perceive this sin than, as a result of sin, he can truly know the revelation in the Creation. It is only through the historical revelation that man comes to perceive both the revelation in the Creation and his sin, which, for this reason, is without excuse" (1947: 77-80).

> The function of natural theology will henceforth be, not to construe preparatory stages and draw unbroken, continuous lines of religious development ending and reaching their surmount in Christ, but in the light of the Christian revelation to lay bare the dialectical condition not only of the non-Christian religions but of all the human attempts toward the apprehension of the totality of existence. Or, to put it differently, to uncover in the light of the revelation of Christ the different modes of God-, self-, and world-consciousness of man in his religious life. (1938: 125)

Unlike Barth, Kraemer refused to reject the classical terminology, but he insisted on redefining them in a manner that expressed his sympathy with Barth's concerns. For Kraemer, God is revealing himself in all times and places, but such activity can only be discerned in hindsight, in the light of the revelation of God in Christ.

Accordingly, Kraemer's answer to whether or not God is revealed in the non-Christian religions is that all religions, including Christianity, can show an impressive array of cultural, aesthetic, and ethical achievements, yet this is precisely where they may be furthest from God in his revelation. Even at its most sublime, averred Kraemer, humanity is hampered by its apparently constitutional blindness to God as he is in Jesus Christ (1938: 125). Kraemer did affirm that God reveals himself in other religions, albeit with dialectical tension. He does not outline the nature of this revelation, nor does he indicate how it occurs:

> God works in man and shines through nature. The religious and moral life of man is man's achievement, but also God's wrestling with him; it manifests a receptivity to God, but at the same time an inexcusable disobedience and blindness to God. The world fails to know God even in its highest wisdom, although it strives to do so. Man seeks God and at the same time flees from Him in His seeking, because his self-assertive self-centredness of will, his root-sin, always breaks through. God's anger is revealed towards the iniquity of man as manifested in his religious and moral depravity; but nevertheless the entire creation is eagerly longing for the revelation of the "glorious freedom of the children of God" (Rom. viii). Such was and is the contradictory condition of the world and of the religious and moral life of the world in its different forms, and the dialectical relation of God to it. To indicate systematically and concretely where God revealed Himself and wrestled and wrestles with man in the non-Christian religion is not feasible. Every effort to do so is hazardous. Personal concrete experiences,

the meeting of spirit *with* spirit and illumined divination can alone lead on the right track. (1938: 126-27)

On the basis of the previous discussion, it would seem that for Kraemer there are no points of contact: if the biblically realistic world of the revelation in Christ is systematically incommensurate with the similarly holistic worlds of non-Christian religions, then there is no common ground. At the same time, however, Kraemer states that, if "the essential meaning of Christianity is to witness to the world of divine and human realities as revealed in Jesus Christ" (1938: 299), there must be points of contact or common ground to which this witness can appeal in order to be grasped. Kraemer resolved the dilemma dialectically, saying that there are no points of contact between revelation and the non-Christian systems of thought, but there may be many situational encounters between Christians and others.

Kraemer rejected any understanding of points of contact that takes "seemingly kindred elements of other religions . . . as fragments detached from [their] total reality [as] the starting-point of the road that leads to Christ and to Christian truth" (1938: 300). In the first place, such an approach refuses to understand particular beliefs or practices within their holistic framework, thereby rejecting them a priori on their own terms. Kraemer noted that although it "honestly starts from the very laudable and (for a missionary) indispensable desire to show open-mindedness and genuine sympathy for the best in other religions, it starts from the assumption that Christianity is the crown of these religions, and so it evinces a hidden feeling of superiority, that is rightly sensed as condescension" (1938: 301-2). In the second, it ignores the fact that more often than not, such "fictitious similarity acts more as a barrier than as a bridge" to interreligious conversation (1938: 300). While such an approach may uncover elements of the Christian message that are common and therefore relatively unsurprising, its surprising, unique features are the focal points for conversation. "When the word 'approach' is taken in the sense of Christianity as a total religious system approaching the non-Christian religions as total religious systems, there is only difference and antithesis, and this must be so because they are radically different" (Kraemer, 1938: 300). For these reasons, the systematic search for points of contact among the religions was, for Kraemer, to be avoided.

On the other hand, Kraemer was equally adamant that "in practice the religious needs and aspirations that are embedded in these great religious systems often offer, of course, splendid opportunities for practical *human* contact" (1938: 300, emphasis his). Rather than searching for theoretical points of contact, Kraemer preferred a situational approach that "means to have constantly in mind that a missionary is a living human being among other living human beings, whose minds are soaked in the atmosphere of their own religions. This being so, it goes without saying that it is impossible and not permissible to approach them without a thorough knowledge of their religious and general human background" (1938: 303). Kraemer thus highlighted the obligation to strive for the presentation of Christian truth in terms and modes that the audience will understand: the problem of adaptation: "So it is obvious and legitimate that Christian truth must be at present expressed against the background of, and in conflict with, the moral and religious content of the non-Christian religions" (1938: 308). If points of contact were not to be found in theory, for Kraemer, in missionary practice, they abounded.

Once again a dilemma is confronted: if biblical realism is incommensurate with other religious apprehensions of life, then no adaptation is possible; at the same time, however, if faithful Christian witness is to take place, adaptation must occur. Kraemer's solution lies in the focus on situation over system: "Adaptation . . . does not mean to assimilate the cardinal facts of the revelation in Christ as much as possible to fundamental religious ideas and tastes of the pre-Christian past, but to *express* these facts by wrestling with them concretely, and so to present the Christian truth and reveal at the same time the intrinsic inadequacy of man's religious efforts for the solution of his crucial religious and moral problems" (1938: 308). As the New Testament writers neither assimilated nor refuted Judaism, Greek philosophy, and mystery religions, but used them to present and formulate the revelation in Christ, they therefore are paradigmatic for the strategy Kraemer pursues.

Kraemer's situational approach, itself a reminder that the Christian message does not arise within a socio-cultural vacuum, first challenges missionary activity where "Christianity is preached and transplanted in the historical, theological and institutional forms that have been developed in the West, and in the case of Protestant Missions, this is still further aggravated by the fact that the various and often separatist-minded denominational, theological and institutional expressions are the models on which various types of Christianity in Africa and Asia are moulded" (1938: 315-6). However, it also confronts missionary activity that "leads to the weakening of Christianity, for in practice it is not the endeavour to bring Christian truth to its most vigorous and clear expression by indigenous ways, but to recast [it] into an indigenous philosophy of life, in which the dominant elements are the pre-Christian apprehension of existence, coloured and sanctioned by supposedly kindred Christian elements" (1938: 317). Adaptation then, for Kraemer, is neither a simplistic antithesis nor a naïve synthesis but a procedure dependent on concrete situations to determine whether one emphasizes contrasts or commonalities:

> if a synthesis of Christainity and Indian or other elements will ever come about . . . such a synthesis will grow slowly out of the stress and need of life, but never can be the result of a premeditated effort, apart from living and continual contact with the actual situations. . . . In our description of the non-Christian religions, we have repeatedly stressed how rich and how varied are the ways in which man there has tried to give expression to his religious needs and aspirations, in theology, in worship, in art, in forms of organization, in different ways of presentation. . . . It is not at all important that they do not fit in with our Protestant traditions and natural reactions, but it is very important to ask in the light of Biblical realism how they can function so as to foster pure and vigorous Christian life. (Kraemer, 1938: 324-5)

There is therefore no valid objection to using the philosophical terminology of the world religions. To avoid doing so is to despise both the New Testament and a natural means of communication.

At the Tambaram meeting of the International Missionary Council, Kraemer's book was the flash point for controversy. Kraemer held that a Christian interpretation of the religious life of humanity takes its starting point within the Christian revelation. Further, he argued that this interpretation depends on a proper understanding of beliefs and practices in relation to the complex religious totalities in which they arise. Finally, *The Christian Message* contended against the artificial and abstract comparison of religious systems that true points of contact and adaptation were uncovered only in the situational encounters between Christians and others. Each of these elements sparked intense and, as shown, unresolved debate. The conference statement admitted that there was no agreement on whether or how God reveals himself outside Christianity, and a call for further study was issued. This resulted in the publication of *The Authority of the Faith*, in which Kraemer restated his position in an essay entitled "Continuity or Discontinuity" (1939) and invited criticism. I turn now to an examnination of this essay and its criticism.

2. Clarifications, Qualifications, and Criticism

While Kraemer had not changed his mind in "Continuity or Discontinuity," he did introduce a number of important clarifications of his original presentation in *The Christian Message*. Kraemer admits that biblical realism is a "more or less clumsy" term. He had intended it to express "the idea that the Bible, the human and in many ways historically conditioned document of God's acts of revelation, consistently testifies to divine acts and plans in regard to the salvation of mankind and the world, and not to religious experience or ideas" (1939: 2). Troubled by the accusation that the term was "vague and unnecessary," Kraemer challenged his critics to offer a better term:

> provided it conveys more clearly and adequately the idea that the Bible and its contents can only be understood when it is taken as the record of God's thoughts and acts in regard to mankind, and not as a tale about the pilgrimage of the human soul towards God, however moving a tale of that religious pilgrimage might be told by one who surveys the religious history of mankind. (1939: 2)

And, while he continued to stress the sui generis and therefore discontinuous nature of Christian revelation, Kraemer qualified this by noting that there are "longings and apperceptions in the religious life of mankind outside the special sphere of the Christian revelation, of which Christ, what He is and has brought, may be termed *in a certain sense* the fulfilment"(1939: 3, emphasis his). With this admission, he sought to strike a middle way between two extremes. On the one hand, the highest and best of the religions merely serve as a preparation for the gospel, while on the other, such achievements are at best minimized and at worst despised.

Although he thus admitted a limited "fulfilment," Kraemer had avoided the use of the term at Tambaram for three reasons. First, his version—unlike that expressed at Edinburgh and Jerusalem—"never represents a perfecting of what has been before. In this fulfilment is contained a radical recasting of values, because these longings and apprehensions when exposed to the searching and revolutionary light of Christ, appear to be blind and misdirected" (1939: 3). For Kraemer, this does not detract from the significance of such elements, but emphasizes the radical difference of Christ and his message. He also refrained from using his conception of fulfilment at Tambaram lest it be seen as tacit approval of natural theology conceived as an imperfect and introductory form of revelation. Kraemer did not deny God's capacity to work outside the Christian revelation, nor did he dispute the belief that there may therefore be "acceptable men of faith" outside Christianity; on the contrary, he affirms it as following from belief in the grace of God: "God forbid that we mortal men should be so irreverent as to dispose of how and where the Sovereign God of grace and love has to act" (1939: 4-5). But he refused to commend the religions as inferior versions of Christianity, to be completed by Christ, for to do so would reflect both hubris toward non-Christian faith and a misunderstanding of Christian revelation. Third, he declined because even the most cursory investigation into the religions themselves highlights their uniqueness, thereby prohibiting the construction of a relationship of preparation and fulfilment between them and Christianity.

Kraemer insisted that the world religions do not combine to form a coherent whole, nor do they stem from a common core. Drawing from Indian theologian Pandipeddi Chenchiah, Kraemer posited that, rather, they ask and answer different questions.

> "The facile presumption that in Hinduism we have a search for salvation without satisfaction and that Christianity satisfied the longing is untrue to fact." "The supreme longing of the Hindu, to escape from *samsara*, Christ does not satisfy, and the Lord's gift of rebirth does not appeal to the Hindu. Thus the correspondence of longing and satisfaction fails." "Jesus kindles new hopes not felt before and kills some of the deepest and persistent longings of man." These dicta of Mr. Chenchiah . . . stress facts that are generally glossed over in the discussion, because the laudable desire not to overlook or minimise religious insights or aspirations which arrest by their depth and quality blinds the eyes to the real elements of the discussion. Appreciation thus leads towards entirely unwarranted and untenable identifications. (1939: 5-6)

Although on other issues Kraemer was criticized by Chenchiah at length, on this point he was in agreement. Because of the deep differences among the religions, Kraemer felt that it would be a sign of ignorance and condescension to speak glibly of Christ as their fulfilment. If the word is to be maintained with any credibility at all, Kraemer wrote, one must use it sparingly and carefully to convey only the notion of "contradictive or subversive fulfilment" (1939: 5).

A further important clarification in "Continuity or Discontinuity" is Kraemer's explanation for the presuppositions underlying *The Christian Message*. The original work came from a Christian perspective. "In all my reasoning and in all my efforts to formulate my opinion, I take my standpoint within the realm of the Christian revelation. . . . [It] is my authoritative guide and no other principle or standpoint" (1939: 7). Though Kraemer neither required nor expected non-Christian commentators to agree, he was perplexed by the controversy the adoption of such a standpoint aroused among his Christian critics:

> How can I, and how can you ignore the fact that our whole apprehension of religious life is moulded and coloured by our contact with and knowledge of Christ? How can we acknowledge Him as the ultimate

> authority . . . in all things religious, and then try to find a so-called wider and more inclusive standpoint from which to . . . determine the significance . . . of the religious dream of mankind? [Whatever noble motives give rise to such activities, this] simply means that there is another ultimate standard than Christ, a so-called religious *a priori* by which even Christ, who upsets all human standards is measured. At any rate for a Christian this standpoint leads to hopeless confusion. (1939: 9)

Kraemer clarified that his work also presupposed the Bible to be the primary source for developing his Christian frame of reference. Kraemer deplored that the discovery of the "human and historically-conditioned trappings, in which the message of biblical realism is expressed," had caused some to regard the Bible as "an interesting and highly important piece of religious literature, but not . . . as containing the prophetic and apostolic witness to God's dealing with mankind" (1939: 10). He believed this to be an unwarranted conclusion. While accepting the results of historical criticism, he stressed that the Bible must continue to be "recognised as the central orientation-point for our theological thinking" (1939: 10). Finally, he noted that his work presupposed a sympathetic understanding of religious beliefs and practices. This is to say that, for Kraemer, the religions can and should be understood in the first instance according to their own peculiar axes and intentions. Although the Christian interpreter answers ultimately to another authority, Kraemer felt that it was inexcusable simply to allow such a commitment to function uncritically in religious interpretation and evaluation.[6]

Although Kraemer's position in his 1939 paper was attacked from a variety of perspectives, the majority of criticism—in essays published with "Contintuity or Discontinuity"—centred on his concept of revelation. Two critics took issue with his separation of revelation from religion. Farmer argued that Kraemer, by sundering them and regarding the latter as the

---

6 In the remainder of "Continuity or Discontinuity," Kraemer set out his position again, this time by comparing Clement of Alexandria's positive assessment of Greek philosophy with Barth's negative assessment of religion. Kraemer suggested that Clement regarded philosophy as a schoolmaster leading to Christ, "a covenant peculiar to the Greeks" (1939: 17). Kraemer assessed Barth's regard the revelation of God as the dissolution of religion (1939: 18). Not surprisingly, Kraemer finds Barth's account more compelling not because of "better and simpler logic," but because of "deeper and more consistent religious and theological thinking" (1939: 21). In so doing, Kraemer recognizes the modern separation of Greek philosophy from Greek religion to be fictitious. According to Dunn and Mackey, this disjunction is one of the "commonest and most misleading conceits of the history of Christian theology. It is the insistence that the so-called pagan Greek theology with which these early erudite Christians had to deal was really philosophy as distinct from theology, a product of autonomous human reason" (1987: 33).

result of human creativity alone, ignored "the awareness of God as One who makes the sacred and absolute *demand* which can be discerned in varying forms at the heart of the religious life of mankind" (Farmer, 1939: 172, emphasis his). Horton sought to overcome the disjunction by synthesizing the best of Kraemer with the best of Hocking (Horton, 1939: 148-62; Horton, 1966, 234). Chao took a more traditional approach, which defended a version of general revelation and rejected Kraemer's suggestions that salvation may occur without the witness of the Church (Chao, 1939: 40, 58). Moses sought to link revelation with morality by proposing that the Christian revelation was the judge of religious truth not by virtue of its revelatory status, but because of any revelation, it best embodied "universal moral values" (1939: 83). By Kraemer's own admission, however, the most penetrating evaluation was by Hogg.

Hogg argued that Kraemer had failed to distinguish sufficiently "non-Christian faith" from "non-Christian faiths" (1939: 102-25). Hogg sought therefore to distinguish between world religions (i.e., non-Christian faiths) and many of their adherents who, while evincing no desire to leave their spiritual homes, live lives touched by grace (that is, they have non-Christian faith) (1939: 102). Drawing from his long missionary experience in India, Hogg wrote: "I have known and had fellowship with some for whom Christ was not absolute Lord and only Saviour, who held beliefs of the typically Hindu colour, and yet who manifestly were no strangers to the life 'hid in God'" (1939: 110). Hogg argued that, by insisting that the religions were products purely of the human imagination, Kraemer had excluded the possibility of non-Christian faith. In suggesting that the religions were human phenomena, Kraemer had been forced to the conclusion that they were merely, in Hogg's words, "a seeking but not a finding, not an experience of Divine self-disclosure" (1939: 103). For Hogg, this was wholly inadequate. By taking non-Christian faith as his clue, Hogg concluded that all religions in varying degrees combine divine revelation and initiative with both appropriate and inappropriate human responses. Accordingly, for Hogg, the sui generis nature of the Christian revelation lies not, as Kraemer had argued in the fact of revelation, but in its portrayal of God as a loving and forgiving heavenly Father. Hogg concluded: "It is not here affirmed, as Dr. Kraemer's line of discussion at least appears to suggest, that Christianity is unique because it is created by the *occurrence* of revelation. . . . Christianity is unique because of the unique *content* of the revelation of which it is the apprehension and product and to which it bears witness" (1939: 125, emphasis his). In Kraemer's view, despite Hogg's sharp disagreement, only he of all the critics, had substantially understood the issues at stake.

Most post-Tambaram analysis has centred on Kraemer's doctrine of revelation and specifically his separation of revelation from religion. His clarifications have been seen by and large as cosmetic. Despite them, most of his opponents have agreed that Kraemer could neither recognize nor affirm authentic spirituality outside Christianity and, therefore, his stated intentions aside, elevated Christianity above all other religions. Kraemer addressed these concerns in later writings, but his overall starting point remained the same. He concluded "Continuity or Discontinuity" with these words:

> Fundamentally speaking, we have in regard to this problem only to choose between two positions: to start, consciously or unconsciously, from a general idea about the essence of religion and take that as our standard of reference, or derive our idea of what religions is or really ought to be from the revelation in Christ, and consistently stick to this as the sole standard of reference. To my mind, the choice of the second of these our alternatives is inescapable. (1939: 23)

3. The Later Work

Kraemer's most developed statement, *Religion and the Christian Faith*, begins where "Continuity or Discontinuity" ends. Published nearly two decades later, it aimed "to vindicate by a critical evaluation of the attempts of the Science of Religion and of the Philosophy of Religion to understand and explain religion and religions, the scientific and philosophic legitimacy of a Theology of Religion and Religions" (1956: 32). This vindication takes place in four movements, in which Kraemer argues that a theology of religions is justified by appeals to the scientific study of religion, is found in Christian history, and is supported by scripture. To complete his apology, Kraemer outlines how his approach impinges on discussion of general and special revelation, natural theology, and interreligious co-operation and tolerance.

In *Religion and the Christian Faith*, Kraemer responded to those who charged that his openly confessional starting point—what he called biblical realism—was somehow arbitrary or prejudiced by outlining two important insights yielded by the scientific study of religions.[7] In the term "scientific

---

7 Kraemer was especially perturbed by what he perceived to be the near deliberate misunderstanding not only of his starting point, but also of his intentions: "The fundamental difficulty in the [Tambaram] debates was that the 'standing-place' of the writer (namely that the right theological criterion is not a universal Idea of Religion at its highest, but God's self-disclosure in his revelation in Jesus Christ) was misunderstood by many, and misinterpreted as narrowness of mind, dogmatism [and] even fundamentalism" (1956b: 222).

study," he referred to all investigations of religious phenomena, whether anthropological, philosophical, or theological, as they can and should use scientific methods to collect, arrange, and present data. In other words, they are to strive for impartiality, which Kraemer asserted was not to be confused with "neutrality," defined as an attempt to distance oneself from the object studied. For Kraemer, the impartiality after which scientific study strives rests on the undemonstrable assumption that it is worthwhile to investigate religions, thereby recognizing that they must have some meaning (1956b: 49). Furthermore, true understanding inevitably involves a sympathetic and congenial entry into a different universe of discourse. For these reasons, Kraemer averred that neutrality is impossible, but impartiality remains an important goal: this "studious attitude of avoiding judgments of value and truth, is the indispensable condition for having the right attitude, because the aim is to understand a religion or religious phenomenon according to its own intention and structure. It must be done in such a way that a religion or realm of spiritual life can speak for itself" (1956b: 48). For Kraemer, then, impartiality in so far as it is possible could be preserved through a holistic approach to religious beliefs and practices.

These commitments to impartiality and to a more holistic approach led Kraemer to conclude that a universal "essence of religion" was a piece of academic fiction. He therefore opposed both the naturalist and transcendentalist approaches to the study of religions for similar reasons. The naturalist approach—exemplified in the works of Freud, Feuerbach, and Marx—regards religion as a stage in human self-consciousness that is eventually to be transcended. To do so, insisted Kraemer, is ultimately reductionistic. While naturalistic studies can and do expose "historical, psychological and sociological causes of religious phenomena," Kraemer contended that they confuse such exposure with explanation (1956: 56-7). The irony, of course, is that such explanation is ultimately satisfactory only to those who have adopted a naturalistic world view beforehand. In spite of claims to objectivity and neutrality, naturalistic approaches are also founded on undemonstrable assumptions about the nature of humanity—human life can be explained solely in material terms—the universe—it is the result solely of natural proceses—and humanity's place therein—human life is the product of random forces and has no ultimate significance (1956b: 54-71). The transcendentalist approach—ably represented by Kant, Schleiermacher and Otto—regards religion as that realm where the human consciousness encounters the absolute (whether conceived, according to the examples given, as duty, feeling, or mystery). Once again, Kraemer's charge is that this approach is reductionistic. By developing a general idea of religion first and investigating actual beliefs and practices after, the transcendentalist approach runs the risk of ignoring, minimizing, or misrepresenting those who do not readily fit its presuppositions.

Clearly, Kraemer understood naturalist and transcendentalist approaches to be opposing theories about the nature of religious life. The former excludes as a matter of method the possibility of an explanation lying outside the material world, while the latter insists on it. What interested Kraemer, however, was what he saw as their subliminal or foundational agreement. Kraemer charges both naturalism and transcendentalism with positing a universal religious essence functioning either as an axiom from which they begin or the goal toward which they strive. Moreover, he charged both approaches with using this criterion to plot religions along an evolutionary scale:

> The important concept by which they aimed at arranging and classifying the material in different grades is that of the essence of Religion (*das Wesen der Religion*), an all embracing and all-explaining formula. Either one hopes to discover it by persevering research, and formulates provisional working definitions, or more precise ones, of what religion is, or one starts from a philosophical concept of the Essence of Religion, making it the criterion and judgment of explanation. In either case, it is considered to be derived from the religions which are either crude or sublime expressions of it. (1956b: 59)

While this universal essence is easy to presuppose, Kraemer argued, it is impossible empirically to ground or to demonstrate its warrant. Rather, he insisted, as investigation into the diverse religious beliefs and practices continued throughout the world, one ought to be driven precisely to the opposite conclusion. "There are and have been many concrete religions, each with its peculiar structure and character. All general definitions . . . reduce them to such a kind of common denominator that little meaning is left" (1956b: 76). Furthermore, this fundamental denial of difference removes each religion's uniqueness, thereby emptying the scientific study of its interest in the first place. What results is "an intangible, rather void *ens generalissimum* which has nothing to do with the *ens realissimum* which these cultural notions of the concrete religions pretend to be" (1956b: 76).

By presupposing the peculiar nature of each religion, Kraemer undercut all attempts to distill an "essence of religion" (1956b: 76). Rather, following Kristensen, he adopted a holistic approach, which he called "totalitarian," to the study of religions. Each religion, from this view, is assessed according to its own ideals. This approach removes any feelings of cultural superiority, for it uncovers the ambivalence in all religions, including empirical Christianity, as Kraemer stated: "The merit of modern Science of Religion is not that it has discovered this ambivalent character, but that by its meticulous research into all the nooks and corners of religious experience and expression it has demonstrated in a compelling way the evident truth of this common notion, and so forces us to face the implications of the disturbing character of this fact" (1956b: 38). The implications to which he referred apply to the grading of religions according to their "value" and "truth." Kraemer felt that, when examined carefully, no religion can be shown to be better or worse than any other, for there is no universally recognized standard by which to grade them.

One conclusion drawn from these insights is that essentialist approaches—whether naturalist or transcendentalist—coupled with the exposure of the ambivalence of all religions reveal that the objectivity demanded by Kraemer's Tambaram critics is impossible. When assessing religious beliefs and practices, there is no perspective that does not presuppose fundamentally religious attitudes about humanity and the nature of the cosmos. Kraemer argued that understanding religions begins and ends with the taking of sides in the great questions: What do you think of God and humanity? and Which God do you choose? Answers to these are, of course, fundamentally religious themselves. Kraemer therefore concluded:

> the theologian can and must [study and interpret religion and religions] with a good philosophical conscience, by being faithful to his theological conscience. That is to say, in being a faithful interpreter of God's self-disclosure in Christ, and thereby exercising that interpretation of religion which is implied in his primordial, undemonstrable starting-point. In doing so, and in doing it faithfully and methodically, open to all he can learn from the Science of Religion, and delight in the rules of the "scientific" game, he is not prejudiced, but humanly speaking in the same position as any other honest investigator of religion, whether the latter is conscious of his starting-point or not. We are, in saying this, not invoking the right of prejudice. On the contrary, by full recognition and avowal of one's bias one is comparatively speaking better armed against the temptations of partiality, to which every scholar without exception is constantly exposed. (1956b: 52)

Thus, Kraemer vindicated his approach by arguing that, even on the best scientific and objective evidence, an evaluation of religions that is theological is inevitable. His choice, therefore, of an explicitly Christian evaluation was not necessarily arbitrary or obscurantist, as his critics charged.

Kraemer opened the second movement of *Religion and the Christian Faith*—an evaluation of five theological starting points in Christian history—by taking this conclusion one step further. Not only did he advocate that a theological approach is on an equal footing with any other, he contended it is to be preferred, for it declares its biases from the beginning and remains aware of the temptation toward subjectivity. He maintained that:

> on scientific and philosophical grounds, theology is fully entitled to formulate the case and to say its personal word on the problem of religion and religions, on the basis of its peculiar presuppositions. Just when it is frank about its presuppositions, it can be free of a false make-believe of 'scientific' objectivity. It is obliged to give a clear account of its estimate of the value and truth of all religions outside the sphere of Biblical revelation. (1956b: 143)

The bias to which Kraemer alluded is then made plain: "Under all conditions, in all kinds of work . . . [the Christian] remains primarily a disciple, a captive of Jesus Christ in whom God disclosed Himself, full of grace and truth" (1956b: 144). For the Christian, the starting point for a theological study of religions can be none other than the revelation of God in Jesus Christ.[8] To those outside Christian faith, Kraemer could say only that "this theological starting-point is as valid as, for instance, that of the mystical philosophies of religion, which assume axiomatically the identity of God and man as self-evident" (1956b: 144). To the Christian, however, he insisted that this starting point is revelation, one radically different from all others. It cannot therefore be grounded in anything other than itself: "The sole possible response to it is, therefore, that of faith, not a justification by reason; although reason can render Christianity help in understanding it, without believing it. Without faith, the Biblical thesis of revelation will generally be considered a fiction, an illusion, a pretence, or a useful error" (1956b: 145-6).

Having defined his starting point, Kraemer sought to clarify it by comparing it to three historical and two contemporary approaches to the theology of religions. He began with the *logos spermatikos* as set out by

---

8 To say so is simply openly to acknowledge what the label "Christian" entails. For the Christian scholar, the basic assumption is "that Jesus Christ is *the* Way, *the* Truth, and *the* Life, by whom alone man comes to the Father, and by whose light alone all problems can be seen in their proper perspective. . . . Jesus Christ is the centre of history and therefore the religious history of man before and after him, till the end of history, can only rightly be understood in him. He is God's decisive and final act of self-disclosure or revelation, and in Him all divine revelation, past, present and future, has its proper criterion" (1956b: 237).

Justin, developed by the Fathers, and perfected by Clement and Origen (1956b: 148-54).[9] Through their use of this Stoic notion (meaning, "seed of reason"), they argued that all that was good in Greek philosophy prepared the Greek mind to receive the gospel and was therefore, in Kraemer's words, "a basis for a positive attitude towards the spiritual heritage of their forefathers and non-Christian neighbours" (1956b: 150). Kraemer argued that although "fired by sincere conviction," this misrepresents Christian faith as a "philosophical religion, consisting of Greek (especially Stoic) ideas in a Biblical garb, and as a moralist religion, in which man by a moral decision works out his own salvation" (1956b: 150). It therefore obscures "the central point of the Christian revelation, i.e., that it means entering in and through Christ into a new *life-relationship* with God. Instead of that the emphasis is shifted towards attaining a fuller rational knowledge of God" (1956b: 153). This approach, for Kraemer, fails because its Stoic roots, unlike the prologue to John's gospel, have not been sufficiently subverted by biblical realism.[10]

Kraemer next considered the approach of Thomas Aquinas, which separated knowledge of God into natural and revealed categories. In the former lies knowledge of God's existence and certain attributes while, in the latter, the supernatural Christian dogmas are revealed to the faithful (1956b: 161). In a manner similar to the Fathers, Thomas regarded the former knowledge as the "*praeambula fidei* and *preparatio evangelica*" (1956b: 161).[11] Although there is much insight to be gained from careful study of Thomas's work, Kraemer found his balance between the natural and the revealed to be artificial. While Thomas's system will always supply "new discoveries of old truths," Kraemer felt that Thomas failed to present the Christian revelation as the crisis of religion (1956b: 164-65).

Indeed in Kraemer's view, Christianity's approach to other religions and philosophies was largely mistaken until the Reformation, the third historical period he considered. The Fathers and the Medievals generally acted on

---

9 See also Justin (1953: 231-5), Clement (1954: 96-7), and Origen, (1954: 238ff).
10 Similarly, Kraemer believed Augustine, "the great genius who for the first time formulated evangelical Christianity with its emphasis on sin and grace," whose *City of God* was the last "great Apology for Christianity . . . indulges too much in the luxuries of metaphysical thinking entirely alien to Biblical religion." From the Augustinian corpus, Kraemer preferred the *Retractiones*, where "greater reserve is expressed. He recognized more and more, notwithstanding similarities and affinities, the unbridgeable gulf between the non-Christian religions and the *vera religio*, yet felt that the religious consciousness of classical paganism had something to do with God." Kraemer was more sympathetic to another North African theologian, concluding that the "merit of Tertullian is that he seized the dialectical condition of man: God-conscious, yet unfaithful, and therefore in his natural condition far from the truth" (1956b:156-8).
11 See Thomas Aquinas (1954: 35-7;1955: 61-78).

the questionable assumption that Greek philosophy and Christian revelation were by and large in agreement: "They did not and could not delimit philosophy and theology sufficiently" (1956b: 168). It was not until the Reformers that this assumption was cast in a critical light. Calvin, for instance, recognized the consciousness of God that lies behind all religious life, but because of sin, "man who could be a worshipper of the true God produces a great variety of fictitious religions. . . . Man's erring finds its origins in man's disoriented religious consciousness so that the light afforded by the *sensus divinitatis* is insufficient for the *vera notitia Dei*" (1956b: 170).[12] Kraemer presents Luther as following similar lines, but where Calvin is dispassionate, Luther is a "volcanic genius" (1956b: 174). Whether dispassionate or explosive, Calvin and Luther, along with many of their followers, agreed that, because of human sinfulness, the vast majority of the human race would remain unreconciled to God. This was not, however, a unanimous judgment. Kraemer urged readers also to consider Huldrych Zwingli, who, because he "was not fixed on the dilemma of faith and works, but on God as the only Saviour" (1956b: 174) displayed a greater optimism with regard to the final salvation of those not sharing Christian faith. Classical Protestant theology need not necessarily be restrictive in its understanding of final salvation. Although he is generally positive toward what he perceives to be the first serious attempt at theology of religions, Kraemer went on to remark that the Reformers were handicapped by their lack of interaction with other faiths at any significant level (1956b: 176).

This impairment is overcome in the first contemporary approach. While the Reformer's goal was lost during what Kraemer calls "The Liberal Period," (1956b: 177-8) and though a recovery was foreshadowed in the writings of Hamann (1956b: 179-81), Barth and Brunner were the first to reclaim and build upon the perspective of the Reformation. For them, the Christian revelation is radically different from all other religious expressions. Of their writings Kraemer said:

> The revelation in Christ stands apart from all religions—not as a unique individual case of a common species, but as a different genus. It is *sui generis*. There is no continuity between what becomes manifest in the data of the different religious structures and the Christian message with its view of the human condition, the character of God and His relation to man and the world. In the doctrine of the justification of the sinner all religion appears to lose its real basis, because from God alone comes salvation. The Christian revelation is the crisis of all religion. (1956b: 182)

---

[12] See Calvin (1960: 39-47).

Kraemer regarded the two as the "outstanding representatives of a fully *theological* understanding of religion and religions" (1956b: 189). Nevertheless, even they did not escape Kraemer's criticism. In their desire to avoid the *logos spermatikos* error, Barth and Brunner both "ignore entirely the Logos doctrine, whose sole interpretation is not necessarily that of the Fathers" (1956b: 189). Moreover, neither employs all the biblical material available; Kraemer felt that they were excessively Pauline.

Finally, Kraemer considered the approaches of contemporary Anglo-American and other European contributors. Although he felt that one may learn much from the philosophical assessments of Brightman (1946), Söderblom (1943), Farmer (1954), and Hocking (1912), Kraemer noted that each falls "back again in the fatal vicious circle of all philosophy of religion, which recognizes theoretically the transcendence in religion, and yet elevates the purely historical and psychological element...into the criterion of the transcendent, which practically means the personal religious taste of the philosopher" (1956b: 202-3). He was more sympathetic to missionaries because of their cross-cultural experience (1956b: 214-15), but even their best examples, Farquhar (1971) and Macnicol (1936), have "either hardly any articulate theology or a weak one, focused on comparing 'religious experience', and reducing the Christian message to some 'general principles'" (1956b: 216). The legitimate desire to be generous "seduces them into fatally blurring the true issues" (1956b: 216).

From the summary it is clear that Kraemer intended to follow the route proposed by the Reformers and blazed by Barth and Brunner. He was not content, however, with recapitulating their arguments. He hoped to present a model that makes better use of biblical material than either Barth or Brunner and is better acquainted with the religions than the Reformers.

Before examining Kraemer's theological interpretation of other religions, I turn to his biblical exegesis, arranged as it is around three doctrines. The first, theological anthropology, is rooted in the narratives of the Creation and the Fall, the Noahic Covenant, and Babel, as found in the first eleven chapters of Genesis. Kraemer opened with a reflection on the meaning of the "image of God" as it arises in the first story (Genesis 1:1-3:14). Where past exegetes have distinguished "image" from "likeness," Kraemer countered that this misunderstands the text: "there is, it seems, not one jot or tittle of all these constructions in it" (1956b: 248). With Kraemer's more straightforward and contextually sensitive reading, "image" and "likeness" are simply parallel terms, both meaning "copy," or "figure" (1956b: 249). Combining this understanding of image with the command to take dominion over the earth, Kraemer interpreted this narrative to signify that human beings are divine creations with a divine mandate to represent God's rule. Hence, conjecture about what aspects of the image have been lost or retained after the Fall fails to grasp the narrative's purpose: to describe the fragmentation resulting from sin:

> [The] breach of the communion with and obedience to God . . . has as its immediate implication the total disturbance and corruption of all human relations (man-woman, man-man . . .), of the relation to the world (animals, soil, work, etc.). The usurped autonomy of man through his repudiation of the theonomy, under which he began his career, turns out to be the polynomy of his fancies, passions and self-fabricated gods. (1956b: 250-1)

For Kraemer, the Creation and the Fall together paint a dialectical picture: in all activities, including religious ones, human beings remain God's creatures, uniquely chosen to care for all that God has made, while God, in his gracious act of creation, has bestowed upon human beings a fundamental dignity that remains regardless of race, gender, culture, or history. As a result, for Kraemer, all humans everywhere have the potential to create beauty and perceive truth; yet human beings are fallen creatures, alienated from God, from each other, and from the created order itself. Thus, humans are equally liable to confuse beauty with ugliness and exchange the truth for a lie. For an authentic anthropology to be developed, argued Kraemer, both poles need to be held together, for only then will one see humanity in its proper light.

This idea is reinforced by Kraemer's discussion of the Noahic Covenant (Genesis 9:1-17) and Babel (Genesis 11:1-9) narratives. The former recounts the divine dialectic of judgment on sin and mercy to humanity; furthermore, Kraemer contended, it "is striking and deeply significant that before God's special revelational experiment with Abraham and his Covenant with him . . . the 'everlasting Covenant between God and every living creature' is stated as an established and irremovable fact governing the spiritual destiny of mankind as a whole" (1956b: 253-4). Babel, on the other hand, expresses the dialectic in human terms, as it speaks of human cultural and religious creativity in grand terms, but they remain nevertheless tainted by corruption and pride. For Kraemer, the Babel story presents human beings as designed to be God's representatives, but corrupted by sin into tyranny. On the one hand, humanity's religious life is affirmed and preserved through the Noahic Covenant, while on the other, it is restrained by the Babel narrative.

The second doctrine on which Kraemer centred is that of the Logos. Before considering the Johannine Prologue directly, however, Kraemer turned to its forerunner—the wisdom literature of the Hebrew Bible. After noting the "pure delight" accorded to "wisdom" in Job and Proverbs, he observed that, along with the condemnation of Gentile religion, there are also affirmations of wisdom as a gift from God wherever it is found:

> it is evident that alongside the broad stream of negative and condemnatory judgments of pagan religions . . . there are also traces, slight, but undeniable, of a positive attitude toward human Wisdom . . . esteemed as a great, universal human value, essentially a gift from God, and on a par with the God-given nature of man. . . . The attitude, implied in these passages, can be formulated in a simple sentence: God is at work in man's spiritual aspirations and achievements. (1956b: 265)

Although the Johannine Prologue has been the victim of much speculation, Kraemer's exegesis of the passage is simple: "the Logos, from eternity with God and Himself God, is the fact Jesus Christ, the man of Nazareth" (1956b: 275). If this interpretation has merit, he cautioned, then this passage can no longer be used to affirm that non-Christian religion and philosophy culminate in the Christian gospel. On the contrary, while God is indeed at work in the religious life of human beings, this work is not the result of a universal Logos, but of the Logos incarnate in Jesus Christ:

> The Prologue states in an uncompromising way that man's condition is such that he is unable to know God as He really is, or himself, by his own powers. It can only happen through faith and the work of the Holy Spirit, i.e. through revelation, through divine self-disclosure. The truth about God is not, either in the Prologue or in any other part of the Bible, a lofty conception about His being and nature, monotheistic, mystic or what not, but it is the incomprehensible fact that He became flesh in Jesus Christ, that God is self-giving, self-forgetting love, as was manifested in the scandal of the Cross. (1956b: 277)

For Kraemer, God is indeed at work throughout the world, making himself available to be known everywhere, including other religions. Testimony to such divine self-disclosure is found in the wisdom which, although a gift from God, is not the exclusive possession of any one community, religion, or race; wherever found, it is affirmed. And yet, Kraemer reminded, because of the noetic consequences of human sinfulness, those who have encountered the revelation of God in Jesus Christ more accurately discern this wisdom because, in Christ, the wisdom of God has come in the flesh.

Kraemer saved his more extensive exegetical work for the third doctrine: the Pauline understanding of the righteousness and wrath of God. Beginning with Paul's speech in Lystra (Acts 14:8-18), he draws three points: first, the goal of Paul's preaching is conversion (v. 15); second, God has abandoned people to their own ways (v. 16); yet, third, God continues to testify to them through creation whether or not they recognise it (v. 17). These points are underscored by three more drawn from Paul's sermon in Athens (Acts 17:16-34). First, all have sinned in their religions (vv. 22-23, 30); second, people continue to demonstrate an awareness of God (vv. 27-28); and, last, God never completely abandons people, but redeems them by converting them (vv. 29-31).

Kraemer then moved to Romans 1:18-2:16, arguing that Paul's understanding of the righteousness of God, while an act of love, nevertheless manifests itself as wrath (v. 18). Kraemer noted that the righteousness of God is a "terrible . . . *yet* saving, gracious reality" (1956b: 292) and elaborated that God has never been inactive with respect to humans; his self-disclosure is so plain that no one has an excuse (vv. 19-20). For Kraemer, the problem lies not with the adequacy or inadequacy of God's self-communication, but with the human response to it; instead of glorifying the true God, new gods are invented (vv. 21-23). Therefore, God expresses his wrath by giving people over to the consequences of their actions (vv. 24-32). In these verses, Kraemer contended that:

> Paul uncovers the appalling drama between God and man which underlies this perverted lust and anti-social destructivity. God's wrath is revealed in a double movement which can be defined by using the words of [Hebrews] 10:31: "It is an awful thing to fall into the hands of the living God", and by saying at the same time that it is a terrible thing to fall ought of the hands of the living God. . . . God did not leave men to themselves, but gave them up, so that the falling away of men from God into their self-willed autonomy draws them into a world of evil which is animated by its own severe logic of increasing self-destruction. (1956b: 297)

Kraemer noted that Jews and Gentiles both find themselves in this predicament (2:1-16); no one is excused. The final four verses (2:13-16) are not intended as an argument for salvation by works, but a further indictment against those who believe that simply having the Law is proof of God's favour (1956b: 302-3).

On the basis of this exegesis, Kraemer drew several conclusions. First, humanity is God's creation intended for divine fellowship. Second, God is present in other cultures and other religions. Third, all religions belong to unredeemed humanity and, therefore, no matter how marvellous in appearance, stand under judgment. Yet, fourth, their attempts to deal with the ultimate problems of human existence cannot be ignored by those who live by God's revelation (1956b: 256-271). The great cultural, spiritual, philosophical and other achievements in religions are to be valued, while recognising that they take on their true significance only in the light of Christ. In summary, For Kraemer, all religions, including Christianity, can and do represent a simultaneous search for and a flight from God.

To complete his vindication in *Religion and the Christian Faith*, Kraemer outlined how his approach shapes discussions of general and special revelation, natural theology, and interreligious co-operation and tolerance. He sought to mediate between "systasis (harmonizing, synthesis)," and "diastasis (keeping a distance)" (1956b: 322). While both are needed, an over-emphasis on either excludes real dialogue and communication: in this way, "the attitude of open, congenial understanding of other religions and alien spiritual worlds," is combined with the "theological understanding and interpretation on a Biblical basis" (1956b: 338). While discussing general and special revelation from this perspective, two foci are introduced: "The first is a strong, determined unequivocalness in regard to the truth, that is to say that the knowledge and honouring of God, the God of Abraham, Isaac and Jacob, the God and Father of the Lord Jesus Christ, is the sole *religio vera*, and that all the other religions, of whatever quality and value they may be, are . . . *religio falsa*" (1956b: 340). On its own, this focus may in fact fall to the criticism of obscurantism. Such a charge, however, would ignore the second focus: that "there are manifestations in this religious and spiritual life and witness in the realm outside the revelation of Christ that are acknowledged as evidence of God's uninterrupted concern" for humans (1956b: 340-41). Thus, religions must be regarded as "idolatry, spiritual adultery, manifestation of the divine wrath," and a "response to God in various ways, but never in the sense of an autonomous faculty or achievement of man; always as evoked and wrought by God" (1956b: 341). This perpetual dialectic rebuts the view that Christianity is the result of special revelation while other religions at their best arise from general revelation.

This separation devalues revelation in nature, history, and conscience. All revelation, all disclosure, of God, is special for Kraemer: revelation is "objective divine action, decisively in the person and work of Jesus Christ, the 'Word made Flesh' " (1956b: 345). The distinction between general and special revelation is therefore a false one. Revelation is not a combination of natural and supernatural propositions, but "God's judgment *on* man . . . God's active relationship *to* man, and his long-suffering dialogue *with* man. He, God, is taking the initiative in the dialogue, from which man spontaneously tries to escape" (1956b: 347). General revelation, then, for Kraemer, is a misleading term. "The initial difficulty is that, when we take seriously the Biblical way of speaking of revelation as God's active self-disclosure out of direct personal concern for man, and directed towards the creative re-establishment of the relation of God with man, every kind of revelation is a 'special' revelation" (1956b: 353). The revelation of God in nature, history, and conscience, for Kraemer, is special revelation and other religions combine positive and negative responses to it. Nevertheless, a Christian by definition regards God's revelation in these ways, as capable of explanation only in the light of the revelation in Christ (1956b: 354). For this reason, Kraemer prefers the terms *Uroffenbarung*, "original revelation," or *Grundoffenbarung*, "fundamental revelation," to general revelation.

When applied to natural theology Kraemer's dialectical approach produces a similar outcome. Classically defined, natural theology is an attempt to discern what may be known about divine existence and nature apart from any appeal to a special instance of revelation, whether a vision, a sacred text, or some other kind of divine encounter. Thus, natural theology deliberately limits its investigations to the external world it believes all human beings to share. When Christians apply natural theology they can be led to an investigation of the Christian scriptures and, it is hoped, to an encounter with Christ. Natural theology could, in this way, wrestle with such problems as whether it can be shown that God is (either by empirical investigation or logical argumentation), that God is the ultimate source of all that is, that God is personal or non-personal, and so on. With noblest of intentions, Kraemer noted, many have pursued this activity in an attempt to "build theories which function as preambles or stepping stones or bridges . . . which lead gradually to what is called, in the context of such constructions, the fullness of Christ" (1956b: 360). So defined, however, natural theology can, as Kraemer stated, justify "what the Bible considers one of the root-sins and fundamental blindnesses of man, i.e. that man is able to arrange his relation with God" (1956b: 360). Kraemer proposes not the rejection of natural theology, however, but a reversal in priority: truly natural theology, he wrote, is illuminated and judged solely by the "central revelation in Christ" (1956b: 363).

Kraemer asserted that, between the wisdom of God and the wisdom of humanity, "there is no point of contact. . . . Only the Holy Spirit can open the eyes for God's word. Understanding and accepting the gospel means conversion, nobody excepted. This is unambiguous Biblical teaching." (1956: 363). At the same time, Kraemer said, there are points of contact for which there is no systematic method of discernment: it rests in the concrete situation of communication between people. Kraemer explained: "Different spiritual worlds in which the abortive positive responses, often in a deeply moving way, and also the negative responses to God's ongoing dialogue with man, are frequently crystalized in myths, aspirations, expectations, demonic distortions, etc." (1956b: 364). These responses would necessarily be used "in the spirit of humble service [by] the ordinary bearer of the gospel message . . . when encountering non-Christian fellow-beings or particular manifestations of spiritual reality" (1956b: 364).

Kraemer argued strongly for interreligious tolerance and co-operation, but cautioned against a tolerance rooted in the belief that the religions are ultimately one. Not only would this fail to reckon with the differences among religions sufficiently, Kraemer contended that it "practically means that except for the tiny minority of philosophies and first class mystics, the overwhelming majority of mankind has had to live in all ages in a delusive fiction" (1956b: 375). If tolerance and co-operation are rooted in a respect for difference, then they are to be furthered. True co-operation and tolerance, for Kraemer, should be approached by people who are at once "sincerely religious [and ready] to take a candidly self-critical view of the *empirical reality* of their *own* religion" (1966: 244-5). Furthermore, such activities can and should be conducted on a pragmatic basis that does not include common worship: co-operation and tolerance "on a pragmatic basis and with a pragmatic goal in mind, out of a common feeling of responsibility and concern for man and his needs, is a very important thing to strive after. This can be done if one does not seek first for a common religious basis which transcends or presumably unites the religions" (1966: 249). For Kraemer, activities presuming or aimed at demonstrating the fundamental unity of all religions, such as common worship, is misguided and ultimately counter-productive:

> We are quite aware that this sounds extremely harsh and intolerant, but it is the only way to look matters in the face, to stop blurring the issues and to arrive at a really tolerant attitude, born from a real concern for the cause of co-operation and mutual sincere esteem of adherents of different religions. . . . Why is [common worship] wrong . . . ? For the simple reason that it is spiritual quackery to maintain that one is praying to the same God named alternatively God, Ram, Allah. . . . It is not allowable to experiment with God. This softheartedness leads to a corruption of truth and loss of identity and spiritual character unintentional though this may be. Christians should be the first to point out and keep to the rules of sound inter-religious co-operation. To accomplish common worship is overstepping the boundaries and creating . . . newly constructed gods, unwittingly used as toys. (1956b: 369-70)

For Kraemer, such practices have more to do with a yearning for human solidarity than one for common religious truth and experience (1956b: 370-72). For the Christian, any model of tolerance and co-operation cannot be built on anything other than Christian faith itself, for tolerance is the only right response to the revelation in Christ.

> The Christian Faith is only a right response to the revelation in Christ, if it is tolerant. It is against God's character and His whole way of dealing with men, it is against the life, work and death of Christ, to be intolerant. God's way, Jesus' way is not the fight for truth, either by power or violence, but by love. Therefore, Christian tolerance should have nothing to do with a smiling attitude towards the finiteness and relativity of human workings of truth, including the truth which is in Christ and which is Christ. This finiteness and relativity are facts—and not at all disturbing facts—for those who live by faith in God's righteousness in Christ, and not theological doctrines or ecclesiastical prescriptions. This should make us humble, modest, patient and open with others. (1956b: 372)[13]

Religion and the Christian Faith was Kraemer's endeavour to rebut the charge that an openly Christian interpretation of the religious life of humanity is somehow arbitrary or unscientific. He insisted that a proper theology of religions is justified by appeals to the scientific study of religion and is indeed more legitimate than other, allegedly neutral, approaches, which simply mask or refuse to acknowledge their own theological biases. He argued that theological assessments are found in Christian history and contended that such interpretations are supported by scripture. To complete his defence, he outlined how his approach impinges upon discussions of general and special revelation, natural theology, and interreligious co-operation and tolerance.

Kraemer's 1956 work culminated in the development of his theology of religions begun in *The Christian Message in a Non-Christian World* and clarified a year later in "Continuity or Discontinuity." With this summary of Kraemer's work, I close Part One.

In Part One, I have argued that there are no compelling reasons to dismiss Kraemer a priori solely on the charge that he is most often associated with "exclusivism." I have shown that, while his thought overlapped with

---

13 This is a belief from which Kraemer never wavered. For him, commitment to interreligious tolerance and dialogue was a necessary implication of commitment to Christ. Toward the end of his life, he reiterated this position eloquently when he wrote, "The Christian mission, fully conscious of its role and responsibility in the serious matter of interreligious relationships, partakes or has, in my opinion, to partake in this matter, just because it is the embodiment of the most essential expression of the nature and calling of the Christian church, that is to say to proclaim by word and deed the universal Truth in Jesus Christ" (Kraemer, 1966: 243).

that of dialectical theology on several points, Kraemer was highly influenced by his education and cross-cultural encounters; it is, therefore, inappropriate to place his work under the Barthian label. Through a close exposition of his major works, I have demonstrated that Kraemer is a figure worthy of historical interest, especially in missiological circles. His pioneering work as a missionary, theologian, and ecumenist helped shape Protestant thought in Europe and North America, and it is unfortunate that his influence is being overlooked outside highly specialized circles.

In Part Two, I show that Hendrik Kraemer's position has more than emotional inspiration to offer to those contemporary Christians wrestling with religious plurality.

PART TWO

RADICAL DIFFERENCE

5

THE RADICAL DIFFERENCE OF THE GOSPEL

Biblical Realism

In Part One, I sought to overcome two obstacles. The first was the widespread assumption that confessional theologies of religions—that is theologies of religions conducted from within Christian faith—are either theologically deficient or ethically insensitive. The second was the lack of scholarly exposition of the context and content of Kraemer's thought. Having addressed these, I now turn to a critical examination of his work. In Part Two, I hope to show that Kraemer's theology of religions is theologically and ethically sound. Once this is demonstrated, Kraemer's work can be recognized as an invaluable resource for those Christians seeking to account for other faiths unapologetically, that is, from within their Christian faith.

In this chapter, I examine what Kraemer called "biblical realism," or the contention that a Christian, qua Christian, should be influenced by his or her Christian commitment when seeking to understand and assess other religions. I do not discuss whether such a position can or need be epistemically justified; although important, this highly philosophical issue falls outside the scope of this study.[1] Rather, I focus on the theological issues raised. I summarize Kraemer's position, than analyze the concern that such a position fails to take into account the rise of the historical-critical method, resting instead on what is described as a naïve biblical hermeneutic. I show that this criticism not only misunderstands Kraemer but is itself highly problematic. In a third section, I deal with a cluster of criticisms focused on Kraemer's contention that the revelation of God in Christ—the starting point for biblical realism—is sui generis, or absolutely unique. Finally, I show that Kraemer's position defends the explicitly Christian nature of the theology of religions adequately, while affirming religious diversity as part of the Christian narrative.

---

[1] Consider, for example, the work of Alvin Plantinga (1998).

1. Kraemer's Biblical Realism

Kraemer developed his theology of religions in response to what he (and other theologians) perceived as theological misunderstandings of the nature of the Christian Church and its mission in the world. According to the first, the world religions including Christianity are thought to be equally valid expressions of the human encounter with Ultimate Reality. The Christian Church is simply the corporate expression of those who have experienced this reality through the person of Jesus Christ. The goal of Christian mission, in turn, is not the proclamation of the gospel, but the pursuit of interreligious understanding, appreciation, and truth, however that may be defined. Kraemer had in mind here the work of the American philosopher and mystic W. E. Hocking (1932). The British philosopher of religion John Hick ably defends a persuasive version of this position, holding that all religions potentially provide saving contact with Ultimate Reality and can and should be assessed according to their ability to produce exemplary human lives, or saints (1989). To draw a biological analogy, this view suggests that religion is a genus of which the religions are the species.

This biological analogy can do further service to characterize another misunderstanding Kraemer addressed, namely, that religion is a genus, with Christianity as the most advanced species. According to this position, Christianity represents the highest stage of human religious evolution. What is hidden and incomplete in Hinduism, Buddhism, tribal, and other religions is rendered explicit and complete with the coming of Christianity. Here, a more or less traditional sense of mission is maintained: the gospel is to be proclaimed, and all who believe are to be baptized. Although their visible incorporation into the Christian Church may entail a rejection of certain beliefs and practices once held, the new converts can and ought to incorporate the highest and best elements of their previous religious lives into their newly embraced faith. Those holding to a version of this position seek nobly to affirm other beliefs and practices, while at the same time maintaining the uniqueness of Christ and his Church. Intentions aside, however, Kraemer felt that this position also runs the risk of reducing other religious expressions to mere preparations for the gospel, having no significance in and of themselves. Dominant in missionary circles at the time Kraemer was writing, this understanding was best defended by J. N. Farquhar, a Christian missionary to India (1971). The early liberal Protestant theologian Friedrich Schleiermacher (1989: 31-76), along with the modern Roman Catholic Karl Rahner (1966) have propounded similar theories in contemporary systematic theology.

Kraemer also responded to modes of thinking that insisted that "the generating factors of religions [exist] in some region of man's consciousness, a certain psychological attitude or social necessity, a lack of adequate knowledge of the world" (1956b: 54). According to this view—propounded by Sigmund Freud (1964), Ludwig Feuerbach (1957), and Karl Marx and Friedrich Engels (1964)—the religions can and should be reduced to, and described in, strictly this-worldly terms. For Freud, religion is simply a sophisticated form of wish-fulfillment; Feuerbach sees it as the projection of human ideals onto the universe; and, for Marx and Engels, it is a means to distract the working class from their present economic plight and thereby to control them. For all three, religion generally, and Christianity specifically, represents an infantile stage in human development and must, among members of a human race come-of-age, be transcended. In some cases, the religions are arranged on an evolutionary scale and, as with the previous position, Christianity is often found at the top. This is unsurprising, given the cultural influence of Christianity in Europe and America when these positions initially grasped intellectual imaginations. Kraemer's assessment was that where fulfilment theology sees Christianity as the highest and best of all that has preceded it, here Christianity is but the highest and last of many mistakes. The Church, in this view, is regarded as redundant and/or obsolete; ironically, a strong sense of mission is often retained, as in the expansionist vision of Marxism.

Prima facie, these three positions are very different. As Kraemer presents them, the first two are broadly religious accounts, while the third is strictly naturalist; for the first, Christianity is one among equals; for the second, Christianity perfects the highest and best of the rest; for the last, Christianity is regarded as the end of a string of errors. Nevertheless, Kraemer regarded all three as fundamentally similar for despite their clear differences, each posits an essence of religion against which all religions can and should be evaluated. Kraemer contended that this was precisely the root of their error. For him, all three positions err in their seeking to understand Christian faith and life according to a set of criteria foreign to that faith and life. Truly to understand Christian faith, indeed any religion, countered Kraemer, one must sympathetically enter into the universe of discourse that it occupies. More specifically, if the Christian faith is to be understood at all, it must be understood first and foremost from within on its own terms.

Furthermore, once such a sympathetic approach is undertaken, one cannot but conclude that Christian faith is not one among many, superior to the rest, nor an emotional prop to be overcome, but something radically different. Kraemer encapsulated this contrariety in the term biblical realism (1938: 32). For him, one can begin to understand the uniqueness of the Church and its mission only from the perspective of the Bible, "the tale of God's self-disclosure and of the disclosure of the genuine condition of man and the world in the light of the divine Self-disclosure" (1939: 2). For Kraemer, the Bible is not simply a piece of classic literature or a record of human religious experience; rather, it is the record of God's self-disclosing activity (1939: 2). This is, of course, not the only text claiming such authority. For the Christian—certainly for Kraemer—it is the primary text, for it alone has as its climax the life, ministry, death, and resurrection of Jesus Christ.

This is a bold assertion to be sure, but it may be countered by the important argument that there are other texts purporting to record the acts and sayings of Jesus. Why then ought Christians to consider only those texts found in the Bible to be authoritative? This problem of canon is not a new question. The institution of a final authority in matters of doctrine, a point of orientation for the Church's faith and practice, is almost as old as Christianity. Kraemer addressed this issue, first, by defending such an approach to the Bible. From a strictly historical perspective, it may be argued that the constitution of the Christian canon was both arbitrary and accidental. This is precisely all a historian can say, replied Kraemer, along with the possible admission that, while arbitrary, it proved to be of enormous significance in the shaping of European culture for nineteen centuries. Nevertheless, Kraemer stated, a "member of the Christian Church cannot and ought not to be satisfied with this external judgment. Standing in the stream of the fellowship of believers, he sees in this act not only a right intuition, but the guidance of the Holy Spirit" (1956b: 276-7). There is a sense, in other words, in which a defence of biblical authority is ultimately internal to Christian faith. It is not that there are no external criteria to validate this understanding of the Bible but that, in and of themselves, they are insufficient. Archaeological discoveries confirming biblical accounts, for example, cannot, in themselves, bring human beings to trust in the Bible as an account of God's revelation; they show only that it is more or less historically sound in certain cases. Belief in the authority of scripture is finally dependent on the illumination of the Christian by the Holy Spirit.

Externally, the most that can be said is that, while there are other texts purporting to describe the deeds and teachings of Jesus, throughout history none has proven as sustained or fruitful as those compiled in the Christian Bible. The Christian Bible, for Kraemer, is authoritative for Christians because it gives its readers access to Jesus Christ, it records the self-disclosing acts of God that culminate in Jesus Christ. It is as the climax of the biblical narrative that Kraemer designated the revelation in Christ as sui generis—in a class alone. Without denying either the possibility or the reality of God speaking or revealing outside Christ or the Bible, he affirmed that, for the Christian, it is the criterion by which all claims to revelation are to be judged. The Bible is normative for Christians, in other words, because it links them to Jesus Christ.

Kraemer held that, in order to discern the nature of the Church and its mission to the world, one must be founded on the only authority to which the Church can be held accountable: the revelation of God in Christ as recorded in the Bible. This is his biblical realism. Still, this might suggest that an individual alone stands on this foundation. For Kraemer, however, proper discernment also requires situation within the Church, the structure erected on the biblical foundation. My exposition of biblical realism would therefore be incomplete without a brief examination of Kraemer's understanding of the role of the Church in biblical interpretation.

Kraemer regards the Church as a divine-human society founded on the revelation of God and erected by humans in history. From the divine perspective, it is unique in the world and among religions because it is "a fellowship rooted in God and His divine redemptive order, and therefore committed to the service and salvation of the world" (1938: 30). Uniqueness derives from its commission to be a "bearer of the witness to God and his decisive acts and purposes" (1938: 2). Regardless of its position in geography and history, the Church, for Kraemer, is an apostolic body called to testify to what God has done in Christ. Yet, were it to be defined simply in terms of this essential nature, the understanding of the Church would be incomplete. For the Church does not exist above history, but in its midst. It is a human institution and therefore shares in human limitations and sin. It is embodied in particular times, at particular places and reflects particular historical temperaments and cultural predispositions (1938: 419). From the human perspective, the Church can and ought to be seen, as Kraemer said, as "a specimen of human effort in the field of religion, and therefore to be brought into line with the other expressions of human spiritual life" (1938: 285). This divine-human dialectic is inevitable for the divine essence always and everywhere works through human institution.

When this dialectic is applied to Kraemer's understanding of scripture, an interesting tension results. From the divine side of his dialectic, the Church is called into existence by God to preserve and proclaim the divine self-disclosure as it has been recorded in the Bible. Accordingly, the interpretation of scripture is an inherently communal activity. Individuals undertake it, to be sure, but ones formed and informed by the peculiar practices of the peculiar ecclesial communities to which they belong. There is a sense in which the interpretation of the Church provides a control for the interpretation of the individual. From the human side of the dialectic, a different picture emerges. For the empirical Church—the Church embodied in history—has continually to confront itself with the message of the Bible, Kraemer averred, in order to be inspired, cleansed, and renewed (1938:

418). The Church both interprets and is judged by the revelation of God recorded in the Bible.

To summarize, through biblical realism, Kraemer held that the relationship of the Church to the world and, accordingly, to other religions, is properly discerned only when the inquirer is deliberately and explicitly situated within the realm of the Christian revelation. For Kraemer, the foundation is the Bible, and its climax is the narrative of Jesus Christ; the Christian Church is built upon this foundation, testifies to and interprets it and stands under its judgment. If this foundation is rejected for another, the result is hopeless confusion. Thus biblical realism attempts to situate the theologian explicitly within the tradition through which he or she comes to the problem of other religions. "The seriousness of true religion," Kraemer concludes, "demands that one shall be one's true religious self" (1960: 356).

2. Biblical Realism and Biblical Criticism

Kraemer's insistence on the foundational and communal nature of the Christian scriptures for theological reflection has, however, invited criticism. "Historical studies," wrote Alan Race, "have made us so aware of the nature of the biblical material and how it has come to us that Kraemer's reliance on the Bible, in its particular form, now seems over-simple and naïve" (1993: 30). The unsophisticated and even stubborn nature of biblical realism is particularly evident in its orthodox affirmation of the incarnation. Bluntly put, Kraemer's critics charge that traditional understandings of the incarnation cannot withstand the scrutiny of historical/critical scholarship and are no longer binding for contemporary Christians (Race, 1993: 33). Consider, for example, the questions posed by Paul Knitter concerning traditional language about the incarnation:

> [Is it] part of the *essential message* of the New Testament or does it belong to the *medium* used to get that message across? Further is it *philosophical* language about the structures of the relationship between the infinite and the finite, meant to *negate* all relationships apart from Christ? Or is it *confessional* language meant to affirm the importance of what God had done in Jesus? (1985: 92-3)

According to these critics, Kraemer cannot account for the historically conditioned nature of the Bible because he "depends too heavily upon a literal reading of the biblical texts. . . . [He] interprets God as operating in the world in a limited historical, geographical and cultural context" (Gillis, n.d.: 267). Dependent as he is on a pre-critical and naïve hermeneutic,

BIBLICAL REALISM   93

Kraemer's understanding of scripture cannot withstand biblical criticism; the historically, geographically, and contextually bound biblical documents cannot provide the foundation biblical realism requires.

Race, Knitter, and Gillis appear to agree that it is the task of biblical criticism to disclose the pre-textual essential message by abstracting the kernel of meaning from the husk of human accretions in the medium. Such an approach relocates the meaning and, accordingly, the authority of the text from its received form to what actually happened. The result of this strategy is ably expressed by Daniel Migliore: "What is authoritative is not the text, but the 'facts' behind the text as reconstructed by the historian" (Migliore, 1991: 44). Hans Frei has shown that such an approach to the biblical texts has been on going since the eighteenth century. In his landmark work, *The Eclipse of Biblical Narrative* (1974), he further argues for a break with this methodology. At its outset, liberal hermeneutics located the meaning of the biblical story either in universal experience or reason, or in a world behind the text accessible only through historical reconstruction. Although conservative responses rejected the first option, they shared the fundamental presuppositions of the second, differing only in the conclusions reached:

> [In both,] real events of history constitute an autonomous temporal framework of their own under God's providential design. Instead of rendering them accessible, the narratives, heretofore indispensable as a means of access to the events, now simply verify them, thus affirming their autonomy and the fact that they are in principle accessible though any kind of description that can manage to be accurate either predictively or after the event. (1974: 4)

Since the eighteenth century, biblical hermeneutics has posited a gap between the biblical narratives and that to which they refer, and has located the meaning in the latter. Hence, the meaning of the Bible is sundered from its literary form and the facts are set within a different interpretive grid—one provided by the biblical scholar.[2]

As a result, the Bible is meaningful only within the limits of the "assumptions about the nature of history brought by the interpreter to the

---

[2] Frei wrote, "the bond of continuity, the meaning of the narrative, has to be discovered at a level more remote than that of depiction or cumulative rendering through the interaction of character and incident. The meaning of the narrative is something other than the narrative shape itself. There is, for this whole point of view, simply no way of dealing with descriptive or narrative shape without shifting the meaning to a more profound stratum. The documents mean something other than what they way" (1974: 318).

text" (Migliore, 1991: 45). Issues of meaning and authority, however, are inevitably interwoven in the interpretation of sacred texts. By reducing the meaning of the text to the world behind the text, critical hermeneutics is forced to account also for the authority of these texts. Conservative hermeneutics has typically resorted to doctrines of inerrancy or infallibility—for instance, that the Bible preserves the world behind the text without error or in a manner incapable of error—to render such an explanation. Liberal hermeneutics, on the other hand, tends to reduce authority to a matter of historical and cultural contingency.

In contradistinction to both, Frei offers a postcritical hermeneutic that locates meaning neither in psychologically reconstructed authorial intentions nor in historically reconstructed worlds, but in the biblical text itself. He therefore opposes both a critical separation of text and meaning and a precritical equation of intra-textual meaning and extra-textual reality.

> [It is] reading with that second naïveté which is done in correspondence with a hermeneutics of restoration . . . the kind of reading that might well wish to be of a "revised literal" sort. It distances the text from the author, from the original discourse's existential situation and from every other kind of reading that would go "behind" the text and "refer" it to any other world of meaning than its own, the world "in front of the text." And yet, this kind of reading has been through the mill of critically transcending that first naïve literalism for which every statement on the printed page "means" either because it refers not only ostensively but also correctly, naming a true state of affairs each time, or else because it shapes part of a realm of discourse whose vocabulary one can finally understand by repeating it and in that sense (if sense it is) taking it at face value. (Frei, 1993: 130)

Frei proposes to close the gap in hermeneutics, both liberal and conservative. For him, there is no interpretative breach between texts and their meaning; rather, the biblical narratives most resemble realistic novels "where meaning is most nearly inseparable from the words—from the descriptive shape of the story as a pattern of enactment. . . . [T]here is neither need for nor use in looking for meaning in a more profound stratum underneath the structure (a separable 'subject matter') or in a separable author's 'intention,' or in a combination of such behind-the-scenes projections" (1993: 30). The biblical narratives can, but need not, describe actual historical events in order to be meaningful for Christian theology.

Rather than criticize or build on Frei's proposals here, I employ him to challenge the unstated assumption of Kraemer's critics that historical-critical methodology is the only scholarly way to approach the biblical or any other text in order to access its meaning. Clearly, this is not the case. Frei, for one, makes a compelling case that the meaning of the text is in the text and is accessible apart from appeals to authorial or historical worlds behind it. Second, if Frei's argument has merit, then beginning with the biblical text, as Kraemer does, is not necessarily hermeneutically naïve. As a result, the onus is on Race, Knitter, Gillis, and others who assume that to begin at a place other than historical reconstruction is somehow uncritical or arbitrary.

This criticism is easily dismissed, first of all because it is marked by a lack of reference to Kraemer's understanding of scripture. Even a cursory glance at his writings indicates a position with greater nuance that welcomes the findings of critical biblical scholarship. Consider these words:

> Thanks to the remarkable results of modern Biblical research our possibilities of faithful interpretation (of various elements of the Biblical literature as well as of these elements in the context of the whole of the Bible) have enormously increased. These results of Biblical research have set us freer on the one hand, and on the other hand have taught us that we should be very serious in accepting the fact that the Bible speaks the Word of God in definite historical situations and wholly by means and in terms which were products of the situation. (1956b: 267)

Kraemer does not found biblical realism on a rigid, literalistic hermeneutical approach to the scriptures but, rather, refers to their "human and in many ways historically conditioned" nature (1939: 2). This seems to introduce an inconsistency, for if chapter 3 has summarized Kraemer's position accurately, then he has a high view of biblical authority. However, the previous excerpts suggest that he also accepts historical-critical scholarship as a legitimate and helpful enterprise.

Historical-critical methodologies clearly do have a place in biblical studies. Properly employed, historical critical hermeneutics discern how the biblical texts have come to their present form, addressing—among others— issues of authorship, redaction, and historical context. Though the methodologies cannot disclose the one true meaning of the text, they provide boundary markers against false or poor ones. They cannot deal with questions of revelation, authority, and canon because they are not designed so to do. Biblical realism, on the other hand, can wrestle precisely with these dilemmas. The question that concerns Kraemer—*Why has this text come to be?*—is theologically prior to the historian's question *How have these texts come to be?* It appears then that the concerns expressed by Race, Knitter, and Gillis confuse two different questions, while Kraemer rightly separated them. As a result, he could accept on the one hand the findings of biblical criticism and affirm on the other the authority of scripture as the revelation of the word of God:

> The Bible is a book which, being composed of many writings . . . reflects various historical, cultural and religious situations. Only when the collections gathered under the names Old and New Testament gradually became canonized . . . did it begin its career as a solid authoritative unity. . . . The remarkable thing is that, from the time it was made into one book, it not only functioned as one book, because the Church's canonization made it so, but that, independently of this canonization, it proved to have on the whole an intrinsic unity, because, in spite of its multiform composition, it was held together by its great theme: God, the Creator, the God of Abraham, Isaac and Jacob; the God of the Covenant with Israel, His chosen people; God the Creator and Redeemer though His Son Jesus Christ, who entrusts His "people", the *ekklesia*, to the guidance of His Holy Spirit; God the Consummatory, who leads His world towards His end, which is the full manifestation of His Kingdom. Both this intrinsic unity, which witnesses consistently to a wholly transcendent conditioning of the book in all its aspects, and the multiform historical conditioning of the gook in its many parts, must be seriously kept in mind if the material is to be used in the right way. (1956b: 238-9)

By pointing to the thematic unity of the documents, Kraemer located authority—rightly in my view—not within historically reconstructed, pretextual facts but within the text itself, within the larger pattern of the biblical narrative and its climax: the life, ministry, death, and resurrection of Jesus Christ. Biblical realism is an attempt to articulate the authority and indispensability of the Bible, not only for a Christian interpretation of religions but for all Christian faith and life. Thus, Kraemer's biblical realism recognizes the limits of biblical criticism overlooked by its opponents.

3. The Sui Generis Nature of Revelation

Other criticisms centre on Kraemer's persistent description of the revelation in Christ as sui generis. One is directed against a perceived weakness in his doctrine of the Church, contends that Kraemer's focus on the primacy of the revelation in Christ as the evaluative criterion creates a disjunction not between Christianity and other religions but between Christ and all religions. Hence, the sui generis in Christ provides an equally damning judgment on what Kraemer called "empirical Christianity." He stated:

"Christianity as a historical religion has to be distinguished very sharply from the Christian revelation because Christianity, as the well-known historical phenomenon which belongs to world history and church history, has in very many respects to be put on the same plane as the other religions of mankind" (1939: 13). To divorce the Christian revelation from Christianity in so sharp a way has been criticized by Lesslie Newbigin, who observes that the Christian revelation cannot be abstracted from the communities that receive, remember, protect, and proclaim it: "The claim that . . . Christ is decisive for all human life is a meaningless claim except as it is interpreted in the life of the community which lives by the tradition of the apostolic testimony. There cannot, therefore, be a *total* disjunction between the Gospel and 'Christianity' " (1969: 77). It cannot be denied that Kraemer's writings, both early and later, make this distinction (e.g., 1938: 108-9; 1956b: 82). Still, the objection fails to consider the context of Tambaram and the ecclesiological framework of Kraemer's argument.

When taken into account, these factors show that Kraemer's distinction was not to disparage the Christian Church but to preserve and better articulate its mission. It must be remembered that Kraemer separated empirical Christianity from the Christian revelation in the aftermath of the International Missionary Council meeting in Jerusalem 1928 and its preoccupation with the values of non-Christian religions. This discussion distracted participants from the central issue: the mission of the Church in the world. Adherents to the fulfillment school spoke of Christianity as the completion of the highest and best of the religions. Kraemer felt that such an attitude, however well intentioned, was both condescending and mistaken—as he stated in *The Christian Message*—for the "non-Christian religions can just as well as Christianity show up an impressive record of psychological, cultural and other values, and it is wholly dependent on one's fundamental axioms of life whether one considers these . . . achievements of higher value for mankind than the Christian" (1938: 106). Those following Hocking took the values argument to its logical conclusion and spoke of an interreligious alliance aimed at enriching an increasingly secular world. Kraemer argued that this strategy ignored the nature of the Church as an apostolic body witnessing to the revelation of God in the world. Each case presupposed that Christianity was one species in the genus of religion. By distinguishing between Christianity and revelation, Kraemer countered that the Church's uniqueness derives not from its ability to complete non-Christian belief and practice, but from the message it has been commissioned to proclaim. His Christianity/revelation distinction, far from detracting from the uniqueness of the Church, was a means to underscore it against those who misunderstood it.

Furthermore, the criticism overlooks the overtly ecclesiological model within which Kraemer worked and about which he was explicit: "The Church and all Christians, if the have ears to hear and eyes to see, are confronted with this question: What is its essential nature, and what is its obligation to the world?" (1938: 1). This is the question that *The Christian Message* proposed to answer. Moreover, it is also the central problem tackled two decades later in *Religion and the Christian Faith*:

> Independent of any circumstances or historical situations, the problem of the relation of the Christian faith to the many other religions is inherent in the nature of the Christian Church. . . . As an apostolic body, the Church is commissioned to proclaim—by its *kerygma* of God's acts of salvation in Christ, by its *koinonia* as a new community, living in the bonds of peace and charity—the message of God's dealings with and purpose for, the world and mankind. (1956b: 17-8)

It was Kraemer's position that any theology of religions that strictly limits the discussion to problems of general revelation or natural theology without addressing ecclesiology neglects that the conversation is "embedded in the all-embracing problem of the Christian religion or the Christian Church in its relation to the world" (1938: 103). This position both preserves and is set within a strong doctrine of the Church. Nowhere is this more apparent than the closing chapter of *The Christian Message*: "Just as the prophetic religion of Biblical realism is a religion *sui generis*, so the Christian Church, according to the conception of the New Testament is a community *sui generis*. . . . It is . . . not a voluntary society but God's act through Jesus Christ, called into being by His redemptive purpose" (1938: 415-6). In this light, it is clear that Kraemer does not so much sharply separate Christianity from revelation, as emphasize that the Church's uniqueness lies not in any inherent value but in the message it proclaims and by which it is judged.

Another criticism challenged Kraemer's dual affirmation of the revelation of God in nature, history, conscience, and the universal religious consciousness and, simultaneously, that all religious life is misdirected in the light of the Christian revelation. In what sense, asks Gavin D'Costa, "can Kraemer claim a *sui generis* status for the *event* of God's revelation in Christ, in the light of his own admission that God works outside this revelation?" (1986: 65). He pursues this question further with Israel as a test case.

> Israel's understanding, acceptance and faith in Yahweh, although faltering, provides a test case for examining the coherence of Kraemer's . . . assertions that salvation is only possibly through explicit confession and surrender to the revelation of God in

Christ. If this exclusivist contention is taken seriously, then it must imply that the revelation of God in Israel's history was (a) not revelation after all, or (b) a revelation, but somehow inadequate for salvation. (D'Costa, 1986: 66)

According to D'Costa, Kraemer opts for (b) thereby contradicting his own position. D'Costa notes that, since Kraemer allowed that there is revelation outside Jesus Christ, "then it cannot be claimed that Jesus is the only or *sui generis* event of revelation" (1986: 66). While the contents of the Christian revelation may have normative status, it is self-contradictory to admit other revelatory events while asserting that the Christ event is sui generis. Further, D'Costa points to an even more perplexing contradiction: "How can it be maintained that the only way to salvation is explicit confession and surrender to God in Christ, if God has truly revealed Himself in Israel's history before the coming of Jesus Christ?" (1986: 67). If a study of Israel shows that God's revelatory activity is not limited to Jesus Christ, then the same is true for God's saving activity. D'Costa notes a third contradiction that is an expansion of the second:

What of the many pious Jews before the time of Jesus; those who did submit entirely to God's self-disclosure within Israel's history? What of Abraham and Moses and the many holy men and women Israel listed so eloquently in the Letter to the Hebrews, chapter 11? Relatedly, we may ask what of the countless millions of non-Christians who lived before the time of Jesus who have never heard the gospel, often through no fault of their own? . . . Can we really accept that the God revealed in Christ, a loving father of "generous unlimited Divine love" has denied so many millions the means to salvation—through no fault of their own? (1986: 68)

The success of the criticism depends on what Kraemer means by the phrase sui generis when applying it to the Christ event.

D'Costa contends, above, that Kraemer's phrase means both that the revelation in Christ is the only revelation and that salvation is possible only by responding in faith to this revelation. If this interpretation is correct, then the charge of self-contradiction is justified. It can be shown, however, that in his use of sui generis, Kraemer intended neither. Rather, he used the phrase to emphasize that a properly Christian evaluation of other religions takes as its ultimate criterion the revelation in Christ. In this way, he sets himself against the fulfilment theology predominant at Jerusalem 1928 and Tambaram 1938 and Hocking's nascent pluralism. "Natural theology of that sort," Kraemer wrote, "which conceives the Gospel as essentially the fulfilment, the highest development and budding forth of the religious forces and seeds in mankind overlooks—we repeat—the *sui generis* character of the revelation of Christ" (1938: 123). To do otherwise subjects the revelation in Christ to yet another, higher standard. Kraemer asked: "Is Christ the measure of true religion, or is it some general religious *a priori* by which Christ has to be measured? Christians cannot behave as if there is an ultimate religious *a priori*, under which Christ is to be subsumed. For them Christ is the religious *a priori*" (1956b: 145). The sui generis nature of the Christian revelation, as Kraemer characterized it, does not deny the working of God outside it but posits it as the standard by which such divine activity can be measured.

To leave the matter there, however, rasies the question of self-contradiction, for it can yet be argued that Kraemer's affirmation of extra-Christian revelation contradicts his evaluation of the "world which is manifested in the whole range of religious striving" as discontinuous with the revelation in Christ (1939: 2). Here, his notion of subversive fulfilment must be further explored. In Kraemer's view, to represent "the religions as *somehow*, however imperfect and crude it may be . . . a schoolmaster to Christ," fails to account for the "essential 'otherness' " both of the religions and the Christian revelation (1939: 5). If the religions are indivisible totalities, each with their own distinctive doctrines, practices and ultimate aims, then Kraemer reasoned to regard them as "preparation or a leading up to a so-called consummation or fulfilment in Christ," is to fail to take them seriously (1939: 3). In the light of Christ, they are "blind and misdirected" because they do not share the goal of the Christian revelation in the first place. For example, of the missionary experience in Africa, Kraemer wrote that, often, it is "not the consciousness of sin [that] brings men to Christ, but the continued contact with Christ [that] brings them to consciousness of sin" (1938: 112). Later, he clarified that: "Only an attentive study of the Bible can open the eyes to the fact that Christ 'the power of God' and the 'wisdom of God' stands in contradiction to the power and the wisdom of man. Perhaps in some respects it were proper to speak of contradictive or subversive fulfilment" (1939: 5). Thus, the dual affirmation of the Christian revelation as sui generis and the revelation of God outside it is not necessarily self-contradictory. By sui generis Kraemer does not mean to say that the revelation in Christ is the only revelation, but that it is the criterion by which Christians are to judge all religious activity.

By rejecting the fulfilment theology of many of his contemporaries, Kraemer did not withhold salvation from those who have not heard or responded to the gospel, as D'Costa's criticisms have suggested. Consider these remarks by Kraemer, intended for the Tambaram meeting:

> This rejection of a *theologia naturalis* as affording the basic religious truths on which the realm of the Christian revelation rises as the fitting superstructure does not, however, *include* denying that God has been working in the minds of men outside the sphere of the Christian revelation and that there have been, and may be now, acceptable men of faith who live under the sway of the non-Christian religions—products, however, not of these non-Christian religions but of the mysterious workings of God's spirit. God forbid that we mortal men should be so irreverent as to dispose of how and where the Sovereign God of grace and love has to act. (1939: 4-5)

Kraemer, like Newbigin later, refused to pronounce on the eternal fate of non-Christians. He never asserted that salvation is possible only through explicit faith in Christ. D'Costa, however, is unhappy with Kraemer's agnosticism: "This answer seems painfully inadequate . . . and it is not clear, if we use our test case of Israel, where there are supposedly inadequate grounds for attempting to probe the issue further" (1986: 68). With these words, D'Costa implies that God's covenant with Israel is a limit-case for all non-Christian or pre-Christian religions. For Kraemer, however, as the Old Testament records the revelation of God to Israel—the revelation that finds its fullest expression in Jesus Christ—both are themselves unique: "Christianity is a child of the religion of Israel, the religion of Moses and the prophets. Jesus stood deeply rooted in this ancestral heritage and breathed in this atmosphere of God's revelation through His dealing with, and his spiritual gifts to, the people of Israel" (1938: 237). As a result, the religion of and revelation to Israel was and remains an important part of the world of Kraemer's biblical realism. This neither demeans the religious quality of non-Christian sacred texts nor implies that the Old Testament is immaculate. What he did say was that: "The crucial point is that religiously speaking, the Jewish Old Testament is not primarily the document of Jewish religious experience, but of God's revelational dealings with the people of Israel and through them with the world, as an introduction to His decisive and revelational dealing with Israel and the world in Jesus Christ" (1939: 329-30). Of course, the uniqueness of the revelation of God to Israel is not peculiar to Kraemer but a postulate central to orthodox Christian doctrines of revelation.

If Israel is a unique case in the history of God's dealings with humanity, then D'Costa's use of Israel and the Old Testament as a salvific test case can be questioned. Can he legitimately argue that remaining agnostic on the fate of those who have never heard of Jesus Christ through no fault of their own is tantamount to being skeptical about the eternal destiny of the many faithful people listed in Hebrews 11? I think not. Alternatively, if, as

DiNoia has persuasively argued, religions offer "distinctive teachings about the true aim of life, the reasons for pursuing it and the means of attaining and enjoying it" (1992: 35), must we not be cautious about affirming the final salvation of members of other religious communities? At the same time, however, given the eschatological hope for the renewal of all creation comprising a redeemed Israel and a restored human race (e.g., Romans 8:18-11:36), must we not also refrain from denying it? Kraemer's avoidance of a priori judgments, in this light, appears to be justified. D'Costa rightly admits that, when debating "the salvation of non-Christians, or Christians, for that matter, we cannot confidently assert that this or that person is saved or not—ultimately all rests within the 'mysterious workings of God's Spirit' " (1986: 68). Just as Kraemer's emphasis on the sui generis nature of Christian revelation does not necessarily contradict his affirmation of extra-Christian revelation, neither does it necessarily withhold salvation from those who are not visibly incorporated into the Christian Church.

This soteriological debate leads directly to a third major criticism of Kraemer. This criticism by D'Costa makes three charges, the first being that Kraemer risks reducing all religious activity to human achievements and failures. D'Costa further charges that Kraemer assumes there is an unbridgeable gulf between God and humanity that prohibits any and all natural theology, and that his christology is reductive. D'Costa argues that "Kraemer's stark emphasis on the *sui generis* nature of Christ's revelation assumes a deep and unbridgeable gulf between God's grace and fallen humanity.... That is, salvation is constituted and brought about by Christ who is the sole bridge across the gaping abyss between God's grace and fallen humankind's sinfulness" (1986: 69). D'Costa contends that in so doing, Kraemer risks reducing all events other than the revelation in Christ to "human achievements and failures, despite his protestations to the contrary" (1986: 69). Further, D'Costa notes that this is also the source of his opposition to all natural theology: "according to Biblical realism, the opposite of grace is not nature or reason, but sin" (Kraemer, 1938: 115). D'Costa takes this admission that such a gulf seems to contradict another of Kraemer's contentions: that God has given all human beings a universal religious consciousness. D'Costa counters, "If a person's ability to respond to revelation is not by means of reason or through any faculty possessed by that person, but by the initiative of God, however misused and misdirected, is not this basic orientation towards God a gift of grace? What else can it be called? And if it is, can such an absolute rift between grace and sinful nature be maintained?" (1986: 69-70). To the charges of this criticism, I offer responses.

While I have shown that Kraemer's emphasis on the Christian revelation does not deny extra-Christian revelation, I feel that D'Costa is justified in his first charge. Consider, for example, Kraemer's remark in *The Christian Message*: "Surveying *human endeavour* towards spiritual expression over the whole range of life, the obvious statement to be made is that all religions . . . are the various *efforts of man* to apprehend the totality of existence" (1938: 111). Not only does he stress the human element in religions in *The Christian Message*, but, while criticizing Barth for a similar shortcoming, Kraemer remains vague on the workings of God outside Christ (1938: 120). This can be attributed to his desire to "throttle"—to quote Kulandran (cited in Ariarajah, 1991: 86)—Hocking's naïve endorsement of religious activity. In a later clarification, Kraemer sought to right the balance by over-emphasizing that the "most sincere representative of the most impressive forms of piety or quality of life may happen to be the farthest from the kingdom of God. There is at least, no guarantee whatever that sincerity, or, humanly speaking, superb expressions of spiritual calibre mean necessarily openness or nearness to the understanding of God's 'foolishness in Christ' " (1956b: 365). In this light, his overemphasis on the human nature of all religious activity, while perhaps unjustifiable, is understandable.

Religion and the Christian Faith as a whole reflects this greater sense of balance. There, Kraemer asserted that remaining true to "dialectic character of the Biblical revelation . . . means saying in one breath 'yes' and 'no' to the world in all its spheres of life, which precludes the programme of synthesis, and yet impels toward true 'communication' " (1956b: 322). For instance, Kraemer reported that a myth central to the religious life of a tribe in Indonesia "conveys the idea that the life of the world is established in the death and sacrifice of a god, and that it has to be re-established constantly therein by re-enacting this primordial event in the ritual actions of the whole tribe" (1956b: 323). Kraemer discerned a deep *Ahung* (intuition): "It is striking that this dramatization of myth contains an apprehension akin to the Biblical one that all life and existence rests in the activity of God" (1956b: 324). This positive analysis, however, is follwed by the insight that: "The dialectical condition manifests itself in the fact that this re-enactment of myth is perverted into a magical human act. With all his sacral awe, man behaves as a usurper of God's domain, which is exactly what is meant by 'Original Sin' " (1956b:324). Therefore, while D'Costa is right to point out a possible extreme in Kraemer's work, the force of the charge is turned aside by a contextually sensitive reading of his early work coupled with a careful analysis of his later work.

The gravity of D'Costa's charge regarding Kraemer's apparent prohibition of natural theology depends on what is meant by natural theology. If the term designates "the process whereby persons can, by their own natural powers arrive at belief in God" (D'Costa, 1986: 58), then

Kraemer as a Reformed theologian is quite willingly guilty. He opposes any natural theology conceived as a universal foundation for revelation because it rests on what Kraemer contended is "a fundamental religious mistake. . . . [Its] starting-point is the ontological conception of Greek philosophy about God, that God is Pure Essence and the Unity of all Being—and not the prophetic voluntaristic conception of the Bible" (1938: 115). In this system, Kraemer argued, revelation and its content becomes "logically speaking, a much-needed supplement to the insufficiency of reason in the realm of supernatural truth, and not the crisis of all religions and all human reasoning, which it is in the sphere of Biblical realism" (1938: 115). Moreover, that which Kraemer sought was not a rejection of natural theology, but its redefinition and reappropriation. In *Religion and the Christian Faith*, his opposition to natural theology remains undiminished, for it makes "the God and father of our Lord Jesus Christ . . . a subordinate idea which can fit in with a philosophy of religion" (1956b: 361). Rather than repudiate it altogether, Kraemer subverted the traditional relationship between the natural and the revealed where "a Biblically based doctrine of God's revelation in nature, history and conscience [can be treated as] modes within the one central revelation in Christ, which illuminates the real meaning and is the criterion of these modes" (1956b: 363).

If, by their own natural powers—for instance, through some kind of natural theology—people cannot respond to revelation then they must do so by the gracious intervention of God. If the source of this response is Kraemer's religious consciousness, then this consciousness is a gift of grace. If it is a universal gift of grace, however, then, according to D'Costa's final charge, the rift between God and humanity does not seem as severe as Kraemer's sui generis definition of the revelation in Christ seems to indicate. The impact this final charge is dissipated when one remembers that Kraemer did not require the explicit confession of and surrender to Christ as a precondition to the enjoyment of final salvation. He was not an Arminian; he did not believe—as much evangelical thought does—that people are saved by their explicit faith in Christ. To Kraemer's ears, such a proposition would sound like soteriological synergism, a denial of the sola gratia central to Reformed Christianity. On the contrary, Kraemer is a Reformed theologian who refused to limit arbitrarily the saving grace of God. The sui generis does not deny that God saves outside Christianity, but affirms that any salvation willed by God is always the salvation won by Christ.

D'Costa's final charge presents Kraemer's christology as reductive in so far as it "tends to absolutize only one aspect of Christ's revelation of God (concerning humankind's sinfulness), which is excessively Pauline. . . . Time and time again, Kraemer dismisses the value of non-Christian insights because they lack the consciousness of sin and the need for forgiveness" (D'Costa, 1986: 72). In so doing, D'Costa argues that Kraemer denies a priori the possibility of learning what M. M. Thomas calls "new truths in Christ" which, while standing outside the categories of sin and salvation and orthodox christology completely, do not contradict them (1969: 304-5). Thus, despite his profession of openness to learning from other religions, it is difficult to see how Kraemer can be open given his christological criterion. In rejecting Hocking's both/and religious epistemology, Kraemer went to the opposite extreme, opting for an equally simplistic either/or model. D'Costa's criticism is not without foundation: "Clearly what is needed is a judicious use of both the either-or and the both-and models, whenever appropriate, rather than the *a priori* adoption of one rather than the other. In this way, it seems possible to remain committed, while truly open to whatever riches are discovered in the lives and religions of non-Christians, both past, present and to come" (1986: 73). Although Kraemer does speak of the plurality of approaches within biblical realism (1938: 84), he goes on to focus explicitly on "this inexplicable but patent fact . . . that man wanted to be 'like God'. Man, whose natural relation to God, his Lord and Maker, is obedience and love, has become a rebel" (1938: 75-6; see also 1956b: 235-318). The world religions and philosophical systems, even in their most sublime and beautiful expressions, for Kraemer are attempts at self-justification. This overstatement can be accurately interpreted as Kraemer's effort to right the balance of missiological thought after Hocking.

The attitude that Kraemer felt he had to overcome was an unsophisticated reductionism positing an Ultimate Reality as the common goal of the religions. Kraemer countered that even a cursory examination of the religions revealed a plurality of distinct and sometimes opposing ultimate aims. Therefore, to ascribe to them the *telos* of the Christian revelation—justification by grace and renewed fellowship with God—would once again fail to take their own claims seriously. However, there are many examples within Kraemer's work that can counter without repudiation what was in context another overemphasis: his commendation of many biblically realistic themes and motifs which can be used legitimately in evaluation, his belief that God's revelation extends beyond the borders of visible Christianity—albeit in a broken and troubled way—and, his refusal to pronounce on the eternal fate of non-Christians because of God's constant work in the religious life of humanity, provide avenues of openness to Thomas's new truths in Christ, without compromising Kraemer's central belief that the revelation in Christ was for Christians the only legitimate evaluative criterion.

4. Theological Implications of Biblical Realism

Kraemer's position, despite the criticisms, continues to offer avenues of insight that remain relevant for contemporary Christian thought as it defends the explicitly Christian nature of theology of religions adequately, while affirming religious diversity as part of the Christian narrative.

Biblical realism, as shown, is Kraemer's attempt to address the problem of authority in theology generally and theology of religions specifically. He contended here that a Christian is and should be influenced by his or her Christian commitment when reflecting on the problem of religious plurality. Furthermore, Kraemer insisted that such influence need not be grounded in anything outside itself; it is fine just as it is. Based on this position, Kraemer opposed what has been called essentialist phenomenologies of religions, that is, any attempt to grade religions according to some concept of religion. Whether they were graded according to some mystical essence—as in the work of W. E. Hocking, according to Christianity—as in the theologies of mission of many of Kraemer's contemporaries, or naturalistic criteria—as in Freud, Feuerbach, or Marx—for Kraemer, such approaches fail to grapple with the radical difference of Christian faith because they refuse from the start sympathetically to enter into the world of Christian discourse, the world of the biblical realism. Christian theology generally, and the theology of religions specifically, for Kraemer, are rooted in the internal logic of the Christian language. By so articulating an internal authority, Kraemer's biblical realism entails both that the theology of religions recognizes the explicitly Christian nature of theology of religions and that it appreciates religious diversity as a part of the Christian story.

Because the Bible is neither classic literature nor *a* sacred text, but *the* sacred record of the revelation of God to humanity, biblical realism redescribes "reality within the scriptural framework rather than translating scripture into extrascriptural categories. It is the text, so to speak, which absorbs the world, rather than the world the text" (Lindbeck, 1984: 118). It is chiefly though appeals to the Bible and to the history of its interpretation, that the Christian community tests, restates, and reforms it beliefs and practices. Christian theology of religions, therefore, can and should begin with the biblical language and its various interpretations throughout history in order to make sense of other faiths. In this sense it is as much an exercise in self-understanding and self-description as it is one of understanding and describing the faith and life of an other. To the degree that this strategy is undertaken, scripture is "not simply a source of precepts and truths, but the interpretive framework for all reality" (Lindbeck, 1989: 75). Kraemer appears to anticipate what has become a central claim among contemporary postliberal theologians like George Lindbeck: the world of the Bible is the Christian's real world; there is no outside.

Of course, the obvious danger of such language, focussed as it is on social demarcation and self-description, is sectarianism. A theology of religions focussed internally, it could be contended, seeks first to define the boundaries of the believing community and then, systematically, to ignore the outside. In extreme cases, this may result in a refusal to engage in any way with others, for they are lost. They do not have the truth. At most, these others are seen to be the objects of missionary activity. They are worthwhile only insofar as they can be brought within the communal limits. It is a sad and tragic reality that this criticism does have historical bite. A prime and tragic example is the treatment of Jews by Christians during the days of Christendom. Even though the early heretic Marcion, who judged that the God of the Christians and the god of the Jews were two entirely different beings, was defeated, Christian theologians have from Irenaeus to Schleiermacher almost universally regarded Judaism with suspicion. At best, the result of such suspicion was the Church's silence in the face of anti-Semitism; at worst, it was its active approval (Perry, 1999: 69-78). Similar suspicions spawned similar reactions in countries where Christian missions have been active. On the basis of the Church's own tragic history, it can be argued that this tendency toward violence is rooted "in thinking the Christian story a master narrative that positions all other stories. It is the violence of having the last word" (Loughlin, 1996: 24). These realities ought to give those who seek to construct a more confessional theology religions pause.

While this criticism stands forever as a warning against sectarianism and the feeling of cultural superiority that can arise from it, it appears to confuse a historical charge with a logical one. While it is no doubt true that confessional theologies of religions have led to sectarianism, it by no means follows that they must do so. A theology of religions conducted along confessional lines can avoid the sectarian charge through a reinterpretation of natural theology. At first glance, such an assertion seems ironic or inconsistent with what has previously been argued. After all, Reformed theology and philosophy have always been suspicious of the project (Plantinga, 1980: 49-62) and Kraemer, as a Reformed theologian, shares this suspicion (1956b: 361). As a result, two types of natural theology must be distinguished.

The natural theology that Kraemer rejects purports to describe a universally available set of reasons or evidences that grounds particular Christian beliefs and practices. Laura Garcia defines it well: "Natural theology is the attempt to demonstrate certain truths concerning God's existence and nature, operating from premises that are knowable by any rational person independently of divine revelation" (1993: 112-13). The natural theology that Kraemer could accept, however, starts not with allegedly universal grounds but with particular beliefs and practices, as they are embodied in particular religious communities. It moves from there to the universal, by seeking to locate these beliefs and practices on as large a conceptual map as possible. Such a move necessarily takes place only at specific times and places as the adherents of Christian communities become familiar with the beliefs and practices of those of other communities and vice versa.

Consider the following hypothetical account (adapted from DiNoia, 1992: 127-41). A Buddhist monk participating in a monastic exchange with a Dominican monastery in the United States, sharing in its life and worship, hears the word "God" mentioned. As time passes, he understands that "God" signifies the person whom his Dominican hosts worship, love, and to whom they pray. Moreover, in these prayers, God is named Father, Son, and Holy Spirit. This experience of particular beliefs embodied in the particular practices of a particular Christian community may lead him to ask, Who is this God whom you worship and to whom you pray? to which a brother, well-versed in Aquinas, might reply, "God is the Cause of all that is." The move from the particular to the universal is clear.

Reconceived in this manner, the language of natural theology, including the classical theistic arguments, demonstrates the universal scope of particular Christian claims. It does not and cannot provide universal grounds for ways of life embodying the Christian story, but does presuppose its indwelling as "canonically and narrationally unified and internally glossed . . . centred on Jesus Christ, and telling the story of the dealings of the Triune God with his people and his world in ways that are . . . applicable to the present" (Lindbeck, 1989: 75). It sustains the "broadest possible context for Christian affirmation" (DiNoia, 1992: 131), and enables Christian theologians to render these affirmations in an understandable way to those outside the Christian community. Kraemer put it this way: "The function of natural theology will henceforth be not to construe preparatory stages and draw unbroken continuous lines of religious development ending and reaching their summit in Christ, but . . . to uncover in the light of the revelation of Christ the different modes of God-, self- and world-consciousness of man in his religious life" (1938: 125). By fundamentally reorienting natural theology, one may recognize the explicitly Christian nature of theology of religions without thereby becoming sectarian.

Furthermore, it is for the sake of the biblical story itself that any final judgment, either positive or negative, must be resisted. Kraemer employed the story of the Noahic Covenant (Genesis 8:8-17) to develop this point. God's Covenant with Noah, Kraemer stated:

> is a Covenant with mankind as a whole and with every living creature. The rainbow, as a symbol of peace and harmony after the storm is the token of the everlasting (!) Covenant between God and 'every living creature of all flesh that is upon the earth'. . . . It is striking and deeply significant that before God's special revelational experiment with Israel begins in Chapter 12, in the story of God's election of Abraham and His Covenant with him (which is a Covenant with the people of Abraham, with a universal perspective—12:1-3), the "everlasting Covenant between God and every living creature" is stated as an established and irremovable fact, governing the spiritual destiny of mankind as a whole. This is of the greatest significance for a Biblically-based theology of religion. (Kraemer, 1956b: 253-4)

For Kraemer, the Noahic Covenant is a reminder that all evaluations of the religious life of humanity are not final for it reveals God's concern not for one nation or religion but for the entire human race. Thus, the Bible itself prohibits any final declaration about how God must act toward humankind and, accordingly, any final judgment on religions. The last word, just as the first word, belongs only to God.

The religions, for Kraemer, all remain a part of God's providential plan for the human race in such a manner that does not threaten central Christian doctrines or detract from the uniqueness of Christ and/or the Church. On the contrary, DiNoia argues that the "notion that other religions play some part in the divine plan accords with traditional Christian doctrines about other religions, in which it has been affirmed that they . . . may be the instruments of some divine purpose" (DiNoia, 1992: 90). Still, it must be made clear that other religions are to be valued neither because they are anonymous channels of Christian salvation nor because they offer independently authentic ways of relating to Ultimate Reality. Rather, according to the Christian scriptures, their value lies in their real if as yet unspecifiable role in the one "divine plan to which the Christian community bears witness" (DiNoia, 1992: 91). To say more than this, either a priori affirmations or negations, is to presume for oneself a God's-eye-view of history—a presumption rooted in Original Sin—the desire to usurp the place of God.

In this context, questions of salvation arise, for if other-believers are part of God's plan to which the Church testifies, it would seem to follow that they share in the salvation it proclaims. This conclusion, however, is rendered suspect by its failure to give sufficient weight to the internal nature of the debate thus far. If Kraemer's biblical realism is the attempt to understand the Christian faith from within the Christian faith, only then turning outside to the problem of other religions, then such terms as "salvation" and "damnation" can be understood only from the inside. This is to say that one must be fluent in the Christian language in order to understand and experience Christian "salvation" and "damnation." If this is so, then Christians can say very little about those who remain completely outside the Christian universe of discourse. Here, I have argued that while there are biblical grounds for locating the religions within the realm of God's sovereignty, any final judgment on them is premature. Much the same conclusion, I cannot help but think, obtains here. The problem of the final destiny of other-believers is one that finally cannot be answered. It can and should provoke thought on the nature and degree of God's mercy and holiness, but eschatological destiny should remain solely with God.

To summarize, a theology of religions beginning with Kraemer's biblical realism takes the Bible as its authority for interreligious evaluation. This entails both that Christian theology of religions is a Christian enterprise and that the religious diversity is an integral part of the Christian story. This approach need and should not resort to hermeneutical, or indeed physical, violence in its assessment of those who stand outside it.

6

THE RADICAL DIFFERENCE OF OTHER RELIGIONS

THE HOLISTIC APPROACH

In the previous chapter, I noted Kraemer's insistence that any attempt to grade Christianity according to some supposed essence of religion failed to account for the radical difference of the gospel. Kraemer felt that, if the core (at least) of the gospel was constituted by a revelatory act of God, then Christians (at least) could not treat it as equal to other religions and remain logically and theologically consistent Christian inquirers. On the contrary, the world described by the Bible—Kraemer's real world—is the place where the Christian, by virtue of the label, begins to discern the relationship of the Church and its message to the world and all its spheres of life, especially its religions. Kraemer was, therefore, puzzled by the accusation that erupted at Tambaram and continued elsewhere that this argument was narrow-minded or arbitrary. To look for another point of orientation—a starting point other than Jesus Christ—was, for Kraemer, to cease to regard him as the full and final revelation of God: this was tantamount to no longer thinking as a Christian. However bewildered by his Christian critics, Kraemer was unfazed by the potential criticism of naturalist scholars of religion because, he countered, these, just as much as the Christian, incorporated fundamentally religious assumptions about the nature of humanity and its place in the cosmos into their inquiries. The Christian inquirer was, therefore, not necessarily more biased that the naturalist inquirer, nor was the latter necessarily more scientific that the former. Indeed, quite the opposite is more likely for, as Kraemer observed, the openly religious inquirer is better able to discern the role of his or her religious commitments in the investigation.

Kraemer not only asserted the radical difference of Christianity. He also argued for the radical difference of other religions, as this chapter shows. To begin, I offer a summary of Kraemer's argument for treating world religions as holistic apprehensions of humanity's place in the universe, for to do any less fails to consider the beliefs and practices of other religions within an interpretative grid that renders them intelligible. Then I consider a very serious objection raised by Gavin D'Costa, namely that such an approach tends to treat religions statically, thereby ignoring development arising both intrareligiously and interreligiously. This criticism, I believe, is fundamentally accurate, but it can be overcome through a close study of Kraemer's own work. Finally, I conclude that this position better preserves the otherness of other religions than exclusivism, inclusivism, and/or pluralism as popularly defined.

1. The Holistic Approach[1]

In *The Christian Message* and "Continuity or Discontinuity," Kraemer rejected two phenomenologies of the alleged essence of religion. According to the first, Christianity fulfils the religions, while the second posits a transcendental source behind all religions, including Christianity (1938: 111-13; 1939: 1-7). To these, in *Religion and the Christian Faith*, Kraemer added naturalist phenomenologies where he also rejected "the generating factors of religions in some region of man's consciousness, a certain psychological necessity, a lack of adequate knowledge of the world" (1956b: 54). At first glance, as discussed earlier, the phenomenologies he rejected are very different. For the first, Christianity perfects the highest and best of the rest, while the second posits Christianity as one among equals, and the third suggests that it is the highest and last of many mistakes. Nevertheless, all three hold the common notion that there is an essence embodied by the various worlds of religions that can be uncovered and used as a means to evaluate them.

Whether it is explicitly Christian, broadly religious, or overtly naturalistic, for Kraemer, essentialism in any form is an artificial abstraction that fails to take seriously the plurality and diversity of religious beliefs and practices. He stated: "concretely there is no such thing as religions in the singular. There is only a multitude of religions" (1956b: 73). Essentialism, for Kraemer, says either too little or too much about the actual religions it seeks to place; either it so reduces particular beliefs and practices to fit the universal essence that little worth investigation is left, or it so stresses those features common to many religions that it ignores others where it is marginal or absent. Kraemer countered that the more one seeks sympathetically to enter into and understand the different religions, the more one is driven to conclude that they constitute their own worlds, with their own axes and structures. As a result, they cannot be reduced to each

---

1 The term "holistic" is one that does not arise in Kraemer's writing. Rather, he chooses to use "totality" and its cognates. This leads to the unfortunate, but regular appearance of the word "totalitarian." Because of its negative connotations, I have chosen to use the synonym, "holistic" where "totalitarian" arises.

other or to a common denominator expressing their inner core (1956b: 76). "All religions," Kraemer insisted, "if taken seriously according to their true soul and body are distorted and misrepresented when stretched on the Procrustean bed of some general Idea of Religion" (1956b: 77).

This misrepresentation results from the failure of essentialist phenomenologies to consider the role their own subjectivity plays in the investigation. All scientific inquiry is at least partly conditioned by the world of the scientist—a fact confirmed by the ongoing disagreement over what comprises the religious essence. Kraemer declared:

> The patent fact is that there is no unanimity as to what the Essence of Religion is. . . . [There] can be none because every philosophical approach rests on an attitude and a decision as to what to think about man and his attitude in relation to the Beyond, which cannot be cogently and universally demonstrated. Hence, a universally and compellingly valid concept of the "Essence of Religion" is not to be expected. Here again, we have to accept our human condition, which requires that the search for scientific and metaphysical truth will go on as a spiritual contest—full of risks and precious results to be sure—and not as a march towards intellectual unanimity. (1956b: 60)

Regarding comparative religion, Kraemer averred that it "constructs for the religions a hierarchical scale, according to their content and truth-value, from 'lower' to 'higher' and even 'highest' . . . religions" (1956b: 58). Scaling religions not according to revelation but to philosophical thinking, Kraemer contended that comparative religion "claimed to develop the right doctrine of the Essence of Religion which is present in all religions. These religions can then be demonstrated as more or less imperfect embodiments of it" (1956b: 59). He felt that the discipline had bifurcated into opposing transcendental and naturalist approaches that not only disagreed with each other but also failed to speak with one voice. Against Otto's mystery (1959), and Schleiermacher's feeling (1989: 31-76), for example, stand Freud's wish-fulfilment (1964), and Feuerbach's projections (1957). Kraemer argued that these disagreements are rooted in fundamentally incommensurable starting points: if the premises differ, it is no wonder that the conclusions do also.

Every avenue of theological research begins with fundamental assumptions about God, human beings, and the universe. Kraemer noted: "One may also call it a faith, a decision. At any rate, there is a starting point of which no account is given. This belongs to our human condition, happily preventing man from becoming, in the absolute sense of the word, a mere onlooker, a mere observing intellect outside" (1956b: 46-7). Furthermore, this is not to endorse a form of relativism or subjectivism but a realistic assessment of the human condition that Kraemer believed would guard against just such extremes. By recognizing the peculiar historical and cultural limits within which all theological research takes place, Kraemer hoped to guard against unwarranted subjectivism, reducing it to the smallest proportion.[2] As a result, Kraemer followed his teacher, W. Brede Kristensen, proclaiming that "the only way to understand these religions and to be just to them is to take them according to their peculiar fundamental motives and meaning" (1938: 62-3). Kraemer's holistic approach, therefore, begins not with a theoretical essence of religion but with particular beliefs and practices as they arise in concrete situations. Rejecting the separation of secular from sacred, Kraemer's approach contends that a sympathetic understanding of religious belief and practice rests on the perception of both world and tribal religions, not as philosophical speculations but as totalities encompassing epistemology, ethics, and aesthetics, extending to include community and culture.

Perceived in this way, religions offer fairly complete and coherent ways of interpreting humanity's place within the cosmos. While many areas may overlap—for instance, in organizational details, theological and philosophical pronouncements, and ethical practices—for Kraemer, religions are marked by different experiences, emphases, and most importantly, starting points. Further, just as Kraemer rejected talk of religious values on the theological ground of biblical realism, he rejected it on phenomenological grounds here. To speak of values, for Kraemer, was to speak in terms according to which all religions exhibit tendencies toward the sublime and the aberrant. Rather, he felt that all religions can and should point to significant cultural achievements, high philosophical traditions, and satisfying spiritual experiences. Thus of Hinduism, Kraemer can write: "it is indeed a fact that in Hinduism, many people have found salvation and satisfaction" (1956b: 84), but no satisfying, indeed saving experiences, profound philosophies, or majestic art should conceal their "incommensurable peculiarity" (1956b: 78).

As totalities that do not respect the secular/sacred distinction, religions for Kraemer are fundamentally incommensurable and complete apprehensions of the universe and humanity's place therein. Accordingly, when questions of interpretation arise, it is unsurprising to find Kraemer insisting that one cannot abstract a particular doctrine or practice from its

---

2 At this point, Kraemer's position strongly resembles that of Michael Polanyi in philosophy of science and epistemology (1957).

The Holistic Approach

religio-cultural matrix to treat it in isolation and expect accuracy. To equate surface similarities is both inappropriate and inaccurate for Kraemer:

> [every] religion is an indivisible . . . unity of existential apprehension. It is not a series of tenets, dogmas, prescriptions, institutions, practices, that can be taken one by one as independent items of religious life, conception or organization, and that can arbitrarily be compared with, and somehow related to, and grafted upon the similar item of another religion. Every religion is a living, indivisible unity. Every part of it—a dogma, a rite, a myth, an institution, a cult—is so vitally related to the whole that it can never be understood in its real function, significance and tendency, as these occur in the reality of life without keeping constantly in mind that vast and living unity of existential apprehension in which this part moves and has its being. (Kraemer, 1938: 135)

Even the most cursory examinations bear out this contention. For example, Kraemer provided the following clarification in his later work:

> Buddhism and Christianity are both, in a very emphatic way, religions of salvation. . . . Yet, however sublime these conceptions may be, both cannot be true. The Buddhist salvation means salvation from existence as such, because existence is suffering, which is necessarily evil. In Christianity it means salvation from sin. Another example: It is impossible to equate as one and the same Reality the God and father of Jesus Christ and the unconditioned and pure essence of the Vedanta. Sublime and profound . . . they are both, but either one of them is true, or neither. Therefore the claim of adherents of non-Christian religions, which impresses certain Christian theologians and missionaries very much, namely that these religions lead people often into a deep and satisfying religious experience, may be wholly justified; but this undeniable fact does not guarantee that there is Truth or the same Truth in them. It is philosophically superficial to equate the psychic experience of satisfaction with the certainty that it is therefore true, or is related to realities which are true. (1956b: 85)

In response to the various phenomenologies positing a universal essence with which to grade particular religions, Kraemer insisted that, rather, religions encompass all areas of life and, as they are internally complete and coherent, they cannot be analyzed as collections of doctrines, symbols, or practices. For Kraemer, the parts must be interpreted in relation to the organic whole.

2. The Holistic Approach and Religious Development

A serious phenomenological difficulty with Kraemer's holistic approach as described is ably pointed out by Gavin D'Costa. He asks the following question: although Kraemer's "emphasis on the totalitarian nature of religion provides a salutary check against surface similarities and comparisons, does he not neglect the dynamic nature of religion as well as the creative interaction between beliefs and practices which result in the development of traditions?" (1986: 61). In other words, D'Costa infers that, by insisting on an internal approach to evaluation, Kraemer fails to account for either intrareligious or interreligious change.

Considering intrareligious development as D'Costa presents it, he insists that "Kraemer underestimates the dynamic and changing nature of religions because of his emphasis on their totalitarian [i.e., holistic] nature" (1986: 62). Specifically, D'Costa charges that Kraemer fails to comprehend, for example, that Hinduism is at best an umbrella term best abandoned in favour of more precise terms to delineate Indian religious life, such as "Advaita Vedanta, Visistadvaita or Samkhya Yoga and so on" (1986: 62). All too often, D'Costa contends, Kramer neglects this complexity, especially in his analysis of bhakti traditions in Indian religions, where he drew an unnecessarily negative conclusion, that because these movements are part of Hinduism, "they are fundamentally anthropocentric, as all good monistic, mystic Hindu religion is" (Kraemer, 1938: 171). D'Costa finds this to be historically and phenomenologically reductive, as well as limiting; he notes that because Kraemer accepted the fundamental axis of Hinduism as monism, he alleged that, therefore, all aspects of Indian religious life can and should be interpreted in, and only in, this sphere of discourse. D'Costa argues that this precludes a priori the possibility of any development away from monism and therefore opens Kraemer to the possibility of serious misunderstanding. D'Costa further shows that, likewise, in his account of Japanese Buddhism, Kraemer's dismissal of the "almost Lutheran insights of Shinran's Japanese Shin-Shu Amida, where the principle of faith in grace alone, as against effecting salvation by works, is strongly emphasized [is insensitive]. Kraemer discards this phenomenon on the questionable grounds that Shin-Shu must be viewed in the light of the 'naturalistic monism [of] Mahayana Buddhism' " (D'Costa, 1986: 63, quoting Kraemer, 1938: 181). D'Costa concludes that, potentially, many points of contact are obscured in this way by Kraemer's reductive hermeneutic.

The Holistic Approach

It is not my intention to debate the specifics of Kraemer's analyses of Indian religions or Japanese Buddhism; rather, my focus is whether such interpretative errors warrant the rejection or modification of Kraemer's holistic phenomenology. Before forming any final judgment, the context of Kraemer's remarks gives rise to certain insights that ought to be considered. As I argued in the previous section, the holistic approach was Kraemer's corrective to the reductive hermeneutic advocated by fulfilment theologians and by the transcendentalist and naturalist phenomenologists. His foremost concern was to preserve the particularities of religious belief and practice by refusing to scale them according to a purported universal idea of religion. Rather, Kraemer maintained that, in order to preserve their uniqueness, individual religious beliefs and practices must be interpreted within their religio-cultural matrix. I doubt whether D'Costa would disagree with at least the intention of attempting to preserve the particularity of religions that underlies Kraemer's holistic approach.

It is also always worthwhile to keep in mind Kraemer's penchant to overstate his case. I have already shown how *The Christian Message* deliberately overemphasizes the human nature of religious activity as a response both to Hocking and fulfilment theology, although more moderate statements are found in later writings. The intense, even extreme, way in which Kraemer sometimes outlines the holistic approach is another instance of rhetorical overemphasis. This is borne out, for example, by his portrayal of Ramanuja as an agent of change within Hinduism. Kraemer regarded the "great bhakti-theologian [as] passionate in his protest against the absolute monism of Shankara" (1938: 166-9). Ramanuja's belief in the reality of a personal Lord, proclamation of divine grace, focus on the necessity of faith for salvation, and struggle over the relation of faith and works all indicate, for Kraemer, that he "just as Pascal, was not satisfied with the God of the philosophers; with passionate religiousness he vindicated a really living God, not merely a theistic conception of God. [Indeed, he breaks] . . . with the classic Hindu ideas about God, the soul and the world. The world is real, not [illusory] . . . the soul and human consciousness are so also. The eternal personal God . . . is the sole and personal God and Saviour, not merely a god-representation necessary for man in a certain stage in his quest for the summum bonum" (1938: 169). Clearly Kraemer did allow that religious totalities can and do change, that they are dynamic and not static entities.

Kraemer's chief concern—reflected in the conclusion about Ramanuja which D'Costa rejects—is that Christians, upon seeing words such as "grace," "faith," and "Lord," in Ramanuja's writings, might immediately equate them with Christian meanings, or as manifestations of an ethereal universal essence of religion. In either instance, Kraemer contended, Ramanuja would not be understood in his own terms. Furthermore, in light of Edinburgh 1910, Jerusalem 1928 and Hocking's *Re-Thinking Missions*, Kraemer's concerns appear to be legitimate. Kraemer countered that Ramanuja is not the Indian Luther, but a deeply religious man reacting against Vedantic philosophy, who must be interpreted as such. This denies neither the reality nor the significance of the changes Ramanuja initiated, but resists any easy equation between them and Protestant pietism. Kraemer felt that, to do so, "makes the religious mistake of overlooking the radical difference between the Christian revelation and other religions. [While] it starts from the very laudable ... and indispensable desire to show openmindedness and genuine sympathy for the best in the other religions, it starts from the assumption that Christianity is the crown of these religions, and so it evinces a hidden feeling of superiority, that is rightly sensed as condescension" (1938: 301-2). With regard to D'Costa's first criticism and Kraemer's context, what is needed is not the rejection of the holistic approach but a modification that can preserve religious particularity without treating the religions as static bodies of belief and practice.

Before setting out this modification, I must consider the second of D'Costa's objections. When confronted with interreligious development, he contends, "Kraemer does not pay enough attention to the way in which a religion's 'classical' doctrines and axioms change in the light of practice. Again, the continual movement of history and the possible surprises it may bring cannot be minimized" (1986: 63). Once again, D'Costa has in mind Kraemer's exposition of Hinduism, specifically the evaluation of *ahimsa*—the doctrine of abstaining from inflicting pain on living beings in thought word and deed. This doctrine, averred Kraemer, must be seen in the context of Hindu soteriology: the refusal to cause pain is rooted primarily in the self-centred desire to be freed from the cycle of reincarnation and only secondarily in the concept of benevolence toward all beings. D'Costa counters that Kraemer's reading of *ahimsa* neglects "the way in which the psychological component here can lead to a deeper rethinking and understanding, as is reflected in some strands of modern Hinduism" (1986: 63). In this second instance, Kraemer's holistic approach has led to an abstract and over-textual analysis of religions.

Once again, D'Costa validly criticizes an extreme in Kraemer's writing, but, in so doing, fails to give sufficient weight to the issues to which Kraemer was responding in *The Christian Message*. D'Costa concludes that Kraemer is abstract and over-textual where I have shown that Kraemer was reacting against similarly abstract and over-textual analyses. I have argued that a holistic approach need not preclude the possibility of genuine internal change nor the possibility of change arising form external influences. Consider Kraemer's remarks in *The Christian Message* concerning the influence of Christian ideas and morals on the non-Christian world:

> The great non-Christian religions have utilized the permeation of Christian ideas and ideals for their own internal and external strengthening. . . . Men like Gandhi, Tagore and Radhakrishnan, who evince each in his own peculiar way a strong permeation with ideals and ideas deriving from Christianity, are no "unbaptized Christians," . . . but rather have become invigorated Hindus by the process, with an unmistakable element of irritation in their attitude toward Christianity. . . . As a matter of fact, in the case of Gandhi and Tagore, however drastically their activist attitude towards life may differ from Hinduism as we know it, and however emancipated many of their leading ideas may be from dominant Hindu conceptions, the crucial fact is that they consciously keep to Hinduism as their recognised spiritual home, and even announce their new interpretation as being for the sake of Hinduism. (1938: 290-1)

Kraemer recognized that ideas imported from outside by influential individuals remaining inside can in fact lead to change within a religious totality. The conclusion that he resists is the argument that such change signifies that the entire body of belief and practice is slowly becoming Christianized. Rather, he observed that such change may produce just the opposite effect, acting as an inoculation against Christian faith. After nearly two millennia of Christian missionary activity, Kraemer pointed out that many people of non-Christian faith recognize "Christ as one of the highest religious figures humanity has produced. To give Him an honourable place in the different pantheons does not meet with serious opposition. But to recognise Him and what He represents as the Lord of life, to whom supreme loyalty is due, is resolutely refused and rejected even by those who revere him" (1938: 289-90). Kraemer's phenomenology does not necessarily preclude the possibility of genuine change within a religious tradition through the influence of internal factors (e.g., the theological thought of Ramanuja) or external factors (e.g., the impact of Christianity on Gandhi, Tagore, and Radhakrishnan).

Based on my analysis, I see no need to reject outright the holistic approach. As D'Costa's criticisms are somewhat valid, some modification is necessary in order to avoid treating other religions as static entities; to recognize particularity without denying the possibility of change over time. And, it can be argued that Kraemer so stringently stressed the former that he lost sight of the latter.

This is especially the case in his early work. In *The Christian Message*, Kraemer's analysis of the "living non-Christian religions" began not by describing actual religious totalities but with the highly theoretical division of "prophetic religions of revelation [from] naturalist religions of transempirical realization" (1938: 142). The former—comprising Christianity, Judaism, and Islam—are rooted in the self-revelation of God to humanity, and are therefore ultimately dualistic as God is separate and distinct from creation. Those comprising the latter, Kraemer stated: "are all mystical in their core, [and] revelation consists of what are in some sense supreme religious experiences" (1938: 143). Including the major religions of India, China, and Japan, these naturalist religions are, Kraemer stated, ultimately monistic, starting "from the fundamental assumption, regarded as selfevident, that man and nature are essentially one" (1938: 155). This a priori division and the categorizing of all non-Semitic religions together necessarily affects Kraemer's conclusions. His account of Ramanuja's innovations argued that although they radically react against Vedanta, they must be purely cosmetic because all Indian religious and philosophical thinking is monistic. In a manner not dissimilar from the transcendentalist and naturalist philosophers he criticizes, Kraemer refused to consider Ramanuja on his own terms. Instead, Kraemer has interpreted him according to the essence of all Eastern religious life and thought, monism.

I believe that the holistic approach can be preserved, if one takes a more pragmatic, local approach than Kraemer did above. Instead of beginning with an a priori account of the fundamental starting point of religions, one could begin with actual encounters with religious totalities in concrete situations. Here Wilfred Cantwell Smith is helpful; despite his talk of a global theology, Smith takes the diversity of religious beliefs seriously—although for reasons very different than Kraemer's. Smith preserves the diversity of religious beliefs by separating belief from faith: "One's faith is given by God, one's belief by one's century" (1979: 96). Beliefs for Smith are intellectual appropriations of faith and vary not only between religions—a word Smith dislikes—but also between any two individuals within any particular religious community. Faith, however, is a quality of religious life. Because of the inherent diversity of belief and, one might add, practice, Smith insists that appropriate observations are prefaced by such phrases as "most Muslims will agree," or "this group of Vaisnatives accepts," rather than "Islam teaches," or "Hindusim holds" (1981: 97). His operational principle is simply stated: "No observer's statement about a group of persons is valid that cannot be appropriated by those persons" (1981: 97). Whether or not this goal is ever actually attained is a contentious issue. Nevertheless, it remains a valid one toward which to aim.

Following Smith, I contend that, in order to take religious particularity as seriously as Kraemer desires, one must begin at the level of the local religious community. In describing beliefs and practices, one ought to speak not in general but in specific terms. This does not subvert the holistic approach, for there are elements within the local communities that render them recognizably Christian, Islamic, or Buddhist. In the words of Paul Griffiths, these communities bear "a historical relationship that they take to be of salvific significance to one or another of those streams of events called 'world religions'" (1991: 6). Neither these communities nor their adherents can be used to speak for Christianity, Buddhism, or Islam, but they can be recognized as belonging broadly within one or another of these entities. Thus, for example, a holistic interpretation of a specific belief or practice in a rural Reformed church could involve a description of its relationship to those of other Reformed communities, to the official documents of their denomination and the various Reformed Confessions, and, from there, to other recognizably Christian bodies. In this way, particularity is preserved but the possibility of development, and/or change is not denied.

3. The Holistic Approach and Radical Difference

In this section I consider what value Kraemer's holistic approach might hold for Christians seeking to give a theological account of religious plurality. In the previous chapter, I argued that Kraemer points Christians to resources within their own tradition when developing such an account. I would add now that Kraemer's holistic approach preserves "essential 'otherness' " by recognizing that any attempt to understand the other is limited by one's own cultural and historical situation and therefore can never be total. This requires explanation. Above, Kraemer was shown to argue that the interpretation of a religious belief or practice necessarily occurs from a standpoint entailing the interpreter's own religio-cultural beliefs and practices. Further, to acknowledge this is not to affirm the validity of all interpretations, but to admit that the interpreter does not occupy a universally accessible standpoint. Kraemer contended that an interpreter remains as culturally and historically bound as that which he or she seeks to understand: "To 'understand' or to 'comprehend' religion or a religion, we conclude, means to interpret it. Interpretation is not solely, nor even mainly, an intellectual activity but an existential activity" (1956b: 51). For this reason, any interpretation of other religions, for Kraemer, can result in genuine but incomplete understanding.

Otherness, or radical difference, then, is preserved because the holistic approach remains aware of its unavoidable bias. Kraemer advocated this approach because it frankly acknowledges the difficulties encountered when an adherent of one religious totality attempts to make sense of another: "In saying this, we are far from recommending or defending an unbridled subjectivity or putting all degrees of subjectivity on the same level. On the contrary, what we need is the clear recognition of the fact that . . . we are always partly conditioned by the world in which we have our roots, and in the selecting of facts we are partly led by our 'subjectivity' " (1956b: 47). To recognize this prejudice is the best way to guard against it; to reduce it to the smallest possible proportion requires not an intellectual act of distancing oneself from the object of study, "but a moral act of respect for what is alien to us" (1956b: 47). The holistic approach preserves this recognition of otherness in non-Christian religions "because it is an evaluating presentation of an alien or different spiritual world according to its own fundamental presuppositions and intentions. It is a congenial entering into a different universe of discourse, that has its own language" (1956b: 49). When so understood, the holistic approach brings to the theology of religions a suspicion of universal and neutral evaluative criteria, a resistance to the meta-critical quest for a common core of belief or experience to the religions, and an allowance that other religions may be successful in bringing "salvation" to their adherents.

A holistic approach to the theology of religions would regard claims to universal and neutral evaluative criteria with suspicion. Criteria conceived to vindicate one religion, for example, would be rejected by Kraemer. This idea is exemplified by Harold Netland, who insists that "some nonarbitrary criteria exist to evaluate various religious traditions and that it is indeed legitimate for a Christian to conclude that other religions which embrace basic beliefs incompatible with central tenets of the Christian faith are false" (1991: 152). Likewise, a holistic approach would reject Keith Ward's suggestion that "a set of fundamental values which are given by the very nature of human being itself, and which are not merely conventional or matters of arbitrary and wholly subjective preference" confirms the major religions (1991: 179). Despite their opposing aims, one might expect to find in their contributions some common criteria or at least an acknowledgement of some overlap; however, one finds neither. Rather, when subjected to a suspicious analysis, the suggestions by Netland and Ward are shown to disguise bias—albeit unintended—behind their use of language for universality and neutrality.[3]

Abandoning the search for universal and neutral evaluative criteria, however, need not culminate in a relativist approach, in which all religious beliefs are equally valid, because it does not necessarily empty these beliefs of their cognitive content. Prima facie, religions make claims about the nature of reality that are capable of being true or false and these claims must be taken seriously. By recognizing that knowledge of the world in the broadest possible sense is mediated by the tradition of the knower, a holistic approach regards suspiciously any list of criteria as an attempt to prejudice

---

3 See D'Costa (1993: 79-95) and Perry (1996a: 487-94).

discussion in favour of one tradition over others. Here, the post-modern criticism of modernity is judged to be essentially correct: claims to privileged epistemic access have led and can lead to the destruction of other rationalities. To reveal such claims to be historically and culturally situated is to deprive them of their universal and powerful status. This approach is not to embrace a radical relativism but to acknowledge in the wake of modernity, a situation of radical relativity where many different and divergent, yet potentially "rational," claims are being advanced. Where claims to universality seem sometimes to mask cultural bias, Kraemer declared his at the outset. His is a recognition of relativity without an adoption of relativism.

A holistic approach also resists the meta-critical quest for a core common to all religions, an example of which is provided by Paul Knitter:

> If an explicit recognition of "sin" and divine "justice and wrath" are defined as prerequisites for admission into the circle of the elect, then admittedly few Hindus and Buddhists would qualify. But are Althaus and Brunner themselves limiting God by laying down such prerequisites? It appears that the reality behind the symbol of sin is caught by the Hindu symbol of avidya ("ignorance") or the Buddhist experience of tanha ("selfish craving"). Even though the Buddha did not speak about an infinite offense against divine justice, he perhaps has another angle on what is wrong with the human condition when he announced that dukkha ("suffering") is universal and is caused by craving. (1985: 118)

In this excerpt, Knitter seems to assume a privileged vantage point from which he can see that sin, *avidya*, and *tanha* are all more or less partial descriptions of the one human predicament. In other words, he assumes that a more accurate insight into the true nature of reality is his, while that of the other—in this example, either "Mainline Protestants," Hindus, or Buddhists—is only partial. While this is not his intention, such an assumption unavoidably leads to the implicit claim that he understands the others' narratives better than they do.

Given the prima facie difference between these various explanations, Knitter's explanation above must be grounded in a theory that purports to uncover the one human predicament underlying them. This is precisely what John Hick attempts with his pluralistic hypothesis (see chapter 2); for him, the religions "exhibit in their different ways a soteriological structure which identifies the misery, unreality, triviality, and perversity of ordinary human life, affirms an ultimate unity of reality and value in which or in relation to which a limitlessly better quality of existence is possible, and shows the way to realise that radically better possibility" (Hick, 1989: 36). Thus the religions variously and partially describe the one human predicament, one Ultimate Reality, and the one way to move from one to the other; these, for Hick, make up the core common to the world religions. Hick's ambitious undertaking is no less than to construct a theory which would make sense of all religious beliefs and practices; his is a meta-critical quest for a common religious core.

From the perspective I have been developing, this strategy, while admirably attempting to preserve the diversity of religions by granting to each a measure of truth, fails to consider sufficiently the very beliefs and practices that distinguish the religious communities from each other. Hick, for instance, is quite right to argue that, in order for Christians to participate in his pluralistic theory, they must first relinquish or radically reinterpret traditional beliefs about Jesus. Islamic belief in the Qu'ran as the one infallible word of God, Orthodox Jewish doctrine of election of Israel, Vedantic belief in Brahman/Atman, and Zen belief in Nirvana must all be recast as—at best partial and at worst mistaken—apprehensions of reality in order to be adopted into Hick's theory. Peter Byrne is a pluralist who supports this necessary reinterpretation:

> someone who affirms doctrinal statements after going through the reflective process which leads to embracing pluralism as a philosophical thesis cannot affirm doctrinal statements to be unequivocally true. "I believe" cannot mean the same for such a person in "I believe Jesus is the Son of God" as it means in "I believe that grass is green." . . . This much must be conceded by the pluralist. It must also be granted that, despite all the cognitive point the pluralist gives to doctrinal affirmations, it does not leave everything as it is. The doctrinal stance is altered by pluralism. (1995: 202)

The question Knitter, Hick, and even Byrne fail to answer, however, is whether or not the radical reinterpretation of such beliefs does not end up denying the religious diversity and particularity they seek to preserve. This point is taken up by S. Mark Heim, who writes: "To accept the affirmation of their faith given by given by the pluralistic theologies, those of other religions need to agree first that it is actually still their faith which is affirmed when it is in the translated form these theologians give it. Second, they need to be willing for their religious life to be cased in the mould pluralistic theology has set for it" (1995: 108-9). He then recounts the following anecdote:

> At one conference a well-known pluralist theologian said, in good humour, to a decidedly non-pluralist Jewish theologian, the veteran of long years of interfaith discussions, "With your views, you shouldn't be involved in dialogue." "Nevertheless, I am," he replied, and suggested that it was perhaps the pluralist theory that ought to be adjusted and not the reality he represented. In any event, the Jewish theologian continued, when liberal Christians and liberals of other traditions get together to talk about their liberalism, he did not call that dialogue. This affable exchange was capped by another pluralist voice in the audience who allowed that though his Jewish compatriot might be able to dialogue "after a fashion," he would be unable to participate in authentic dialogue until he had adopted a thoroughly pluralistic outlook. Here it would seem that the old lamented triumphalist attitudes of Christians remain in vigorous health, if in different forms. (1995: 109)

Pluralistic theories, in other words, hold either explicitly—as is the case with Byrne—or implicitly—as is the case with Knitter and Hick—that the central beliefs that distinguish religious communities from each other are as they stand indefensible. Here Heim is blunt: "Only as demythologised, adapted to the categories of critical historical thought, put in the context of Western understandings of epistemology, and measured against modern conceptions of equality and justice can these religions be pronounced valid" (1995: 109). It seems that the meta-critical approach results in the preservation of a veneer of diversity and particularity that fails to reckon seriously with either.

The holistic approach counters that these very beliefs, precisely because they distinguish religions from each other, make them interesting objects of study in the first place and therefore ought to be preserved. That differences—and sometimes ones of enormous significance—exist cannot be denied. Most Hindus and Buddhists believe in the karmic cycle of reincarnation; orthodox Christians, Jews, and Muslims do not. Although they would differ about its significance, Christians and Jews are likely to agree that Jesus was crucified. Most Muslims would argue that he was not and some—for example, Ahmadi Muslims—would insist further that he moved to Kashmir, where he lived out his days. The question is whether it is more realistic to suppose that these differences are but minor historical and cultural variations on the one soteriological structure pointing to one Ultimate Reality, or that they are both prima facie and ultima facie different and sometimes opposing interpretations of reality. Against the equation of surface similarities, I believe that the latter is the more accurate answer, given the available evidence.

If left here, in spite of the previous qualifications, the argument would again be left open to charges of relativism. More must be said. Hick, Knitter, Byrne, and, one might add, Ward and Netland, have developed theories on the assumption that religions are different ways of relating to the same reality. Netland differs by arguing that only the Christian tradition offers its adherents the proper relationship. A holistic approach, by taking the different descriptions of their various Ultimates at face value, refuses to equate them as partial descriptions of the one Ultimate Reality. The available evidence—whether it is assessed in terms of values, or satisfactory religious experience, or truth claims—is at the very best ambiguous. Furthermore, legitimate conclusive analysis on these bases would require a God's-eye-view that denies human cultural and historical finitude. Still, these difficulties do not require a relativistic solution. One may, as I do, continue to retain a realist view of religious language (i.e., the belief that religious language is capable of referring to the real world). One may also say that the various religious pictures of the real world are more or less tenable on their own terms. What is fragmented is not truth but warranted assertability. The holistic approach is an attempt to describe a situation of radical relativity rather than one to prescribe a solution of radical relativism (Rescher, 1985: 190).

By applying Kraemer's holistic approach in this way, a theology of religions can better preserve religious plurality. Nowhere is this more evident than when looking at their diverse soteriologies. If the preceding argument is tenable, then in soteriological contexts one no longer speaks of "salvation" but of "salvations." As Kraemer has written, "it is indeed a fact that in Hinduism, many people have found salvation, with deep satisfaction" (1956b: 84). Most theologies of religions across the typological boundaries have until now described salvation monolithically. For exclusivists and inclusivists, salvation always means salvation in and through Christ; they diverge over whether other religions are anonymous vehicles of God's grace (i.e., Rahner, 1966) or ordinary ways of salvation (i.e., Küng, 1984: 89-116) or simply varieties of unbelief (i.e., Barth, 1956: 280-361). Likewise, for most pluralist proposals, despite their radical reinterpretation of certain doctrines, salvation remains a simple, unitary point of reference (Heim, 1995: 129).[4] Salvation is the transformation from self-centredness to Reality-centredness (Hick, 1989) or the liberation of the poor and oppressed

---

4 The exception to this observation is Raimon Panikkar: "The center is neither the earth (our particular religion), nor the sun (God, transcendence, the Absolute...). Rather, each solar system has its own center and every galaxy turns reciprocally around the other. There is no absolute center. Reality itself is concentric inasmuch as each being (each tradition) is the center of the universe—of its own universe to begin with." (1987: 109) See also Panikkar, 1993.

The Holistic Approach

(Knitter, 1987). For exclusivists and inclusivists, other traditions may or may not participate in the Christian soteriological scheme while for pluralists, all are partial expressions of a common end. In both, this end is referred to as salvation.

From a holistic perspective, this monolithic description of salvation is highly problematic for it fails to reckon sufficiently with the internal significance of the soteriological claims of other traditions. If the religions do not proffer overlapping descriptions of the one human predicament and one Ultimate Reality, but of radically different predicaments and Ultimates, then it follows logically that their soteriologies cannot be described exclusively or exhaustively in Christian or pluralist terms. Only terms that give full weight to the internal significance of the structures by which the religions seek to overcome their predicament and relate to their reality, will suffice. Thus, speaking of salvations is justified.

Salvation is an elusive concept; it implies that there is something from which to be saved; what this is, is contextually dependent (Jantzen, 1984: 579). One traditionally Christian description of salvation may be the fellowship of a community of believers with the Triune God culminating in the perfection of heaven. As such, it assumes the reality of a personal God distinct from the believing individual. Theravadin salvation, however, culminates in the realization that there is no substantial individual, and is more likely to see the existence of God as irrelevant. In the absence of convincing arguments to the contrary, it is unlikely that these salvations are in some way partial descriptions of the same event (DiNoia, 1992: 47). Rather, Grace Jantzen concludes: "It is therefore important, when we turn to a religious context, that we do not assume without investigation a monolithic concept of salvation, either in terms of its antecedent condition (from what we are saved), or its goal (to what we are saved). This is especially true in the face of the diversity of religions" (1984: 580). I agree wholeheartedly.

This does not yet pursue the issue far enough, for a holistic theology of religions not only acknowledges a plurality of salvations, but also allows that the various religions may in fact successfully bring their concept of salvation to their adherents. Because a holistic approach regards religions as complex systems of doctrines and practices that encompass complete ways of life, salvation can be interpreted within this comprehensive pattern. Therefore, there is no reason not to assume that someone pursuing diligently the soteriological scheme of a religious tradition may be regarded as experiencing the salvation offered by that tradition. Heim puts it this way: "Any particular religious tradition would regard someone as 'saved' whose life had been most fully shaped by the distinctive pattern it fosters" (1995: 162). For example, a Buddhist on the Noble Eightfold Path may experience something in this life that is recognizably enlightenment and, therefore, enjoy salvation in a Buddhist context. Because the soteriological schemes differ markedly, such an experience cannot be described either as an acceptance or rejection of Christian salvation or as a transition from self-centredness to Reality-centredness. The Christian belief that "there is salvation in no one else [than Jesus Christ], for there is no other name under heaven given among men by which we must be saved" (Acts 4:12), then does not necessarily preclude the possibility of other religions being independently authentic ways of salvation. Through a holistic approach, there are many religions, each of which may offer its own concept of salvation. Pandipeddi Chenchiah concludes: "The supreme longing of the Hindu after escape from samsara is not satisfied by Christ. The gift of rebirth as offered by Christ does not appeal to the Hindu. On the contrary, Jesus kindles new hopes not felt before and kills some of the deepest and most persistent longings of man" (Chenchiah, quoted in Kraemer, 1956b: 215-6). A theology of religions informed by the holistic approach gives a more accurate account of the variations in soteriologies by retaining what DiNoia calls the "internal significance" of these doctrines and practices while deliberately and openly transposing them to Christian contexts of discussion. In so doing, it gives a more accurate account of the otherness of other religions.

The difficult issue of the final salvation—in the Christian sense of the word—of non-Christians must be addressed here, as in the previous chapter. If, as Kraemer contended, salvation is a contextually dependent notion, an experience to be interpreted only within a religious community, what can be said about those who, although standing outside the Christian community, evince what most Christians would recognize as the "fruit of the Spirit" (Galatians 5:22-23)? George Lindbeck confronts an analogous problem as a result of his contention that one must be fluent in the Christian language in order to experience either salvation or damnation. As discussed earlier, Lindbeck seeks to resolve this problem by appealing to the possibility of a post-mortem encounter with Christ (1984:59). He seems to assume that, while there are many pre-mortem religions, each with their own language and grammar, in post-mortem encounters, the Christian language will prevail (1984: 60-1). This assumption is, according to Kenneth Surin, highly problematic:

> How, in this "post-mortem" state, will someone who had in "this life" been a Hindu, be able to "interiorize the language about Christ"? Are we justified in hoping that there will be only one such "post-mortem" language? If there is, which one will it be? Will our Hindu speak "about Christ" in the idiom of John Paul II

or Oral Roberts? Or will she speak in the accents of St. Augustine or Jonathan Edwards? Or will there just be one language, albeit an entirely new and pure language, an Ursprache, which all, Oral Roberts and Hindu alike, will speak? What are we hoping for when we are persuaded to think along the lines prescribed by the "prospective fides ex auditu" theory? We cannot even begin to contemplate what the appropriate answers to these questions would be like, and this should be sufficient indication that we have this difficulty because we cease to be faithful to the Judaeo-Christian Bilderverbot when we start to think about the "after-life" in such positive terms. (1989: 175-6)

Heim takes the first half of Surin's warning to heart. He avoids Lindbeck's apparently inconsistent juxtaposition of many pre-mortem salvations with one post-mortem one simply by affirming plurality throughout.

If religions function as languages, enabling adherents to experience the world religiously, and life continues beyond death in some way, there is every reason to believe that the language that shaped life will also shape after-life. Both before and after death, people will experience as saving what they have been conditioned to experience by their religious traditions. Heim clarifies:

> From a Christian perspective, this requires the somewhat unfamiliar admission that other religious fulfillments may be both distinct and quite real. . . . That is, they are not positive evils (though such evils may also be live possibilities), but they are aims different than the best Christians know and hope for. [The Christian warrant for such speculation lies] in the trinitarian vision of God and a notion of divine plenitude. That is, it rests on the conviction that the most emphatic no of the human creature to the end of loving communion with God meets always some variation of God's merciful yes to creation.[5] (1995: 163)

For Heim, there are, according to this eschatology, three possible human destinies: "lostness, penultimate religious fulfillments, and communion with the triune God" (1995: 165). Diversity, it seems, runs (almost) all the way down.

Heim's case is persuasive. It certainly deals with the problem in a manner superior to Lindbeck's. And it addresses the first half of Surin's

---

[5] Heim offers a fully developed account of this view in *The Depth of the Riches: A Trinitarian Theology of Religious Ends* (2001), a work I received too late to incorporate fully into the present research. It expands and clarifies, but does not alter significantly, Heim's 1995 position.

warning, which pointed to an inconsistency in Lindbeck's own position. I feel, however, that Heim does not adequately address the second half, in which Surin cautioned against speaking about the afterlife in too positive a way for fear that one would cease thereby to be faithful to the Christian language. Aware of this charge, Heim seeks to give Christian warrant for his proposal, namely, the gracious nature of the triune God. And yet, Heim does not, in my view, give sufficient weight to those biblical passages—central to the regulation of Christian eschatological grammar—that speak not of three possible human destinies, but of the final reconciliation of all things. The most obvious is the Christ-hymn quoted by Paul in his letter to the Philippians (2:5-11). Its second half describes the exaltation of Christ and concludes "that at the name of Jesus every knee should bow . . . and every tongue confess that Jesus Christ is Lord, to the glory of God the Father" (5:10-11). Others may also be added, among them, Ephesians 1:15ff, Colossians 1:15ff, and Revelation 21:22ff. These passages seem to preclude an indefinitely long period of penultimate religious fulfilment and, therefore, place limits on Heim's proposal—limits that he does not address.

For those seeking to follow Kraemer, the dilemma remains unresolved. Phenomenologically, his approach compels "salvations" because of the diversity of religions. Eschatologically, one must remain hopeful for the final salvation of many who, though not having been visibly incorporated into the Christian Church, have been reconciled by the Holy Spirit through Christ to the Father. This hope is maintained, further, not because the religions are themselves intrinsically saving but because God is a "gracious and compassionate God, slow to anger and abounding in love, a God who relents from sending calamity" (Jonah 3:2b). About the final salvation of non-Christians, Christians who follow Kraemer's approach can and should say very little; anything that is said ought not to be speculative, but clearly founded in the biblical and trinitarian grammar of Christian faith. While there are grounds for locating the religions and their adherents within the realm of God's providence, as with all final judgments regarding them, eschatological destiny is recognized as God's decision alone.

Finally, I want to address potential criticism of this argument. Consider first of all Hick's soteriological criterion: if one can evaluate the saving ability of a religion according to its production of saints, then a universal, empirically verifiable means of equating salvations exists. For Hick, the transition from self- to Reality-centredness can occur within any number of the world religions. It follows, then, that saving ability can be tested according to the lives of its adherents. To be fair, however, one must not focus on just any adherent but on those a given community recognizes as "much further advanced" in the transformation—saints (Hick, 1987: 23). These remarkable individuals can be tested both spiritually and ethically, according to their embodiment of the universal ideal of compassionate goodwill for others—"Agape/Karuna" (Hick, 1989: 299-342). Inasmuch as these tests can be accurately applied, Hick concludes that no religion can claim superiority. Here then is a simple test that, if successful, undercuts my position completely. On closer inspection, however, the criterion of saintliness is deeply problematic, as it assumes that the religions focus on one Ultimate Reality.

I have already shown that it is more reasonable to assume that different realities are being described and pursued by different religions. This impacts on Hick's criterion, as Rebecca Pentz answers through the mundane comparison of an American football training camp and a Sunday school (1991). Both indirectly build character in individuals, even though they are directly focused on the incommensurate goals of creating better football players or worshippers. Therefore, to test them according to the common but indirect goal of building character is unfair. It is worth quoting her at length.

> Though I can't document this, I bet there is a much closer connection between regular worship and character building that there is between football training and character building. Because of this, even if we ascertain that our young worshippers have better characters than the . . . football players, we cannot conclude that there is more transforming power in our Sunday school . . . than in the training camp. The camp may very well have much more power to achieve its goal of producing better football players than our Sunday school has to achieve its goal of producing sincere worshippers. (1991: 100)

Therefore, the football camp would unjustly fail the test. When one compares religions, the same problem arises. It may be that a religion is very good at achieving its goal but places little emphasis on "Agape/Karuna." Or conversely, it may be that a religion produces many compassionate people but fails consistently with respect to its goal. Hick's test works, as Pentz has it: "only if the same degree of positive correlation holds between salvation and saint-production in the various religions to be tested" (1991: 103). Hick has not shown this to be the case and, until he does, saint-production remains an imperfect test of the holistic approach.

It may be objected by traditional Christian theologians that the recognition of salvations appears to undermine the universality and ultimacy of Christian salvation. I must, therefore, clarify that in no way am I denigrating the salvation that comes in and through Jesus Christ. I am saying simply that to reinscribe a non-Christian soteriology in Christian terms denies a priori the possibility that this salvation is radically different; rather, it is beyond inscription in a Christian vocabulary. Here, an important distinction must be made. I am not offering a prescription of eschatological plurality for the reality of multiple human ends. Tom Driver sums up this prescription well:

> If there is a "salvation history" delineated and forecast in Christian scripture, there are other "salvation histories" outside it; and in them God has different names, different identities, and moves in different ways. Inasmuch as God has different histories, then God has different "natures." In pluralist perspective, it is not simply that God has one nature variously and inadequately expressed by different religious traditions. It is that there are real and genuine differences within the Godhead itself, owing to the manifold involvements that God has undertaken with the great variety of human communities. (1987: 212)

On this point, I stand in agreement with Lesslie Newbigin, who lamented that this amounted to a return to ancient polytheism, a triumph of the many over the one. This victory, however, may come at a terrible cost. As Newbigin puts it: "All belief in the ultimate coherence of things has been abandoned. Chaos has come again and there will be nothing left except the will to power of the competing human projects" (1990: 147). Rather, what I have given is a descriptive, historical account. To argue for the possibility of salvations, as I have done, is to counter claims that beliefs and practices of different religious communities are somehow indefensible as they stand. On the contrary, when interpreted within an entire religio-cultural framework, they are defensible. My account likewise opposes those who argue that those outside one's tradition have, because of this, an imperfect experience or revelation. The experiences and beliefs of those from other religions are not imperfect versions of ours; they are different. In pragmatic terms, their beliefs may and often do make sense and the experiences they produce can be deeply satisfying. Neither contention challenges the final universality and ultimacy of Christianity. It simply acknowledges that these claims are being made in a world of religious plurality in which the evidence is inconclusive. In so doing, the wisdom of Kraemer and those who follow him in refusing to pronounce on the eschatological destiny of the adherents of other religions is underscored.

I opened this chapter by condensing Kraemer's holistic approach to the phenomenology of religions. It was his opinion that the religions were fairly complete, coherent understandings of existence which differ radically from each other. From this perspective, essentialist phenomenologies appear to be reductionistic. I tested this position to account for the fact that religious beliefs and practices develop over time, and concluded that the position initially articulated by Kraemer required modification. I argued further that by focusing on religions in a pragmatic, local way, the holistic approach could in fact be preserved so that the dynamic, developing nature of religious communities is not ignored. I concluded the chapter by developing the claim that Kraemer's holistic approach recognizes that any attempt to understand other religions is limited by one's own cultural and historical situation and is therefore never total.

When set side by side with biblical realism, the holistic approach completes Kraemer's understanding of religious evaluation. The search for a common core or a set of universal and religiously neutral criteria providing a vantage point for legitimate evaluation is futile theologically because it would submit the Christian faith to a foreign criterion, subjugating the wisdom of God to what Kraemer affectionately called the "foolishness of humanity" (1938: 326-27). It is therefore irrelevant whether or not biblical realism is accepted as a legitimate authority outside the Christian faith. Following Kraemer, phenomenologically, as apprehensions of the whole of existence, religions are founded on their own ultimate, unprovable presuppositions; there is no universal foundation—only rival claims to finality. This assertion introduces the most serious problem of all: the final, fundamental incommensurability of religious totalities. It is this problem I address next.

7

RADICAL DIFFERENCE AND COMMUNICATION

Adaptation and Points of Contact

In my discussion of biblical realism and the holistic approach, I have been concerned with the fundamental presuppositions that any inquirer into religions brings to an investigation. Although Kraemer seemed to be committed to a radical perspectivalism, religions are, in his words, apprehensions of the totality of existence; as such, they are founded on their own ultimate and unprovable presuppositions. In Kraemer's view, there is no universal foundation of religious knowledge; there are only rival claims to finality. Lest one think that this perspectivalism is the last word, one must also remember that Kraemer insisted that "Christian revelation places itself over against the many efforts to apprehend the totality of existence. It asserts itself as the record of God's self-disclosing and recreating revelation in Jesus Christ, as an apprehension of existence that revolves around the poles of divine judgment and divine salvation" (1938: 113-4). The recognition of a multiplicity of perspectives is softened, in other words, by the Christian's commitment to his or her own perspective.

The question that this appraisal of Kraemer must finally address arises here: Is communication across perspectives possible? Based on the earlier analysis of Kraemer's missionary experience, it would seem that he believes it is. His years of cross-cultural experience engendered concern that indigenous members of the Indonesian churches be able to express faithfully their Christian beliefs in their own languages and cultures rather than regurgitating the vocabulary of Western missionaries. Kraemer expressed this concern in his theoretical work when considering the problems of adaptation—for instance, expressing Christian beliefs in terms understandable to an other-believer—and the point of contact—for instance, whether there are overlaps between the Christian revelation and other religions. This chapter explores several theological implications to which these two problems give rise.

1. Adaptation and Points of Contact

At first glance, the very word "adaptation" seems to introduce an element of discontinuity with this analysis of Kraemer's thinking, which has been concerned with defending a peculiar form of perspectivalism. Under the heading of biblical realism, I have shown that, for Kraemer, the Christian is committed to the perspective given by Christian faith and through the holistic approach I have demonstrated Kraemer's recognition of a multiplicity of such perspectives, each potentially complete and coherent. Adaptation implies, however, the possibility of genuine communication between and among religious worlds. Because of this apparent inconsistency, I begin by defining as precisely as possible what Kraemer meant by "adaptation."

Kraemer opposed a simplistic assimilation of the Christian message with the religious beliefs and practices of one's pre-Christian past. For Kraemer, the problem of adaptation presupposes the clash of radically different conceptions of the world; if the world views were fundamentally similar, then this question would not arise. Adaptation presupposes "a revolution, a total rupture with one's religious past . . . [a] conversion in the deepest sense of the word" (1938: 114). Having said that, however, Kraemer also rejected an equally naïve dismissal of one's former religious life. That some form of interreligious communication is possible is also embedded in adaptation, which requires Christian belief to be expressed both in terms of and in conflict with other faiths. Finally, adaptation presupposes that such expression is not done in a systematic, theoretical way, but as the situational encounters between Christians and others demand; Kraemer puts it this way:

> Adaptation in the deepest sense does not mean to assimilate the cardinal facts of the revelation in Christ as much as possible to fundamental religious ideas and tastes of the pre-Christian past, but to *express* these facts by wrestling with the concretely and so to present the Christian truth and reveal at the same time the intrinsic inadequacy of man's religious efforts for the solution of his crucial religious and moral problems. (1938: 308)

Models of such adaptation abound in the Bible and Christian history. The New Testament, Kraemer noted, is the

> expression of the revelation in its concrete conflict and intermingling with the Jewish and Hellenistic world of religion and civilization . . . [confirms] that the religion of revelation stands in

> revolutionary contrast to this concrete Jewish and Hellenistic world, but at the same time freely uses its ideas and thought-forms to express itself, and so Christian truth experiences its first incarnation. (1938: 312)

Furthermore, the Christian message has taken on various incarnations throughout history, whether in Augustine's philosophy of history, medieval scholasticism, or contemporary Protestantism. Kraemer observed:

> In the course of its history, Christian theology has always freely employed the different thought-patterns that were available, such as Platonic and Aristotelian and Neo-Platonic-coloured Aristotelian philosophy. This was natural, because all speaking to man must be done in his language and in the terminologies and thought-patterns he understands. (1938: 325)

This is not to say that such incarnations are ever infallible. There is, however, no reason to assume in principle that new Asian and African articulations of Christianity are impossible.

To be more specific, if Western Christians have in the past made use of the vocabulary of Greek philosophy and culture, then there is no valid objection to the deliberate use of Hindu, Buddhist, Confucian, or African terminology in the development of Asian and African Christianity. On the contrary, such work is to be affirmed, for Christianity did not and does not arise in a historical vacuum but can only be expressed in the terms of whatever time and place in which it is found (1938: 313). Thus, we may say that adaptation attempts to overcome the "foreignness of Christianity" without recasting it as yet another indigenous philosophy of life.

The Christian message—at least as it was being preached in Asia and Africa in the first half of the twentieth century—was coloured by the theological and personal histories of the Western missionaries who proclaimed it. Such colouring, albeit inevitable, was often uncritically conflated with the unique and final character of the gospel (1938: 316-7). In Kraemer's view, this served only to make Christianity more foreign to the adherents of other religious systems, for, to become a Christian, meant also to adopt the way of life of another culture and to reject uncritically one's own. Nevertheless, Kraemer insisted that the opposite extreme, epitomized by Hocking and the fulfilment theologians, is also to be avoided. That is, the gospel is neither a species of an essence of religion nor the fulfilment of pre-Christian longings and cannot, therefore, be presented as such. To do so, for Kraemer, is to rob the message of its uniqueness. In content and form, Christianity is inevitably foreign to adherents of other religions. In articulating his position on adaptation, Kraemer hoped to pass between these horns. He wanted to distinguish Christian faith from Western culture, to open up the possibility of indigenous expressions of Christian faith without thereby diluting the subversive challenge it poses to all cultures.

Kraemer supported "the genuine translation of Christianity into indigenous terms so that its relevance to . . . concrete situations becomes evident" (1938: 323), not simply as an academic exercise. Institutional experiments in cultural, intellectual, and theological synthesis between the Christian message and non-Christian systems are necessarily artificial and, therefore, rarely last. Likewise, an a priori emphasis that is outside history and criticism on the contrast between the gospel and indigenous cultures denies its universality. Kraemer mediated between these extremes: "It is not a matter of partisanship in bridge-building or contrast-making, but, by concentration on the living Christian truth of Biblical Realism, and on its living expression, of finding out where to build bridges and where to emphasize contrasts" (1938: 323). True adaptation, for Kraemer, was to be founded in biblical realism, for a fully indigenous expression of Christian faith to arise slowly and always within actual cross-cultural and/or interreligious encounters. It is unimportant that such expressions in theology, worship, art, organization, and presentation differ from Western forms of Christianity. What is vital is that they function in agreement with biblical realism, for this alone can foster a vigorous indigenous Christian community (1938: 324-25). Kraemer concluded:

> The great need . . . is to be constantly alive to the necessity that the religious and philosophical heritage should be used to "tell" what Christian truth really is, and not to amalgamate elements of it as harmoniously as possible with this heritage. The tendency to do the latter is very strong. The real programme is not to *relate* the thought of Christianity to the thought of India or China or another civilization, but to *express* it through these different heritages, and then see whether this in various cases may be called a relating or not. This attitude alone guarantees a virtual contact and wrestling both with Christian truth and also with the religious and philosophical heritage. (1938: 328)

Thus, although the introduction of adaptation seems to be inconsistent with Kraemer's biblical realism and holistic approach, a careful exposition of Kraemer's sense of adaptation turns aside any apparent inconsistency.

The holistic approach regards religious totalities as fundamentally complete and coherent apprehensions of existence. With biblical realism, Kraemer's approach affirms internal criteria authorizing judgments about the beliefs and practices of other religious communities. Consequently, Kraemer held that, between and among religious totalities, rational debate on basic issues is impossible. The difficulty Kraemer exposes here has been clarified by Alasdair MacIntyre. If such a situation obtains, MacIntyre has argued: "the protagonists of rival traditions will be precluded at any fundamental level, not only of justifying their views to the members of any rival tradition, but even from learning from them how to modify their own tradition in a radical way" (1988: 348). And given that each totality shapes its own standpoint according to its own criteria, it would further seem that translation from the language of one to that of another is also impossible. Again, MacIntyre is persuasive: a "social universe composed exclusively of rival traditions, so it may seem, will be one in which there are a number of contending, incompatible, but only partially and inadequately communicating, overall views of that universe, each tradition within which is unable to justify its claims over against those of its rivals except to those who already accept them" (1988: 348). Keeping MacIntyre in mind, the first two themes, biblical realism and the holistic approach, seem to require the incommensurability of religious communities. On the other, by arguing that the Christian message can be translated into the terminology of another religious totality in a manner both faithful to the message and understandable to the other, adaptation seems to presume the opposite.

This is an appropriate place to consider the possibility of points of contact between Christian revelation and non-Christian religions. Like Karl Barth, Kraemer rejects traditional distinctions between general and special revelation for risking "the danger of making human religious experience and effort a preamble to faith, which would imply making the realm of revelation and grace continuous to the realm of human religious effort" (1938: 120). Barth most strenuously opposed this language, arguing that discussions of points of contact between the gospel and the world of human affairs is to surrender the gospel's unique claim to revelation.[1] Yet Kraemer is reluctant to embrace Barth's extreme. For Kraemer, both to affirm and to deny that all people share in a limited knowledge of God treats revelation as a static object rather than the dynamic movement of God toward humanity. By refusing to define how or where it may or may not occur, he presented revelation not as a thing to be apprehended but as an event that is taking place always and everywhere.

Kraemer did not affirm all claims to revelation: "The wholesale talking about all religions being the product of revelation results, in fact, either in theological myopia or in a practical relativism or in an indifferentism in

---

[1] This is especially so in his sharp disagreement with Emil Brunner (Brunner and Barth, 1946).

regard to truth" (Kraemer, 1956b: 349). For Kraemer, so-called general revelation can only be discovered in the light of the special revelation of God in Christ. Accordingly, all religious activity is meaningful and is in some sense either a resistance or acceptance of God's constant self-disclosure. Kraemer therefore reintroduces the sui generis nature of the revelation in Christ: "there are manifestations in this religious and spiritual life and witness in the realm outside the revelation of Christ that are acknowledged as evidence of God's uninterrupted concern and of His travailing with man.... Therefore, all religion is meaningful in some sense, as a dim response or as a refusal towards God's working" (1956b: 340-1). Such comments are, further, not limited to his later work. Consider these words from *The Christian Message*: "Whosoever by God's grace has some moderate understanding of the all-inclusive comparison of God and of Christ rejoices over every evidence of divine working and revelation that may be found in the non-Christian world. No man, and certainly no Christian, can claim the power or the right to limit God's revelatory working" (1938: 122). Revelation, for Kraemer, is not a matter of a priori judgments and descriptions, but an event discerned a posteriori in the light of the revelation in Christ. Hence, both traditional concepts of general revelation and Barth's apparent denial are but different ways of prejudging the question. To indicate systematically and finally whether or where God reveals himself to human beings, for Kraemer, denies God's freedom and ought not therefore to be attempted: "Personal concrete experience, the meeting of spirit *with spirit* and illumined divination can alone lead on the right track" (1938: 127).

For these reasons, it is legitimate and necessary to expect points of contact. Humans, irrespective of their religion and in spite of their sin, are God's creatures. Following Calvin and the Reformed tradition, Kraemer insisted that God has created human beings with an indelible awareness of the transcendent, an awareness that has resulted in the world religions, and that is an undeniable point of contact for the gospel. Kraemer observed that: "This tragic contradictory position is [man's] deepest problem and testifies to his indestructible relatedness to God. The quest for God, even when man tries to kill it in himself, is the perennially disturbing and central problem of man. Therefore, there is undeniably a point of contact for the Message of the Gospel" (1938: 130). More significantly, however, for Kraemer, is the affirmation found in the doctrine of the incarnation: that God should become human "means that God wants, even passionately wants, contact with man, and thus through the act of His revelation shows His belief in the possibility of contact" (1938: 131). Finally, points of contact are presumed by cross-cultural missions; without them, the gospel is beyond communication and missions are irrelevant: "The apostolic nature of God's revelation in Christ pre-supposes it. No human reasoning can wipe this out, unless it wants to make the Gospel void and meaningless" (1938: 131).

In spite of these reasons for optimism, however, Kraemer remained reluctant to speak of points of contact in any detailed way for fear of leading to "the delusion of building too great hopes on our methods; that of expecting success surely to come from our psychological and theological approaches or our dogmatic correctness or liberalism; that of taking the term 'point of contact' in the sense of an idea or disposition in the religious consciousness from which faith and conversion to Christ and his gifts and demands can be developed" (1938: 132). This strategy, for Kraemer, mistakenly assumes that a better understanding of points of contact results in more successful missionary activity and misunderstands them as the agents of conversions to Christianity. For Kraemer, this resembles soteriological synergism—the co-operation of grace and works in salvation—and, as a Reformed theologian, he reacted against it. For him, the "sole *agent* of real faith in Christ is the Holy Spirit" (1938: 132). This reluctance in turn renders him sympathetic to the strong denial of points of contact found in Barth's early works. And yet, Kraemer concluded that Barth was too extreme. Siding with the more reflective position of Emil Brunner, Kraemer wrote: "Out of exclusive zeal for the right contention that God and not man himself in any sense whatever is Saviour of the world, [Barth] disregards what really is at stake in the problem of the 'point of contact'; that is to say, the fact that man can respond to the call of God and consequently is held responsible for his doing so or not" (1938: 133). Combining recognition with reluctance in this way culminates in a dialectical understanding.

Where, then, would Kraemer have allowed that points of contact can be found? Kraemer replied both nowhere and everywhere. Consider first the negative pole. Against those aiming to catalogue systematically all points of contact between Christianity and the non-Christian religions, Kraemer argued that such activity is impossible: "Somehow, the conviction is alive that it is possible and feasible to produce for every religion a sort of catalogue of points of contact . . . based on the similarities between Christianity and the non-Christian religions. [Because] religion is nowhere in the world an assortment of spiritual commodities that can be compared as shoes or neck-ties" (1938: 134-5), they cannot be itemized and compared in this way. To do so is to forget that every doctrine, symbol, and rite is vitally related to the totality of concrete beliefs and practices within each religious community and cannot be understood in abstraction from it. While this may be necessary to gain an intellectual command of the material, as a guide to a religion as practised, Kraemer pronounced that "it is less than useless" (1938: 136). Since discerning points of contact must take place in living cultures with thriving religious lives, the attempt to systematize points of contact is destined to fail. One cannot know the real force, value, and function of a religious claim or ritual without considering its relationship to the "fundamental existential apprehension of the totality of life which dominates this whole religion" (1938: 136). For these reasons, Kraemer can say with Barth that there is no point of contact.

If there were no point of contact, it would appear that one is justified in evaluating the religions solely from within the Christian faith. But this is to affirm "the measuring of these religions with the rod of current Christian dogmatism and dogma. That would be one of the worst forms of intellectualism" (1938: 136). For Kraemer, there are many points of contact in "the disposition and attitude of the missionary" (1938: 140). As the person engaged in cross-cultural communication of the gospel, the missionary needs a genuine interest in the religious and cultural life of the people among whom he or she works. Points of contact between the Christian revelation and other religions will be found in concrete situations, as people endeavour to adapt the gospel to their cultures. With this ad hoc, pragmatic approach, there are many points of contact.

Kraemer held, thus, that points of contact do not arise within the encounter of conflicting religious systems: "When the word approach is taken in the sense of Christianity as total religious system approaching the non-Christian religions as total religious systems, there is only difference and antithesis, and this must be so because they are radically different" (1938: 300). There are many in the everyday encounters between people, as Kraemer noted: "Yet although fundamentally speaking there is no point of contact, in practice the religious needs and aspirations that are embedded in these great religious systems often offer, of course, splendid opportunities for practical *human* contact" (1938: 300). On one hand, Kraemer averred that: "There is theologically speaking no point of contact between the world of God's Righteousness and Wisdom in Christ and man's righteousness and wisdom, whatever it may be," while he countered that: there "are points of contact. In saying this, no deviation whatever from the first thesis is implied. We are simply in a different dimension, namely that of communication, which entails two capital things in the reality of life understood as intercourse with fellow beings of different spiritual worlds— fellow beings for whom we are responsible and for whom we know that Christ came also" (1956b: 363-4). When so articulated it becomes clear that Kraemer's dialectical point of contact parallels and resolves the alleged inconsistency between the incommensurability implied by biblical realism and the holistic approach and the commensurability presumed by adaptation. Kraemer's position, therefore, is not inconsistent.

2. Theological Implications of Adaptation and Points of Contact

A strict incommensurability thesis—as set out by MacIntyre above—denies the possibility of the external justification and genuine translation of religious beliefs and practices, and is contradicted by Kraemer's understanding of adaptation. Drawing on the Bible, Christian history, and his own cross-cultural experience, Kraemer argued that the Christian message can be expressed both in terms understandable to and in conflict with those familiar to adherents of other religions. He thereby strove to demonstrate the universality of the Christian language without lapsing into a priori emphases on the continuity or discontinuity of the Christian message with the culture in which it is being communicated. Against both, he insisted that true adaptation, a biblically realistic, fully indigenous expression of Christian faith will arise gradually, always in concrete interreligious encounters. This argument raises significant issues in comparative theology and apologetics.

Earlier, I argued that a contemporary theology of religions based on Kraemer's work would employ the language of natural theology to demonstrate the universal nature of particular Christian claims. To leave the matter there, however, might imply that these claims can be translated into a philosophical language comprehensible to all regardless of religious affiliation. This is not quite correct: it is not that the language of natural theology is somehow religiously neutral and can therefore be understood and employed by anyone; rather, that particular Christian claims, as they are advanced in confrontation and conversation with other traditions, will sometimes occupy the same logical space as some of the claims of those communities. Consider the example adapted from DiNoia in chapter 5. DiNoia observed that theories of causation "play a crucial role in the Buddhist account of the conditions of human existence that need to be transcended if the round of re-births is to be escaped and Nirvana attained" (DiNoia, 1992: 132). Further, such theories are equally significant for the Christian tradition when describing and providing the rationality for theistic belief. It is in the logical overlap, in this instance between Christian and Buddhist theories of causation, that natural theology can be applied.

To recognize this logical overlap requires more than a passing knowledge of the particular claims of one's interlocutor: it demands both an intellectual and an existential familiarity with the beliefs and practices of a given religious community. Therefore, such an activity would also incorporate comparative theology, which, according to Francis Clooney, is marked by "its commitment to the detailed consideration of religious traditions other than one's own" (1995: 521). If this commitment is to avoid charges of reductionism, it must be predicated on a holistic and local understanding of religious beliefs and practices: it must consider beliefs and practices within their religio-cultural framework as it is embodied in actual religious communities. In Kraemer's words, comparative theology in the first instance "is a congenial entering to a different universe of discourse that has its own language" (1956b: 49).

Comparative theology then attempts to adapt the Christian message into this language, that is, to navigate between the Scylla of incomprehensibility and the Charybdis of assimilation. From this perspective, adaptation is neither the simplistic transliteration of Christian claims, nor the co-option of such claims into the life and practice of others. In the hypothetical conversation between the Dominican and the Theravadin, the Christian's goal is not to "adapt" the classical Thomistic argument from causation such that it harmonizes with the Theravadin's understanding—which is likely impossible—but to articulate this classical argument for the existence of God in such a way that his Theravadin partner will understand, though not necessarily accept. Theologies of religions, thus, will be done in critical dialogue with adherents of other religious traditions, where these traditions are shown to overlap in their interpretations of reality.

Finally, the purpose of this dialogue is not to uncover a global theology, as envisaged by Alan Race and Wilfred Cantwell Smith. By this, they appear to mean "a theological 'Esperanto,' to enhance communication and translate [the religions'] discourse into mutually acceptable language and symbols" (D'Costa, 1992: 330). Natural theology, as I have reinterpreted it, is an attempt to secure the universal scope of Christian claims. Comparative theology is the further endeavour to render such claims understandable to those outside the Christian community. In undertaking both of these tasks, one is arguing for the truth of these claims not only for Christians but for all people everywhere. Therefore, a Kraemerian theology of religions will also involve apologetics.

Apologetics can be defined both as a defence of beliefs and practices from external attack and an attempt to show their superiority to those of another community. A theology of religions, as I have been describing it, will involve both. To return to the example, the Theravadin most likely holds the following belief: "the claim that there exists an eternal, uncaused, omniscient, omnipotent being who desires the welfare of the entire human race is both internally incoherent and produces undesirable effects in those who assent to it" (Griffiths, 1991: 60-1). In so believing, he is at odds with the Dominican who likely believes precisely the opposite: namely, that this belief is coherent and desirable. By invoking St. Thomas's argument from causation, he engages himself in both negative and positive apologetics. Negatively speaking, he is attempting to show that this belief in not necessarily incoherent or producing undesirable effects. Positively, he is going further to show that Theravadin theories of causation are, in this respect, incorrect. Both forms of apology will be evidentialist in orientation. Both will appeal to commonly recognized evidence for support.

Here, I must raise an important clarification, for evidentialist, especially positive, apologetics have been dominated by three unfortunate assumptions. Plantinga describes the first: "much of the discussion has taken it for granted that a good theistic argument would have to meet extremely high standards of cogency and indeed be *demonstrative*. . . . Such an argument would start from what is self-evident and proceed majestically by way of self-evidently valid argument forms to its conclusion" (1992: 293). Second, they also assume that such an "argument must have premises accepted by nearly everyone, or nearly everyone who thinks about the topic, or nearly everyone who has a view on the topic" (1992: 294). Finally, they assume that evidence by definition is universally recognizable and available. Each of these assumptions can be challenged. In philosophical discourse, it is very rare that an argument achieves *demonstrable* status. Indeed, most philosophers would agree that such status, while a valid goal after which to strive, is not necessary in order for an argument to be good or convincing. Much the same applies, I would think, to argumentation in apologetics. Furthermore, for such an argument to be conducted, premises and evidence need only be acceptable to those involved in the conversation and not "nearly everyone," as Plantinga rightly points out. Nevertheless, to question these assumptions is not to give up on apologetics as an important theological enterprise.

In the absence of demonstrative arguments with universal premises and evidence, a theology of religions will be marked by the effort to persuade others of the truth of the gospel. Hence, an absence of conclusive evidence lends emphasis to the role of rhetoric in apologetics, as David Cunningham observes: "all we can do is to desire that our most successful moments of persuasion will be moments of *faithful* persuasion—moments for the sake of the God of Jesus Christ, in whom we live and move and have out being" (1991: 257). Kraemer sums up the nature of theologies of religions:

> The encounter between Christian faith and religions, even when deliberately sought on the highest level of spiritual intercourse, always preserves traits of an *apologia*, of a defence, and of an attack or combat. . . . This is more than dialogue. It is the spontaneous manifestation of . . . the dialectical character of the Biblical revelation, which means saying "yes" and "no" to the world and all its spheres of life, which precludes in principle the programme of synthesis, and yet impels toward true "communication." (1956b: 322)

As shown above, the tensions created by biblical realism and the holistic approach—namely, the incommensurate nature of religious traditions—and the presumption of adaptation—namely, the commensurability of religious traditions—was resolved though an appeal to dialectic. Among world religious systems, because of their incommensurable presuppositions, there is no point of contact. Nevertheless, in the concrete encounters between adherents, there may in fact be many.

I turn, finally, to the problems of justification and translation associated with the incommensurability thesis, to show that Kraemer's dialectical point of contact allows for genuine but always incomplete understanding of the beliefs and practices of the other. There are no external criteria capable of evaluating the beliefs and practices of a religious community according to standards of such acceptability or verity that extend beyond the boundaries of a particular community. Such an assertion emphasizes the negative aspect of Kraemer's dialectic so as to render any investigation into another tradition impossible. When held in tension with the positive—that points of contact are exposed in actual interreligious conversations—it still offers an important reminder to a theology of religions. Kraemer's dialectical point of contact compels the realization that there is no one set of universal and neutral criteria entitling judgments agreed on by philosophers and theologians across religious boundaries and that such a set is unnecessary for such activity to take place. Evaluations, according to Kraemer, can and should take place in practical engagement with adherents of other religious communities. During such dialogue, one need not appeal to universal criteria, the adherence to which defines rationality; one may appeal, rather, to criteria that the interlocutors share. This is not to neglect or reject the importance of theory, but to accept the inevitability of being condemned to history; as William Placher puts it: "We cannot find an Archimedean point, a universal standard of rationality. On the other hand, we are not utterly imprisoned within our own current horizons" (1989: 112).

The justification of beliefs and practices need not entail agreement. This does not deny the importance of evidence and argument—be they historic or scientific—but precludes the notion that evidential arguments can and sometimes do constitute conclusive proof for one belief, or even one entire tradition, over others. Speaking historically, that the evidence appears to support a number of traditions is borne out by their continued and flourishing existence throughout millennia in diverse cultural situations. Those traditions unable in some way to adapt to or make sense of these cultures eventually become historical artifacts. Kraemer's dialectic reminds that, in practical situations, Christian beliefs and practices can be rendered rational and justifiable to others, but denies that the individual receiving them is therefore necessarily irrational or somehow unjustified in rejecting them.

With regard to translation, Kraemer insisted that no member of any particular religious community can effectively communicate the meaning of a belief or practice to a member of another religious community. Once more, this seems to emphasize the negative pole of Kraemer's dialectic so as to render any attempt at translation and communication irrelevant. Nevertheless, when held in creative tension with the positive pole—that, in concrete situations, translation and communication take place—it is a reminder of two further caveats. The first is the indeterminacy of meaning in the act of translation. In practical situations, when transposing a doctrine or practice central to the life of one religious community into the language of another, Griffiths observes that "the 'correct' translation will always be underdetermined by the available data" (Griffiths, 1991: 24). There will always be a range of translations apparently equally reflective of an understanding of the meaning of an original. This is not so say that all translations are equally valid, but rather, that the evidence could possibly support several. The safeguard against incorrect translation is the emphasis on attempting to understand a given doctrine or practice as it is concretely embodied in a specific religious community. Further, attempts at theological translation force an acknowledgement of the limits of our understanding. Understanding is not a thing that one simply does or does not have, but is a matter of degrees. In order for one to understand as much as is possible the nuances of a belief or practice in a religion, one must interpret it as it arises within the life of a specific community. Some interpretations may be incorrect, while others may be affirmed.

To summarize, none of the four caveats—lack of universal criteria, plurality of justifiable positions, indeterminacy of meaning, and limits of understanding—demand a strict and inconsistent incommensurability thesis, but affirm the importance of internal consistency as a component in any external truth-claim. Such truth, according to Kraemer's dialectic, cannot be discerned in isolation from actual religious communities but only in practical concrete dialogue and engagement with them.

In response to the question of whether communication between religious traditions is possible, Kraemer answers that there is no way to reconcile them in such a way as to harmonize them. On the contrary, they are radically different apprehensions of human existence. Between people, however, Kraemer remained convinced that communication takes place with varying degrees of success.

8

CONCLUSION

This study sought to reappraise and defend Hendrik Kraemer's theology of religions to demonstrate its appropriateness for contemporary scholars. Kraemer successfully offers to theologians interested in religious plurality a way of theological creativity that is both aware of contemporary issues and faithful to the Reformed Christian tradition. I believe that Kraemer's approach holds out at least three interesting possibilities. It creates a discursive space for theological or otherwise religious phenomenologies of religions. If the quest for a universal and neutral evaluative vantage point is in fact doomed, there is no reason to prohibit theologians from investigating religious phenomena on the grounds their religious beliefs will somehow contaminate the scientific nature of the research. On the contrary, it would seem that those phenomenologists who are openly religious are in a better position that that of nonbelievers, for they will be able to recognize and therefore minimize the negative influence of their theological or religious assumptions rather than overlooking them. This need not necessarily promote sectarianism—for instance, the view that one's own tradition has nothing of value to gain from protracted contact with and study of another. Rather, it would seem to indicate precisely the opposite, that it is only through such interaction that one's own tradition can continue to develop and avoid stagnation.

Second, Kraemer's views on adaptation—that the Christian story can be retold in the terms of another religious totality—and on points of contact—that there are many personal, as opposed to systematic, points of contact—further underscore the importance and inevitability of contextual, comparative theology. As the Christian story is told and retold throughout the world, it is vital that such narration take place in terms listeners can understand, though not necessarily accept. It must therefore be told in terms of, in dialogue with, and, sometimes, in confrontation with, the dominant culture in which it is found. Comparative theology in this sense opposes both those holding that the Christian story always stands over religions and cultures, as well as those attempting artificial experiments in religious and cultural accommodation. The need to emphasize contrasts or common areas will be determined, following Kraemer, only through slow, painstaking cross-cultural contact.

Finally, Kraemer's position also re-emphasizes the need for apologetics undertaken in interreligious contexts. Being convinced of the truth and universality of the Christian story requires that one attempt to bring others to similar conviction. To do so is not necessarily intolerant, but to refrain from it may be a failure of love and concern for the other. Such activity does not require a universally accessible vantage point from which to determine and assess evidence or construct arguments, but presupposes an understanding of another religious community sufficient to determine what evidence and arguments will be recognized by all parties in the dialogue. Moreover, it can focus not on demonstration, but on persuasion.

These very brief remarks indicate that far from ending the Christian conversation with other religions, Kraemer's approach can open new—and expand existing—avenues where it can and should take place.

BIBLIOGRAPHY

Adriani, Nicolaus
    1917   "Spiritual Currents Among the Javanese." *International Review of Missions* 6: 113-25.

Ariarajah, Wesley
    1991   *Hindus and Christians: A Century of Protestant Ecumenical Thought.* Grand Rapids: Eerdmans.

Barnes, Michael
    1989   *Christian Identity and Religious Pluralism: Religions in Conversation.* Nashville: Abingdon.

Barth, Karl
    1956   *Church Dogmatics I.2: The Doctrine of the Word of God.* Edinburgh: T. & T. Clark
    1957   *Church Dogmatics II.2: The Doctrine of God.* Edinburgh: T. & T. Clark.

Brightman, E. S.
    1946   *A Philosophy of Religion.* New York: Prentice Hall.

Brunner, Emil
    1947   *Revelation and Reason: The Christian Doctrine of Faith and Knowledge.* London: SCM.

Brunner, Emil, and Karl Barth
    1946   *Natural Theology: Comprising "Nature and Grace" by Professor Dr. Emil Brunner and the Reply "No!" by Dr. Karl Barth.* London: Geoffrey Bles.

Byrne, Peter
    1995   *Prolegomena to Religious Pluralism.* London: Macmillan.

Calvin, John
    1960   *John Calvin: Institutes of the Christian Religion, volume I.* Philadelphia: Westminster.

Chao, T. C.
    1939   "Revelation." In William Paton, ed., *The Authority of the Faith,* 24-62. London: Oxford University Press.

Clement
    1954   "On Spiritual Perfection." In John Ernest Leonard Oulton and Henry Chadwick, trans. & eds., *Alexandrian Christianity,* 93-165. London: SCM.

Clooney, Francis X.
    1995   "Comparative Theology: A Review of Recent Books (1989-1995)." *Theological Studies* 56: 520-50.

Craig, William Lane
1995 "Politically Incorrect Salvation." In Timothy R. Phillips and Dennis Ockholm, eds., *Christian Apologetics in the Postmodern World*, 75-97. Downers Grove: InterVarsity.

Cunningham, David S.
1991 *Faithful Persuasion: In Aid of a Rhetoric of Christian Theology*. Notre Dame: University of Notre Dame Press.

D'Costa, Gavin
1986 *Theology and Religious Pluralism*. Oxford: Blackwell.
1990 "Preface." In Gavin D'Costa, ed., *Christian Uniqueness Reconsidered.*, Maryknoll: Orbis.
1992 "The End of Systematic Theology." *Theology* 95: 324-34.
1993 "Whose Objectivity? Which Neutrality? The Doomed Quest for a Neutral Vantage Point from Which to Judge Religions." *Religious Studies* 29: 79-95.
1996 "The Impossibility of a Pluralist View of Religions." *Religious Studies* 32: 223-32.
1997 "Theology of Religions." In David Ford, ed., *The Modern Theologians: Second Edition*, 626-44. Cambridge: Blackwell.

DiNoia, J. A.
1990 "Pluralist Theology of Religions: Pluralistic or Non-Pluralistic?" In Gavin D'Costa, ed., *Christian Uniqueness Reconsidered*, 119-34. Maryknoll: Orbis.
1992 *The Diversity of Religions: A Christian Perspective*. Washington, DC: Catholic University Press.

Donovan, Peter
1993 "The Intolerance of Religious Pluralism." *Religious Studies* 29: 217-29.

Driver, Tom F.
1987 "The Case for Pluralism." In John Hick and Paul F. Knitter, eds., *The Myth of Christian Uniqueness*, 203-218. Maryknoll: Orbis.

Dunn, James D. G. and James P. Mackey
1987 *The New Testament in Theological Dialogue*. London: SCPK.

Dupuis, Jacques
1989 *Jesus Christ at the Encounter of World Religions*. Maryknoll: Orbis.

Edwards, David
1970 "Signs of Radicalism in the Ecumenical Movement." In Harold E. Fey, ed., *The Ecumenical Advance: A History of the Ecumenical Movement, volume 2: 1948-1968*, 385. London: SPCK.

Farmer, H. H.
1939 "The Authority of the Faith." In William Paton, ed., *The Authority of the Faith*, 163-80. London: Oxford University Press.
1954 *Revelation and Religion: Studies in the Theological Interpretation of Religious Types*. London: Nisbet and Company.

Farquhar, J. N.
1971   *The Crown of Hinduism.* New Delhi: Oriental Books Reprint Corporation.

Feuerbach, Ludwig
1957   *The Essence of Christianity.* New York: Harper and Brothers.

Frei, Hans
1974   *The Eclipse of Biblical Narrative: A Study in Eighteenth and Nineteenth Century Hermeneutics.* New Haven: Yale University Press.
1993   *Theology and Narrative: Selected Essays.* Oxford: Oxford University Press.

Freud, Sigmund
1964   *The Future of An Illusion.* Garden City: Doubleday.

Garcia, Laura L.
1993   "Natural Theology and the Reformed Objection." In C. Stephen Evans and Merold Westphal, eds., *Christian Perspectives on Religious Knowledge*, 112-33. Grand Rapids: Eerdmans.

Garon, Armand
1979   "Hendrik Kraemer and the Mission to Islam." Ph.D. dissertation, Ottawa University.

Geivett, R. Douglas and W. Gary Phillips
1995   "A Particularist View: An Evidentialist Approach." In D. Ockholm and T. Phillips, eds., *More Than One Way? Four Views on Salvation in a Pluralistic World*, 213-50. Grand Rapids: Zondervan.

Gillis, Chester
n.d.   *Pluralism: A New Paradigm for Theology.* Grand Rapids: Eerdmans.

Gloede, Gunter
n.d.   *Okumenische Gestalten: Druchenbauer der Einen Kirche.* Berlin: Evangelische Verlangenstalt.

Griffiths, Paul J.
1991   *An Apology for Apologetics.* Maryknoll: Orbis.

Hallencreutz, Carl F.
1966   *Kraemer Towards Tambaram: A Study in Hendrik Kraemer's Missionary Approach.* Uppsala: Gleerup.

Heim, S. Mark
1995   *Salvations: Truth and Difference in Religion.* Maryknoll: Orbis.
2001   *The Depth of the Riches: A Trinitarian Theology of Religious Ends.* Grand Rapids: Eerdmans.

Hick, John
1987   "The Non-Absoluteness of Christianity." In John Hick and Paul F. Knitter, eds., *The Myth of Christian Uniqueness*, 16-36. Maryknoll: Orbis.
1989   *An Interpretation of Religion: Human Responses to the Transcendent.* London: Macmillan.

1990	"Review of Glyn Richards, Towards a Theology of Religions." *Religious Studies* 26: 175.
1993a	*Disputed Questions in Theology and the Philosophy of Religion.* London: Macmillan.
1993b	"The Copernican Revolution in Theology." In *God and the Universe of Faiths*, 120-32. London: Oneworld.
1995	"A Pluralist View." In D. Ockholm and T. Phillips, eds., *More Than One Way? Four Views on Salvation in a Pluralistic World*, 29-55. Grand Rapids: Zondervan.

Hocking, William Ernest
1912	*The Meaning of God in Human Experience: A Philosophic Study of Religion.* New Haven: Yale University Press.
1932	"General Principles." In W. E. Hocking, ed., *Re-Thinking Missions: A Layman's Inquiry After One Hundred Years*, Ch. 1-4. New York: Harper and Row.

Hogg, A. G.
1939	"The Christian Attitude to Non-Christian Faith," 102-25. In William Paton, ed., *The Authority of the Faith*. London: International Missionary Council.

Horton, Walter
1939	"Between Hocking and Kraemer." In William Paton, ed., *The Authority of the Faith*, 148-62. London: Oxford University Press.
1966	"Tambaram Twenty-five Years After." In Leroy S. Rouner, ed., *Philosophy, Religion and the Coming World Civilization: Essays in Honor of William Ernest Hocking*. The Hague: Martinus Nijhoff.

Hunsberger, George
1998	*Bearing the Witness of the Spirit: Lesslie Newbigin's Theology of Cultural Plurality.* Grand Rapids: Eerdmans.

International Missionary Council
1928a	*The Christian Life and Message in Relation to Non-Christian Systems of Thought and Life.* London: Oxford University Press.
1928b	*The Relations Between the Younger and Older Churches.* London: Oxford University Press.
1928c	*The Christian Mission in the Light of Race Conflict.* London: Oxford University Press.
1928d	*Christianity and the Growth of Industrialism in Asia, Africa and South America.* London: Oxford University Press.
1928e	*The Christian Mission in Relation to Rural Problems.* London: Oxford University Press.
1928f	*Addresses and Other Records.* London: Oxford University Press.
1939	*The Authority of the Faith.* London: International Missionary Council.

Jackson, Eleanor
1980   Red Tape and the Gospel: A study in the significance of the ecumenical missionary struggle of William Paton (1886-1943). Birmingham: Phlogiston.

James, George Alfred
1995   Interpreting Religion: The Phenomenological Approaches of Pierre Daniël Chantepie de la Saussaye, W. Brede Kristensen, and Gerardus van der Leeuw. Washington, DC: Catholic University of America Press.

Jantzen, Grace M.
1984   "Human Diversity and Salvation in Christ." Religious Studies 20: 579-92.

Jathanna, Origen V.
1981   The Decisiveness of the Christ Event and the Universality of Christianity in a World of Religious Plurality. Frankfurt: Peter Lang.

Jones, Rufus M.
1928   "Secular Civilization and the Christian Task." In The Christian Life and Message in Relation to Non-Christian Systems of Thought and Life, 283-338. London: Oxford University Press.

Jüngel, Eberhard
1986   Karl Barth: A Theological Legacy. Philadelphia: Westminster.

Justin
1953   "The First Apology of Justin, the Martyr." In Cyril Richardson, et al., trans. Early Christian Fathers, 231-5. London: SCM.

Knitter, Paul F.
1985   No Other Name? A Critical Survey of Christian Attitudes Toward the World Religions. Maryknoll: Orbis.
1987a   "Preface." In John Hick and Paul F. Knitter eds., The Myth of Christian Uniqueness. Maryknoll: Orbis.
1987b   "Toward a Liberation Theology of Religions." In John Hick and Paul F. Knitter eds., The Myth of Christian Uniqueness, 178-202. Maryknoll: Orbis.

Kraemer, Hendrik
1921   Een Javaansche primbon uit de zestiende eeuw : inleiding, vertaling enaanteekeningen. Ph.D. dissertation, Leiden University.
1938   The Christian Message in a Non-Christian World. London: Edinburgh House.
1939   "Continuity or Discontinuity." In William Paton, ed., The Authority of the Faith. London: Oxford University Press.
1943   "The Riddle of History: Thoughts on Romans IX-XI." The International Review of Missions 32: 78-87.
1956a   "A Manifold Appraisal of Barth: Review of Karl Barth's 'Festschrift' Antwort." Theology Today 2: 398.
1956b   Religion and the Christian Faith. London: Lutterworth.

1957	*The Communication of the Christian Faith*. London: Lutterworth.
1958a	*From Missionfield to Independent Church: Report on a Decisive Decade of Growth of Indigenous Churches in Indonesia*. London: SCM.
1958b	*A Theology of the Laity*. London: Lutterworth.
1960	*World Cultures and World Religions: The Coming Dialogue*. London: Lutterworth.
1962	*Why Christianity of All Religions?* London: Lutterworth.
1966	"The Role and Responsibility of the Christian Mission." In Leroy S. Rouner, ed., *Philosophy and the Coming World Civilization: Essays in Honor of William Ernest Hocking*. The Hague: Martinus Nijhoff.

Lathuihamallo, P. D.
1959   "Church and World: A Critical Study about the Relation of the Church and the World in the Writings of Hendrik Kraemer." Ph.D. dissertation, Union Theological Seminary.

Lindbeck, George
1984   *The Nature of Doctrine: Religion and Theology in a Postliberal Age*. Philadelphia: Westminster.
1989   "Scripture, Consensus and Community." In Richard John Neuhaus, ed., *Biblical Interpretation in Crisis*, 74-101. Grand Rapids: Eerdmans.

Lochhead, David
1990   *The Dialogical Imperative: A Christian Reflection on Interfaith Encounter*. London: SCM.

Loughlin, Gerard
1996   *Telling God's Story: Bible, Church and Narrative Theology*. Cambridge: Cambridge University Press.

MacIntyre, Alasdair
1988   *Whose Justice? Which Rationality?* London: Duckworth.

Macnicol, Nicol.
1928   "Christianity and Hinduism." In *The Christian Life and Message in Relation to Non-Christian Systems of Thought and Life*. London: Oxford University Press, 3-52.
1936   *Is Christianity Unique? A Comparative Study of the Religions*. London: SCM.

Markham, Ian
1993   "Creating Options: Shattering the 'Exclusivist, Inclusivist and Pluralist' Paradigm." *New Blackfriars* 74: 33-41.

Marx, Karl, and Friedrich Engels.
1964   *On Religion*. New York: Schoken Books.

Migliore, Daniel
1991   *Faith Seeking Understanding: An Introduction to Christian Theology*. Grand Rapids: Eerdmans.

Milbank, John
  1990   "The End of Dialogue." In Gavin D'Costa, ed., *Christian Uniqueness Reconsidered*, 174-91. Maryknoll: Orbis.
Moses, D. G.
  1939   "The Problem of Truth in Religion." In William Paton, ed., *The Authority of the Faith*, 63-89. London: Oxford University Press.
Neill, Stephen
  1960   *Men of Unity*. London: SCM.
Netland, Harold
  1991   *Dissonant Voices: Religious Pluralism and the Question of Truth*. Grand Rapids: Eerdmans.
Newbigin, Lesslie
  1969   *The Finality of Christ*. London: SCM.
  1988   "A Sermon Preached at the Thanksgiving Service for the Fiftieth Anniversary of the Tambaram Conference of the International Missionary Council." *The International Review of Mission* 325-31.
  1989   *The Gospel in a Pluralist Society*. Grand Rapids: Eerdmans.
  1990   "Religion for the Marketplace." In Gavin D'Costa, ed., *Christian Uniqueness Reconsidered*, 135-48. Maryknoll: Orbis.
  1994   "Mission in the World Today." In *A Word in Season: Perspectives on Christian World Missions*, 121-131. Grand Rapids: Eerdmans.
Nicholson, Wayne Isaac
  1978   "Toward a Theology of Comparative Religion: A Study in the Thought of Hendrik Kraemer and Wilfred Cantwell Smith." Ph.D. dissertation, Southern Baptist Theological Seminary.
Niles, D. T.
  1969   "Karl Barth—A Personal Memory." *The Southeast Asian Journal of Theology* 11: 10-11.
Ogden, Schubert
  1992   *Is There One Religion or Are There Many?* Dallas: SMU.
Origen
  1954   "On Prayer." In John Ernest Leonard Oulton and Henry Chadwick, trans. & eds., *Alexandrian Christianity*, 238-329. London: SCM.
Otto, Rudolf
  1959   *The Idea of the Holy: An inquiry into the non-rational factor in the idea of the divine and its relation to the rational*. London: Penguin Books.
Panikkar, Raimon
  1987   "The Jordan, The Tiber, and the Ganges." In John Hick and Paul F. Knitter, eds.,, *The Myth of Christian Uniqueness*, 89-116. Maryknoll: Orbis.
  1993   *The Cosmotheandric Experience: Emerging religious consciousness*. Maryknoll: Orbis.

Pentz, Rebecca
    1991   "Hick and Saints: Is Saint-Production a Valid Test?" *Faith and Philosophy* 8: 96-103.
Perry, Tim
    1996a   "Are Harold Netland's Principles Universal and Neutral?" *Calvin Theological Journal* 31: 487-94.
    1996b   "Beyond the Threefold Typology." *Canadian Evangelical Review* 14: 1-8.
    1999   "The Historical Jesus, Anti-Judaism, and the Christology of Hebrews: A Theological Reflection." *Didaskalia* 10: 69-78.
Pinnock, Clark
    1992   *A Wideness in God's Mercy*. Grand Rapids: Zondervan.
Placher, William
    1989   *Unapologetic Theology: A Christian Voice in a Pluralistic Conversation*. Louisville: Westminster/John Knox.
Plantinga, Alvin
    1980   "The Reformed Objection to Natural Theology." *Proceedings of the American Philosophical Society* 54: 49-62.
    1992   "Augustinian Christian Philosophy." *The Monist*, 75: 291-320.
    1998   "A Defense of Religious Exclusivism." In James F. Sennett, ed., *The Analytic Theist*, 187-209. Grand Rapids: Eerdmans.
Polanyi, Michael
    1957   *Personal Knowledge*. London: Routledge and Kegan Paul.
Race, Alan
    1983   *Christians and Religious Pluralism*. London: SCM.
    1993   *Christians and Religious Pluralism: Second Edition*. London: SCM.
Radhakrishnan, Sarvepalli, and Charles A. Moore, eds.
    1957   *A Sourcebook in Indian Philosophy*. Princeton: Princeton University Press.
Rahner, Karl
    1966   "Christianity and the Non-Christian Religions." In Karl-H. Kruger, trans. *Theological Investigations*, V, 115-34. London: Darton, Longman and Todd.
Rawls, John
    1981   *A Theory of Liberalism*. Cambridge: Harvard University Press.
Rescher, Nicholas.
    1985   *The Strife of Systems*. Pittsburgh: University of Pittsburgh Press.
Richard, Ramesh P.
    1994   *The Population of Heaven: A Biblical Response to the Inclusivist Position on Who Will Be Saved.*, Chicago: Moody.
Robson, George
    1910   "Part I: History of the Conference." In World Missionary Conference, *The History and Records of the Conference together with Addresses Delivered at the Evening Meetings*, 3-20. London: Oliphaunt, Anderson and Ferrier.

Sanneh, Lamin
- 1997   "Theology of Mission." In David Ford, ed., *The Modern Theologians: Second Edition*, 555-74. Cambridge: Blackwell.

Samartha, Stanley
- 1988   "Mission in a Religiously Plural World: Looking Beyond Tambaram, 1938." *The International Review of Mission* 78: 315-24.

Saunders, K. J.
- 1928   "Christianity and Buddhism." In *The Christian Life and Message in Relation to Non-Christian Systems of Thought and Life*, 119-85. London: Oxford University Press.

Schleiermacher, Friedrich
- 1989   *The Christian Faith*. Edinburgh: T. & T. Clark.

Smith, Wilfred Cantwell
- 1979   *Faith and Belief*. Princeton: Princeton University Press.
- 1981   *Towards a World Theology*. Maryknoll: Orbis.
- 1988   "Mission, Dialogue and God's Will for Us." *The International Review of Mission* 78: 360-74.

Söderblom, Nathan
- 1943   *The Nature of Religion*. London: Oxford University Press.

Stockwell, Eugene
- 1988   "Introduction." *The International Review of Mission* 78: 309-10.

Stuart, J. Leighton
- 1928   "Christianity and Confucianism." In *The Christian Life and Message in Relation to Non-Christian Systems of Thought and Life*, 53-82. London: Oxford University Press.

Surin, Kenneth
- 1989   *The Turnings of Darkness and Light*. Cambridge: Cambridge University Press.
- 1990   "A 'Politics of Speech': Religious Pluralism in the Age of the McDonald's Hamburger." In Gavin D'Costa, ed., *Christian Uniqueness Reconsidered*, 192-212. Maryknoll: Orbis

Temple, William
- 1938   "Foreword." In Hendrik Kraemer, *The Christian Message in a Non-Christian World*. London: Edinburgh House.

Thomas Aquinas
- 1954   *Nature and Grace: Selections from the Summa Theological of Thomas Aquinas*. London: SCM
- 1955   *On the Truth of the Catholic Faith: Summa Contra Gentiles*. New York: Doubleday.

Thomas, M. M.
- 1969   *The Acknowledged Christ of the Indian Renaissance*. London: SCM.

Tiele, C. P.
1897 *Elements of the Science of Religion: Part I. Morphological.* Edinburgh: William Blackwood and Sons.
1898 *Elements of the Science of Religion: Part II. Ontological.* Edinburgh: William Blackwood and Sons.

Van Dusen, Henry P.
1948 *World Christianity: Yesterday, Today, Tomorrow.* London: SCM.

van Leeuwen, Arend Theodoor
1962 *Hendrik Kraemer: Pioneer Der Oekumene.* Basel: Basilea Verlag.

Visser't Hooft, W. A.
1973 *Memoirs.* London: SCM.
1974 *Has the Ecumenical Movement a Future?* Belfast: Christian Journals.

Ward, Keith
1991 *A Vision to Pursue: Beyond the Crisis in Christianity.* London: Oxford University Press.
1995 *Revelation and Religion: A Theology of Revelation in the World Religions.* London: Oxford University Press.

Weber, Hans-Ruedi
1966a "Hendrik Kraemer: A man who obeyed the vision he saw (An address given in the Chapel of the Ecumenical Centre, November 15, 1965)." *The Ecumenical Review* 18: 6-9.
1966b "The Mission of the Church on Bali." In *Asia and the Ecumenical Movement*, 170-79. London: SCM.

Wittgenstein, Ludwig
1974 *Tractatus Logico-Philosophicus.* London: Routledge and Kegan Paul.

Wolterstorff, Nicholas
1984 *Reason within the Bounds of Religion: Second Edition.* Grand Rapids: Eerdmans.

World Missionary Conference
1910a *Report of Commission I: Carrying the Gospel to all the Non-Christian World.* London: Oliphaunt, Anderson and Ferrier.
1910b *Report of Commission IV: The Missionary Message in Relation to Non-Christian Religions.* London: Oliphaunt, Anderson and Ferrier.
1910c *Report of Commission VII: Missions and Governments.* London: Oliphaunt, Anderson and Ferrier.
1910d *Report of Commission VIII: Co-Operation and the Promotion of Unity.* London: Oliphaunt, Anderson and Ferrier.

INDEX

Adriani, Nicolaus, 30, 31, 46-7
Ariarajah, Wesley, 36-7, 44, 51
Augustine, 73 n. 10, 137

Barnes, Michael, 13
Barth, Karl, v, vii, 4, 18-20, 29-30, 33, 45, 47, 48-9, 66 n. 6, 74-5, 126, 139, 141-2
Bevan, Edwyn, 41
Brightman, E. S., 75
Brown, David, v
Brunner, Emil, 33, 48, 59, 74-5, 139-41
Byrne, Peter, 27-8, 124-6

Cairns, D. S., 36
Calvin, John, 59, 74, 140
Chantepie de la Saussaye, Pierre Daniël, 30-1, 45-6
Chao, T. C. 41, 67
Chenchiah, Pandipeddi, 41, 65
Clement, 66 n. 6, 72-3
Clooney, Francis X., 3, 143
Copernicus, Nicholas, 15
Craig, William Lane, 20
Crowder, Colin, v
Cunningham, David S., 145

D'Costa, Gavin, v, vii, 5-7, 11, 12-3, 18, 29, 98-106, 111-2, 116-21, 122 n. 3, 144
De Dietrich, Suzanne, 34
DiNoia, J. A. 3, 13, 24, 102, 108-10, 127, 128, 143
Donovan, Peter, 25 n. 10
Driver, Tom F., 132
Dunn, James D. G., 66 n. 6
Dupuis, Jacques, 13 n. 4, 45 n. 14

Edinburgh, 1910, 30, 35-37, 42
Edwards, David, 34
Engles, Friedrich, 89

Farmer, H. H., 69, 75
Farquhar, J. N., 75, 88
Feuerbach, Ludwig, 69, 89, 106
Frei, Hans, 92-4
Freud, Sigmund, 69, 89, 106

Galilei, Galileo, 16
Garcia, Laura L., 107-8
Garon, Armand, 49
Geivett, R. Douglas, 18
Gillis, Chester, 92-3, 95
Gloede, Gunter, 30
Griffiths, Paul J., 120-1, 144, 147
Gunning, J. H. 30, 46

Hallencreutz, Carl H., 11, 30-4, 38, 42, 47
Hamann, J. G., 74
Heim, S. Mark, 3, 22, 124-5, 126, 128, 129-30
Hick, John, 2, 11, 12-5, 22-5, 27, 88, 124-7, 130-1
Hocking, William Ernest, 4, 29, 40-1, 43, 49-51, 67, 75, 97, 99, 105-7, 118
Hogg, A. G., 47, 67
Horton, Walter, 67
Hunsberger, George, 29 n. 2
Hurgronje, Snouck, 30

Idenburg, A. W. F., 31
International Missionary Council, 4, 7, 11, 35-45, 63

Jackson, Eleanor, v, 44

James, George Alfred, 46
Jantzen, Grace M., 127
Jathanna, Origen V., 47
Jerusalem, 1928, 29, 33, 35, 37-42, 97, 99, 118
Jones, Rufus, 39-40
Jüngel, Eberhard, 19

Kant, Immanuel, 69
Knitter, Paul F., 2, 7, 20-22, 45 n. 14, 92, 93, 95, 123-4, 125, 126, 127
Kraemer, Hendrik, v, vii, 3-5, 9-11, 53, 87, 107-8, 109, 111, 120-1, 126, 128, 132, 134
  Adaptation, 62-3, 135-47 (esp. 136-42)
  Babel, 76
  Barth, 45-52 (esp. 48-9)
  biblical realism, 54, 55-6, 63, 65, 69-71, 73, 87-110 (esp. 88-93), 136, 138, 139, 142
  Canon, 91-3
  Christian Message (summary), 53-64
  Church, 56-7, 87, 91-2, 97-8
  "Continuity or Discontinuity" (summary), 63-8
  Creation and Fall, 75-6
  essence of religion, 69-71
  fulfillment, 64-5, 88, 117
  historical criticism, 94-7
  Hocking, 49-52
  holistic approach, 58-9, 65, 69-71, 111-33 (esp. 112-6), 135, 138, 139, 142, 144
  Jerusalem 1928, 40-1
  life and works, 30-5
  Logos, 76-7
  logos spermatikos, 73
  natural theology, 59-60, 80, 96-101, 103-4, 108
  neo-Orthodoxy, 74-5
  Noahic Covenant, 75-7, 108-9
  non-Western Christianity, 53-4
  Paul, 88-9
  phenomenology of religion, 46-7, 88-9, 112-3, 117-8
  points of contact, 60-2, 80-1, 135-47 (esp. 136-42)
  Reformation, 84
  Religion and the Christian Faith (summary), 68-83
  religious values, 57-8, 97-8
  Re-Thinking Missions 43, 43-4 n. 13
  revelation, 46-7, 56-7, 60-2, 65, 72
  salvation, 100-3
  sui generis, 87, 96-105
  Tambaram 1938, 10, 42-25
  tolerance, 81-2
  totalitarian approach (*see* holistic approach)
  Thomas Aquinas, 83
  Wisdom, 76-7
  World Council of Churches, 9
Kristensen, W. Brede, 30, 31, 34, 45-6, 114
Kruyt, A. C., 30
Kulandran, Sabapathy, 51
Küng, Hans, 126

Lathuihamallo, P. D. 31
Lindbeck, George, 18-9, 106, 108, 130
Loades, Ann, v
Lochhead, David, 19 n. 7
Loughlin, Gerard, 107
Luther, Martin, 74

MacIntyre, Alasdair, 139, 143
Mackey, James P. 66 n. 6
Macnicol, Nicol, 38, 43, 75
Markham, Ian, 13
Marx, Karl, 69, 89, 106
Massignon, Louis, 31
Maus, Marcel, 31
Meinhoff, Karl, 31
Migliore, Daniel, 93-4
Milbank, John, 24

INDEX

Moore, Charles A., 22 n. 8
Moses, D. G. 77, 67
Mott, J. R., 31, 36, 43

Neill, Stephen, 35
Netland, Harold, 122-3, 126
Newbigin, Lesslie, v, 12, 18-20, 22, 24-5, 26-7, 29, 97-8, 132
Nicholson, Wayne Isaac, 30-3
Niles, D. T., 29 n. 1

Ogden, Schubert, 13
Oldham, J. H. 30, 36, 38-42
Origen, 73
Otto, Rudolf, 69

Panikkar, Raimon, 126 n. 4
Paton, William, 38 n. 6, 40, 43-4
Pentz, Rebecca, 131
Perry, Tim, vii, 9, 107, 122 n. 3
Phillips, W. Gary, 18
Pinnock, Clark, 25-6, 45 n. 14
Placher, William, 146
Plantinga, Alvin, v, 87 n. 1, 107, 145
Polanyi, Michael, 114 n. 2

Race, Alan, 11-2, 13, 14, 17, 25-8, 29, 92-3, 95, 144
Radhakrishnan, Sarvepalli, 22 n. 8
Rahner, Karl, 20, 88, 126
Raven, Charles, 39
Rawls, John, 22 n. 9
Rescher, Nicholas, 126
Richard, Ramesh, 13 n. 4
Robson, George, 61

Samartha, Stanley, 9
Sanneh, Lamin, 6, 11, 29
Saunders, K. J. 39
Schleiermarcher, F. D. E., 69, 88
Schlunk, Martin, 38
Smith, Wilfred Cantwell, 2, 10, 120-1, 143
Söderblom, Nathan, 75
Speer, Robert E., 36

Stockwell, Eugene, 10
Stuart, J. Leighton, 39
Surin, Kenneth, 13, 128-9

Tambaram 1938, 11, 29, 34, 35, 41-5, 47, 64, 68, 97, 99, 111
Temple, William, 11, 41-2
Tertullian, 73 n. 10
Thomas Aquinas, 73
Thomas, M. M., 105
Tiele, C. P., 45

Van Dusen, Henry P., 44 n. 12
van Leeuwen, Arend Theodoor, 31
Visser't Hooft, W. A., 32-3, 34, 44

Ward, Keith, 11, 122-3, 126
Weber, Hans Ruedi, 33
Wei, Francis, 41
Wittgenstein, Ludwig, 28 n. 11
World Missionary Conference, 35-8
Wolterstorff, Nicholas, 16
World Council of Churches, 6, 7, 34, 35, 36, 39
Zuniga, Diego, 15
Zwingli, Huldrych, 74

Series Published by Wilfrid Laurier University Press for the Canadian Corporation for Studies in Religion / Corporation Canadienne des Sciences Religieuses

Editions SR

1. *La langue de Ya'udi : description et classement de l'ancien parler de Zencircli dans le cadre des langues sémitiques du nord-ouest*
   Paul-Eugène Dion, O.P. / 1974 / viii + 511 p. / OUT OF PRINT
2. *The Conception of Punishment in Early Indian Literature*
   Terence P. Day / 1982 / iv + 328 pp.
3. *Traditions in Contact and Change: Selected Proceedings of the XIVth Congress of the International Association for the History of Religions*
   Edited by Peter Slater and Donald Wiebe with Maurice Boutin and Harold Coward
   1983 / x + 758 pp. / OUT OF PRINT
4. *Le messianisme de Louis Riel*
   Gilles Martel / 1984 / xviii + 483 p.
5. *Mythologies and Philosophies of Salvation in the Theistic Traditions of India*
   Klaus K. Klostermaier / 1984 / xvi + 549 pp. / OUT OF PRINT
6. *Averroes' Doctrine of Immortality: A Matter of Controversy*
   Ovey N. Mohammed / 1984 / vi + 202 pp. / OUT OF PRINT
7. *L'étude des religions dans les écoles : l'expérience américaine, anglaise et canadienne*
   Fernand Ouellet / 1985 / xvi + 666 p.
8. *Of God and Maxim Guns: Presbyterianism in Nigeria, 1846-1966*
   Geoffrey Johnston / 1988 / iv + 322 pp.
9. *A Victorian Missionary and Canadian Indian Policy: Cultural Synthesis vs Cultural Replacement*
   David A. Nock / 1988 / x + 194 pp. / OUT OF PRINT
10. *Prometheus Rebound: The Irony of Atheism*
    Joseph C. McLelland / 1988 / xvi + 366 pp.
11. *Competition in Religious Life*
    Jay Newman / 1989 / viii + 237 pp.
12. *The Huguenots and French Opinion, 1685-1787: The Enlightenment Debate on Toleration*
    Geoffrey Adams / 1991 / xiv + 335 pp.
13. *Religion in History: The Word, the Idea, the Reality / La religion dans l'histoire : le mot, l'idée, la réalité*
    Edited by/Sous la direction de Michel Despland and/et Gérard Vallée
    1992 / x + 252 pp.
14. *Sharing Without Reckoning: Imperfect Right and the Norms of Reciprocity*
    Millard Schumaker / 1992 / xiv + 112 pp.
15. *Love and the Soul: Psychological Interpretations of the Eros and Psyche Myth*
    James Gollnick / 1992 / viii + 174 pp.
16. *The Promise of Critical Theology: Essays in Honour of Charles Davis*
    Edited by Marc P. Lalonde / 1995 / xii + 146 pp.

17. *The Five Aggregates: Understanding Theravāda Psychology and Soteriology*
    Mathieu Boisvert / 1995 / xii + 166 pp.
18. *Mysticism and Vocation*
    James R. Horne / 1996 / vi + 110 pp.
19. *Memory and Hope: Strands of Canadian Baptist History*
    Edited by David T. Priestley / 1996 / viii + 211 pp.
20. *The Concept of Equity in Calvin's Ethics**
    Guenther H. Haas / 1997 / xii + 205 pp.
    * Available in the United Kingdom and Europe from Paternoster Press.
21. *The Call of Conscience: French Protestant Responses to the Algerian War, 1954-1962*
    Geoffrey Adams / 1998 / xxii + 270 pp.
22. *Clinical Pastoral Supervision and the Theology of Charles Gerkin*
    Thomas St. James O'Connor / 1998 / x + 152 pp.
23. *Faith and Fiction: A Theological Critique of the Narrative Strategies of Hugh MacLennan and Morley Callaghan*
    Barbara Pell / 1998 / v + 141 pp.
24. *God and the Chip: Religion and the Culture of Technology*
    William A. Stahl / 1999 / vi + 186 pp.
25. *The Religious Dreamworld of Apuleius'* Metamorphoses: *Recovering a Forgotten Hermeneutic*
    James Gollnick / 1999 / xiv + 178 pp.
26. *Edward Schillebeeckx and Hans Frei: A Conversation on Method and Christology*
    Marguerite Abdul-Masih / 2001 / 240 pp. est.
27. *Radical Difference: A Defence of Hendrik Kraemer's Theology of Religions*
    Tim Perry / 2001 / viii + 168 pp.

Comparative Ethics Series / Collection d'Éthique Comparée

1. *Muslim Ethics and Modernity: A Comparative Study of the Ethical Thought of Sayyid Ahmad Khan and Mawlana Mawdudi*
   Sheila McDonough / 1984 / x + 130 pp. / OUT OF PRINT
2. *Methodist Education in Peru: Social Gospel, Politics, and American Ideological and Economic Penetration, 1888-1930*
   Rosa del Carmen Bruno-Jofré / 1988 / xiv + 223 pp.
3. *Prophets, Pastors and Public Choices: Canadian Churches and the Mackenzie Valley Pipeline Debate*
   Roger Hutchinson / 1992 / xiv + 142 pp. / OUT OF PRINT
4. *In Good Faith: Canadian Churches Against Apartheid*
   Renate Pratt / 1997 / xii + 366 pp.
5. *Towards an Ethics of Community: Negotiations of Difference in a Pluralist Society*
   James H. Olthuis, editor / 2000 / x + 230 pp.

Dissertations SR

1. *The Social Setting of the Ministry as Reflected in the Writings of Hermas, Clement and Ignatius*
   Harry O. Maier / 1991 / viii + 230 pp. / OUT OF PRINT
2. *Literature as Pulpit: The Christian Social Activism of Nellie L. McClung*
   Randi R. Warne / 1993 / viii + 236 pp. / OUT OF PRINT

Studies in Christianity and Judaism /
Études sur le christianisme et le judaïsme

1. *A Study in Anti-Gnostic Polemics: Irenaeus, Hippolytus, and Epiphanius*
   Gérard Vallée / 1981 / xii + 114 pp. / OUT OF PRINT
2. *Anti-Judaism in Early Christianity*
   Vol. 1, *Paul and the Gospels*
   Edited by Peter Richardson with David Granskou / 1986 / x + 232 pp.
   Vol. 2, *Separation and Polemic*
   Edited by Stephen G. Wilson / 1986 / xii + 185 pp.
3. *Society, the Sacred, and Scripture in Ancient Judaism: A Sociology of Knowledge*
   Jack N. Lightstone / 1988 / xiv + 126 pp.
4. *Law in Religious Communities in the Roman Period: The Debate Over* Torah *and* Nomos *in Post-Biblical Judaism and Early Christianity*
   Peter Richardson and Stephen Westerholm with A. I. Baumgarten, Michael Pettem and Cecilia Wassén / 1991 / x + 164 pp.
5. *Dangerous Food: 1 Corinthians 8-10 in Its Context*
   Peter D. Gooch / 1993 / xviii + 178 pp.
6. *The Rhetoric of the Babylonian Talmud, Its Social Meaning and Context*
   Jack N. Lightstone / 1994 / xiv + 317 pp.
7. *Whose Historical Jesus?*
   Edited by William E. Arnal and Michel Desjardins / 1997 / vi + 337 pp.
8. *Religious Rivalries and the Struggle for Success in Caesarea Maritima*
   Edited by Terence L. Donaldson / 2000 / xiv + 402 pp.
9. *Text and Artifact in the Religions of Mediterranean Antiquity*
   Edited by Stephen G. Wilson and Michel Desjardins / 2000 / xvi + 616 pp.

The Study of Religion in Canada /
Sciences Religieuses au Canada

1. *Religious Studies in Alberta: A State-of-the-Art Review*
   Ronald W. Neufeldt / 1983 / xiv + 145 pp.
2. *Les sciences religieuses au Québec depuis 1972*
   Louis Rousseau et Michel Despland / 1988 / 158 p.
3. *Religious Studies in Ontario: A State-of-the-Art Review*
   Harold Remus, William Closson James and Daniel Fraikin / 1992 / xviii + 422 pp.
4. *Religious Studies in Manitoba and Saskatchewan: A State-of-the-Art Review*
   John M. Badertscher, Gordon Harland and Roland E. Miller / 1993 / vi + 166 pp.
5. *The Study of Religion in British Columbia: A State-of-the-Art Review*
   Brian J. Fraser / 1995 / x + 127 pp.
6. *Religious Studies in Atlantic Canada: A State-of-the-Art Review*
   Paul W.R. Bowlby with Tom Faulkner / 2001 / xii + 208 pp.

Studies in Women and Religion /
Études sur les femmes et la religion

1. *Femmes et religions**
   Sous la direction de Denise Veillette / 1995 / xviii + 466 p.
   * Only available from Les Presses de l'Université Laval
2. *The Work of Their Hands: Mennonite Women's Societies in Canada*
   Gloria Neufeld Redekop / 1996 / xvi + 172 pp.
3. *Profiles of Anabaptist Women: Sixteenth-Century Reforming Pioneers*
   Edited by C. Arnold Snyder and Linda A. Huebert Hecht / 1996 / xxii + 438 pp.

4. *Voices and Echoes: Canadian Women's Spirituality*
   Edited by Jo-Anne Elder and Colin O'Connell / 1997 / xxviii + 237 pp.
5. *Obedience, Suspicion and the Gospel of Mark: A Mennonite-Feminist Exploration of Biblical Authority*
   Lydia Neufeld Harder / 1998 / xiv + 168 pp.
6. *Clothed in Integrity: Weaving Just Cultural Relations and the Garment Industry*
   Barbara Paleczny / 2000 / xxxiv + 352 pp.

SR Supplements

1. *Footnotes to a Theology: The Karl Barth Colloquium of 1972*
   Edited and Introduced by Martin Rumscheidt / 1974 / viii + 151 pp. / OUT OF PRINT
2. *Martin Heidegger's Philosophy of Religion*
   John R. Williams / 1977 / x + 190 pp. / OUT OF PRINT
3. *Mystics and Scholars: The Calgary Conference on Mysticism 1976*
   Edited by Harold Coward and Terence Penelhum / 1977 / viii + 121 pp. / OUT OF PRINT
4. *God's Intention for Man: Essays in Christian Anthropology*
   William O. Fennell / 1977 / xii + 56 pp. / OUT OF PRINT
5. *"Language" in Indian Philosophy and Religion*
   Edited and Introduced by Harold G. Coward / 1978 / x + 98 pp. / OUT OF PRINT
6. *Beyond Mysticism*
   James R. Horne / 1978 / vi + 158 pp. / OUT OF PRINT
7. *The Religious Dimension of Socrates' Thought*
   James Beckman / 1979 / xii + 276 pp. / OUT OF PRINT
8. *Native Religious Traditions*
   Edited by Earle H. Waugh and K. Dad Prithipaul / 1979 / xii + 244 pp. / OUT OF PRINT
9. *Developments in Buddhist Thought: Canadian Contributions to Buddhist Studies*
   Edited by Roy C. Amore / 1979 / iv + 196 pp.
10. *The Bodhisattva Doctrine in Buddhism*
    Edited and Introduced by Leslie S. Kawamura / 1981 / xxii + 274 pp. / OUT OF PRINT
11. *Political Theology in the Canadian Context*
    Edited by Benjamin G. Smillie / 1982 / xii + 260 pp.
12. *Truth and Compassion: Essays on Judaism and Religion in Memory of Rabbi Dr. Solomon Frank*
    Edited by Howard Joseph, Jack N. Lightstone and Michael D. Oppenheim
    1983 / vi + 217 pp. / OUT OF PRINT
13. *Craving and Salvation: A Study in Buddhist Soteriology*
    Bruce Matthews / 1983 / xiv + 138 pp. / OUT OF PRINT
14. *The Moral Mystic*
    James R. Horne / 1983 / x + 134 pp.
15. *Ignatian Spirituality in a Secular Age*
    Edited by George P. Schner / 1984 / viii + 128 pp. / OUT OF PRINT
16. *Studies in the Book of Job*
    Edited by Walter E. Aufrecht / 1985 / xii + 76 pp.
17. *Christ and Modernity: Christian Self-Understanding in a Technological Age*
    David J. Hawkin / 1985 / x + 181 pp.
18. *Young Man Shinran: A Reappraisal of Shinran's Life*
    Takamichi Takahatake / 1987 / xvi + 228 pp. / OUT OF PRINT
19. *Modernity and Religion*
    Edited by William Nicholls / 1987 / vi + 191 pp.
20. *The Social Uplifters: Presbyterian Progressives and the Social Gospel in Canada, 1875-1915*
    Brian J. Fraser / 1988 / xvi + 212 pp. / OUT OF PRINT

Series discontinued